SMiLE

by

MARK LYNCH

EXISLE
PUBLISHING

Mark Lynch was the former editorial cartoonist for *The Australian*, but his first love is the cartoon genre known as the single gag. This is a simple panel cartoon aimed directly at the funny bone and designed to turn the sides of the mouth upwards!

Mark is the recipient of over thirty Australian and international cartooning awards, including twice winner of the National Cartoon of the year and a Stanley Award for best single gag artist of the year.

Mark lives in Sydney with his wife Jennifer and two sons Patrick and Jack.

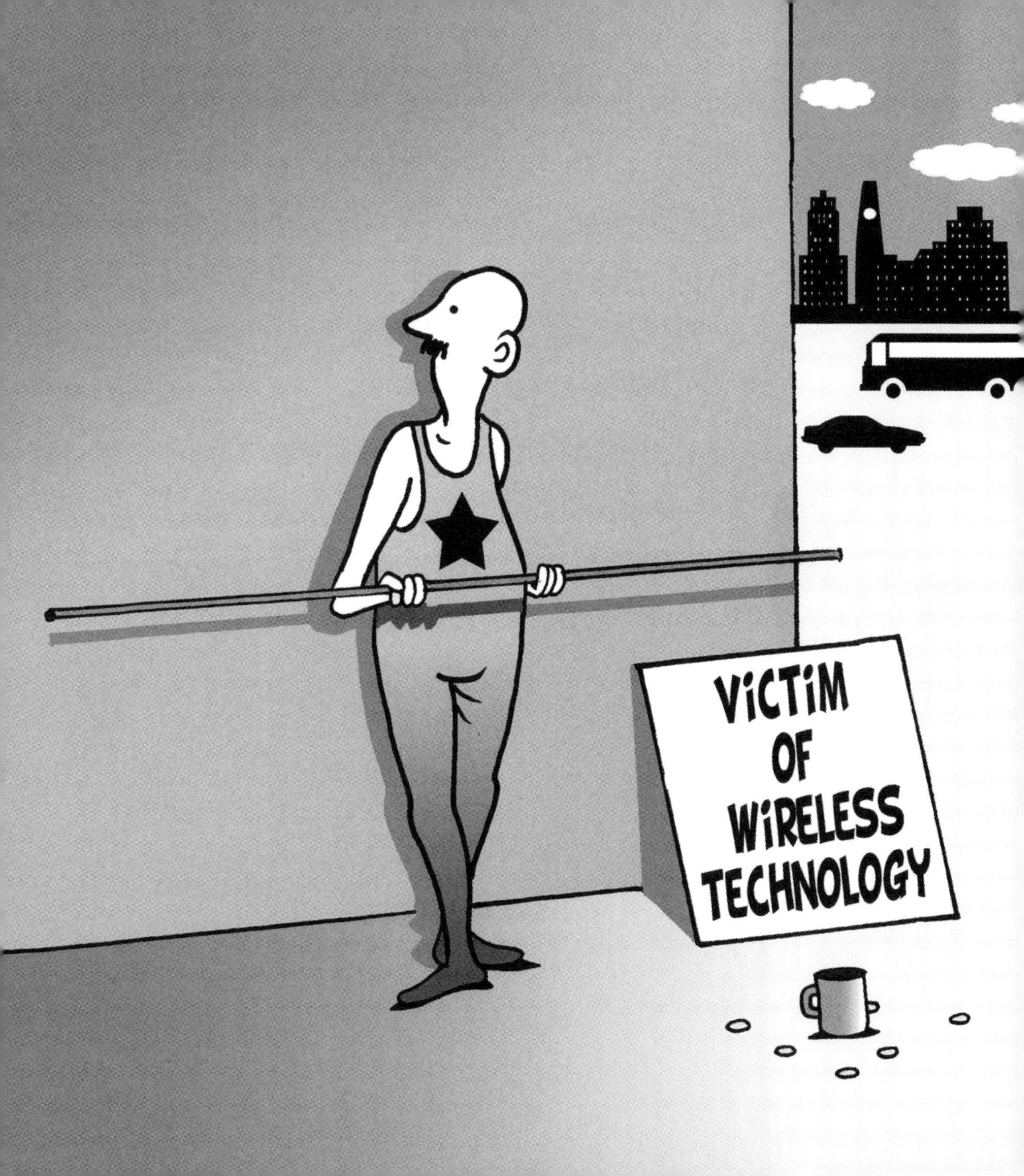
VICTIM
OF
WIRELESS
TECHNOLOGY

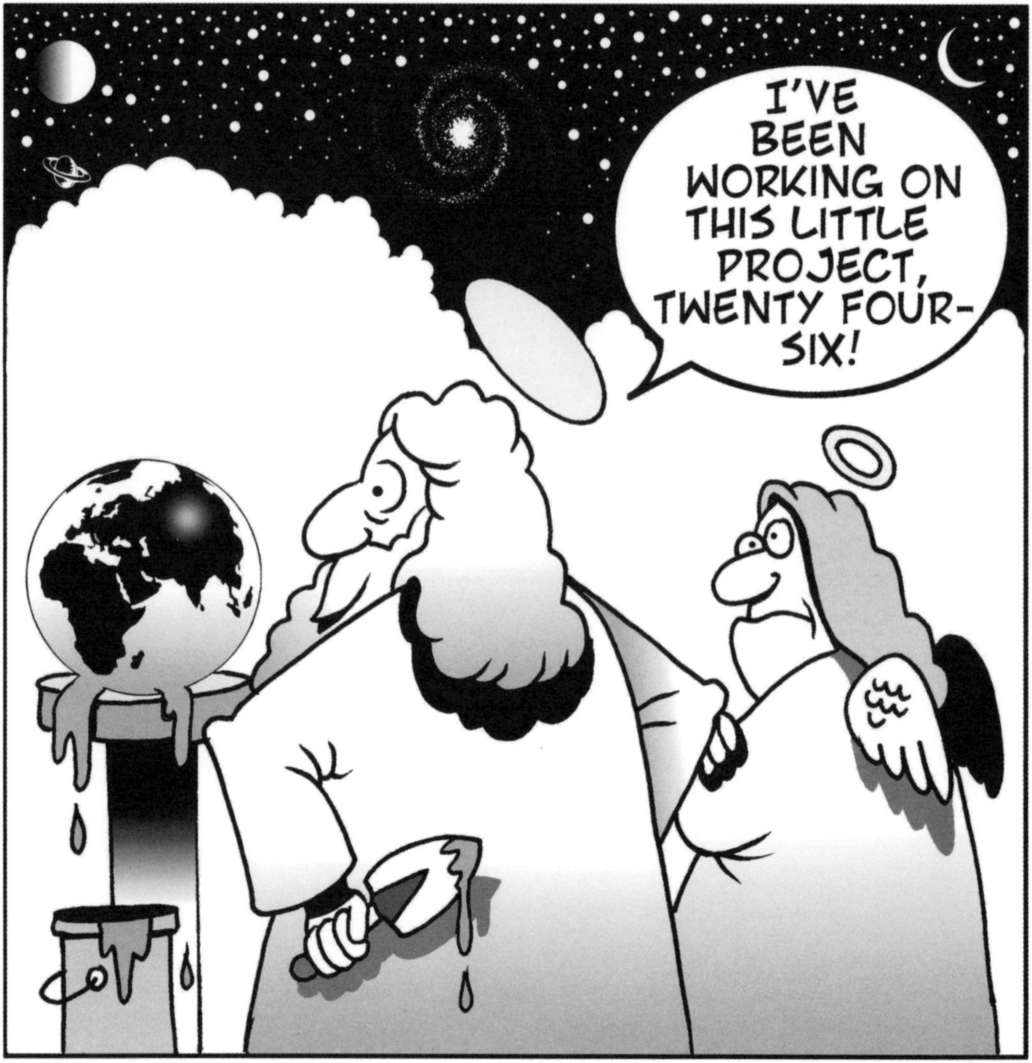
I'VE BEEN WORKING ON THIS LITTLE PROJECT, TWENTY FOUR-SIX!

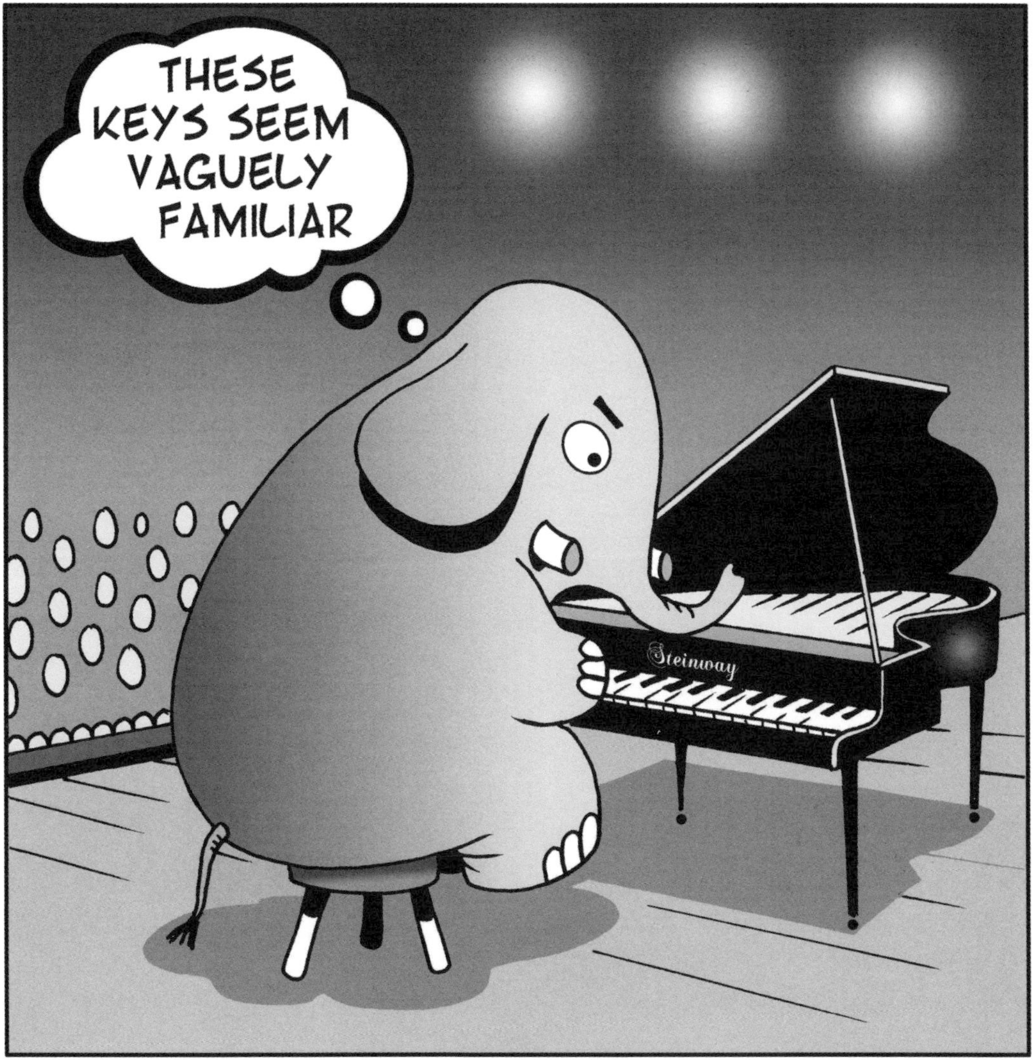
THESE KEYS SEEM VAGUELY FAMILIAR
Steinway

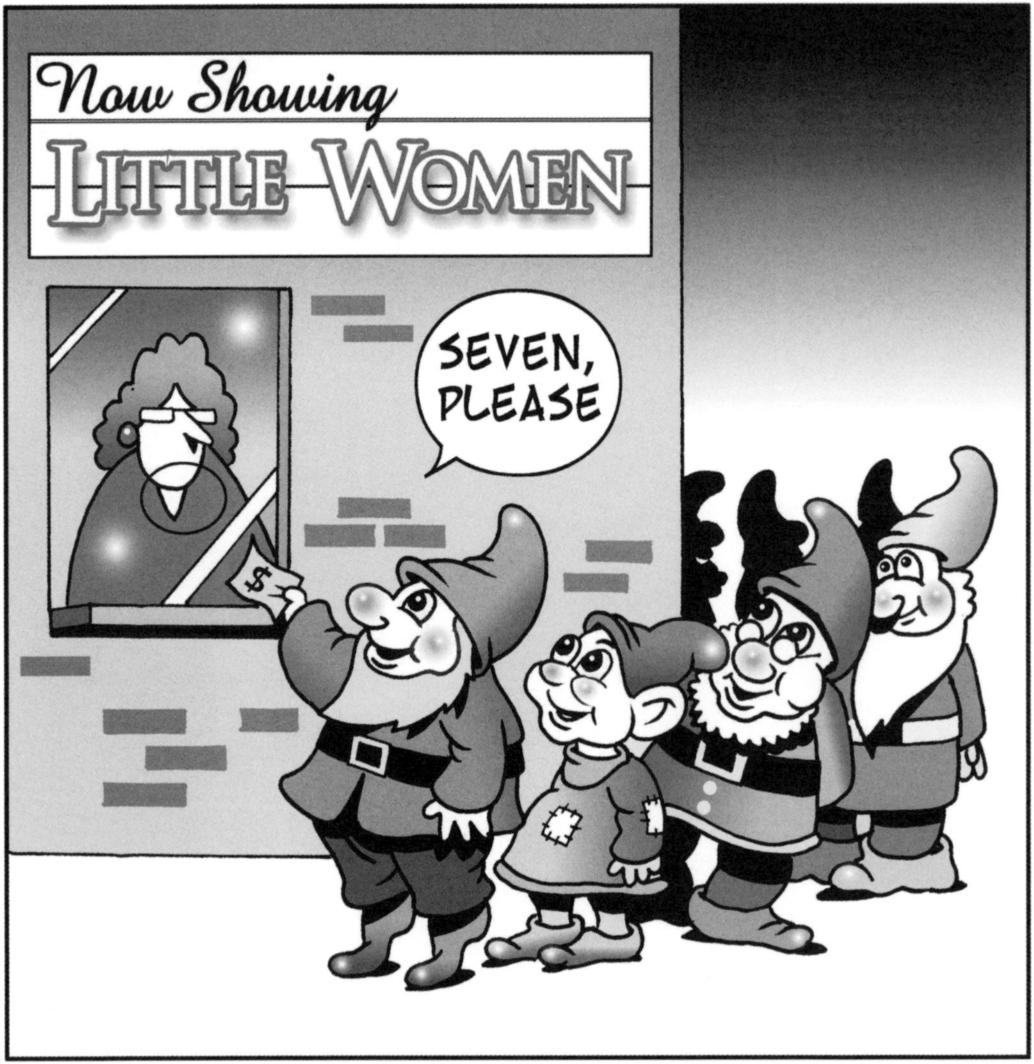
Now Showing
LITTLE WOMEN
SEVEN, PLEASE
$

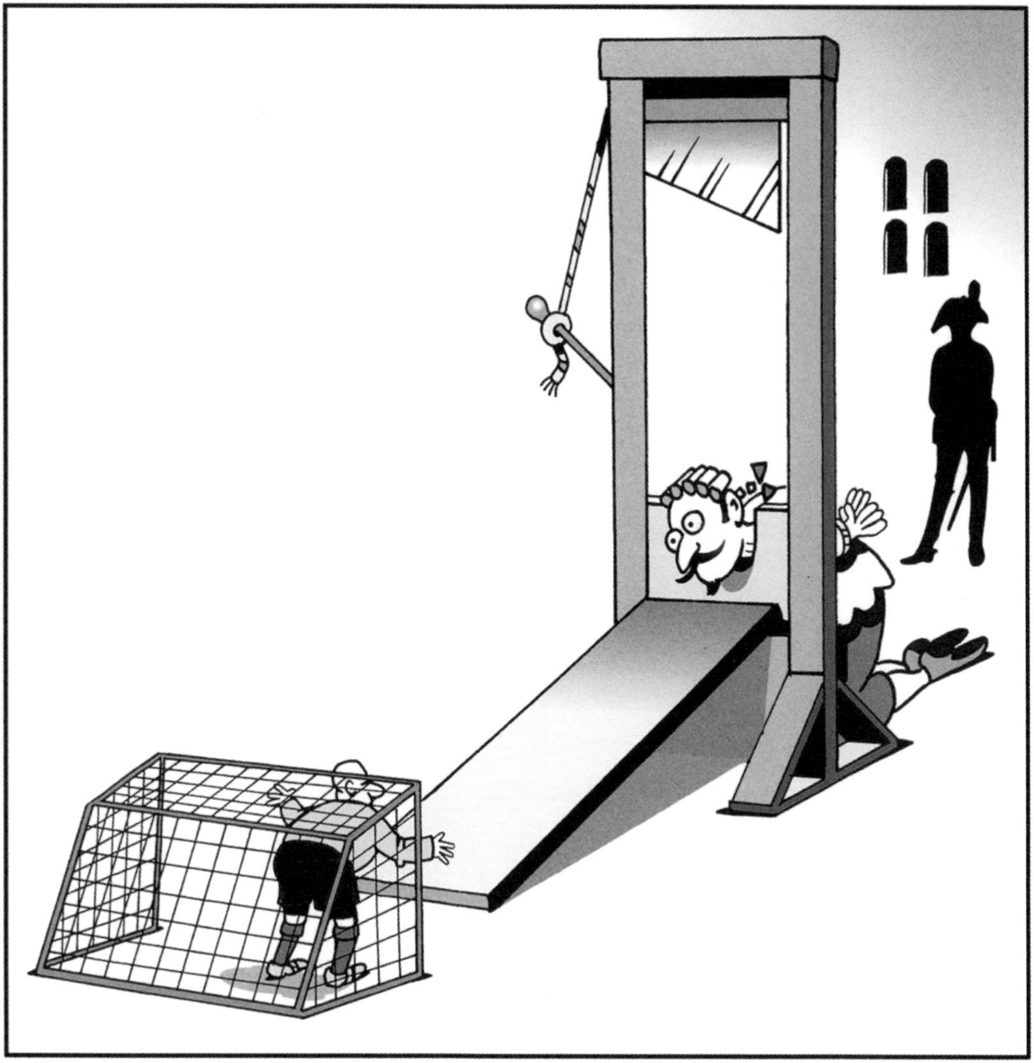

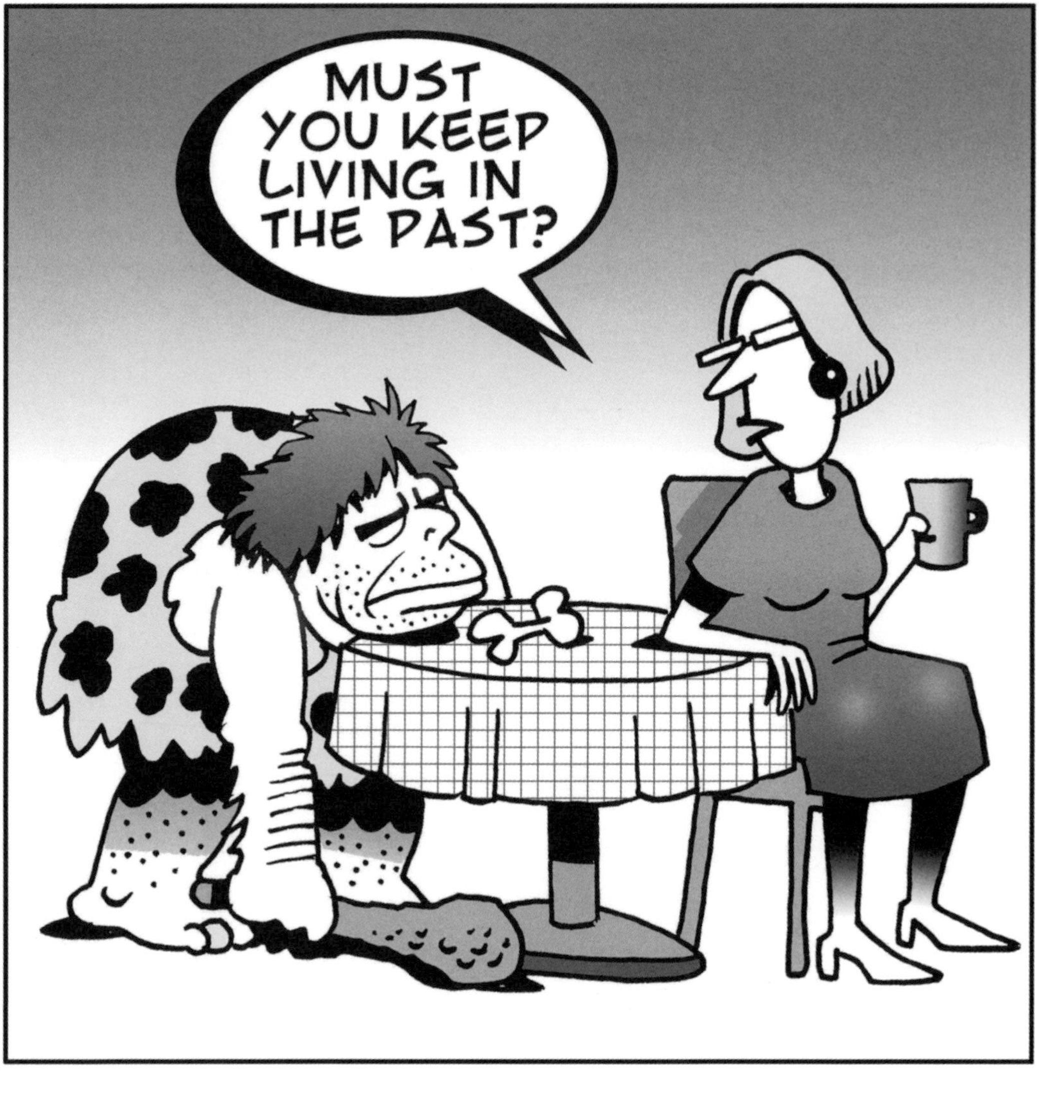
MUST YOU KEEP LIVING IN THE PAST?

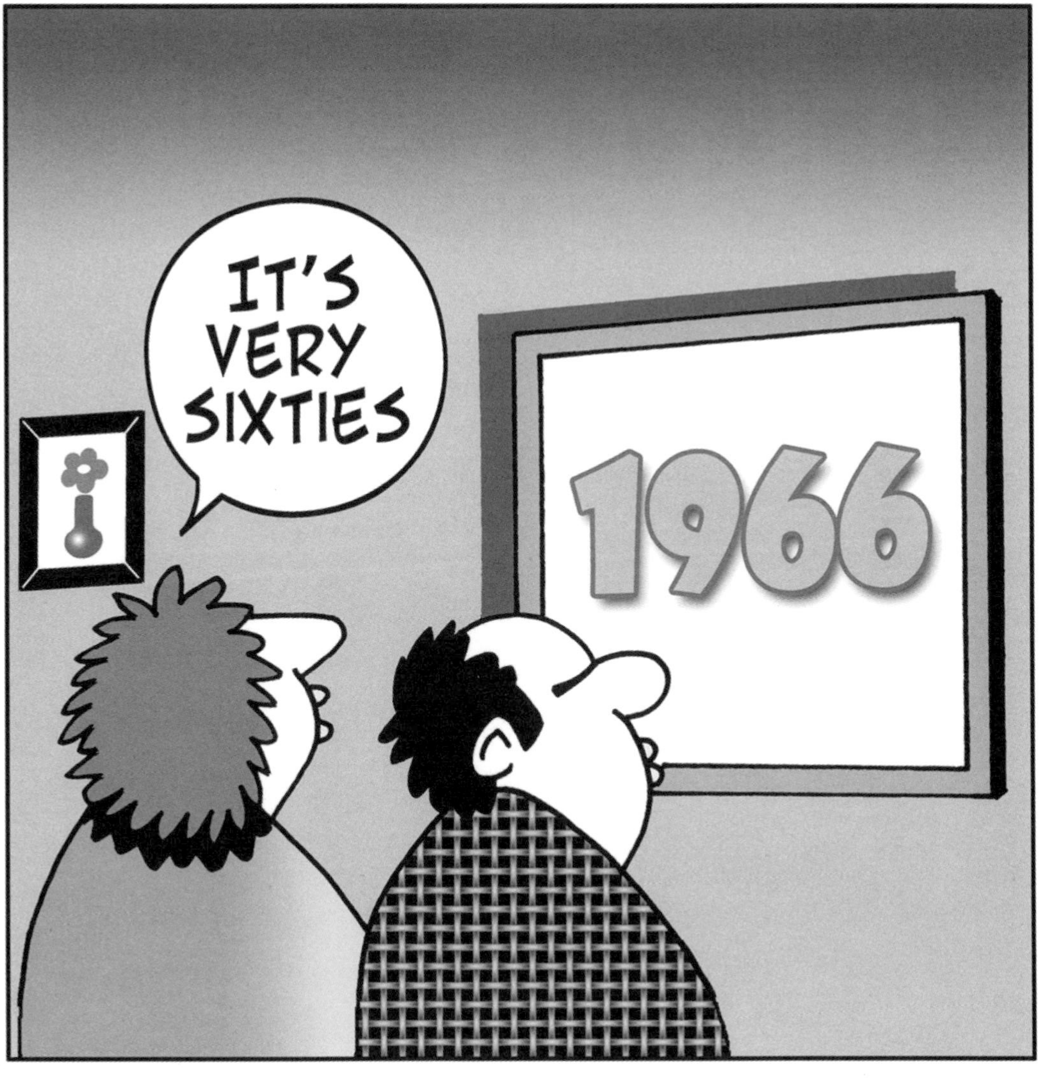
IT'S VERY SIXTIES
1966

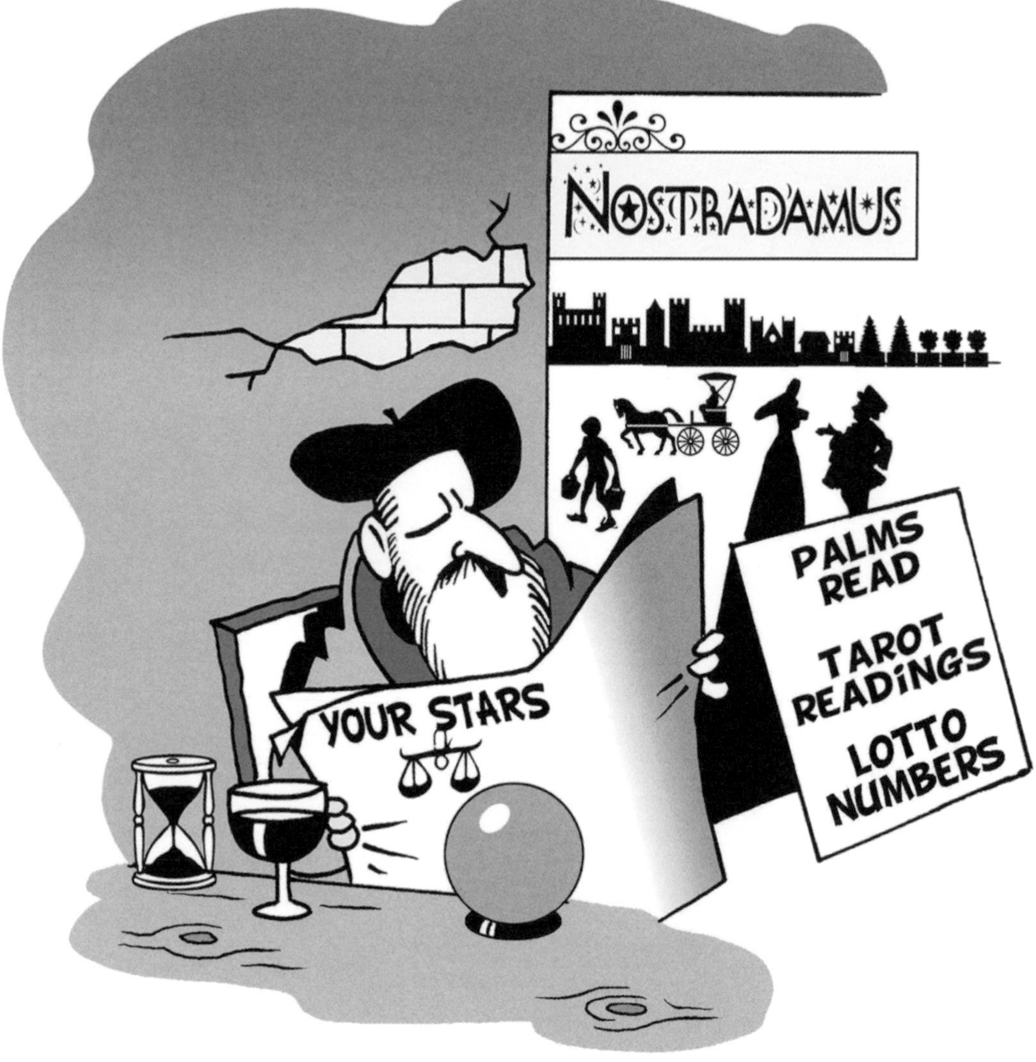
NOSTRADAMUS
PALMS READ
TAROT READINGS
LOTTO NUMBERS
YOUR STARS

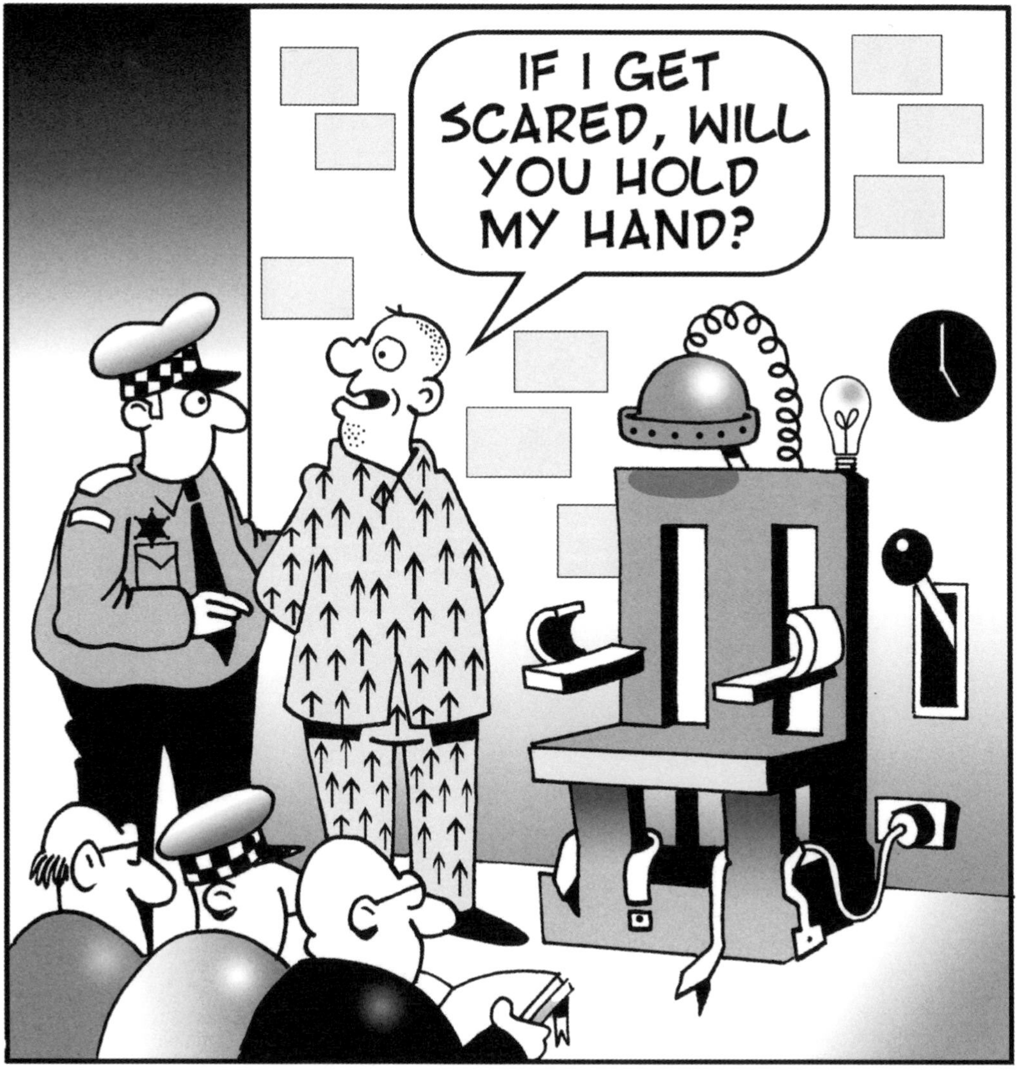
IF I GET SCARED, WILL YOU HOLD MY HAND?

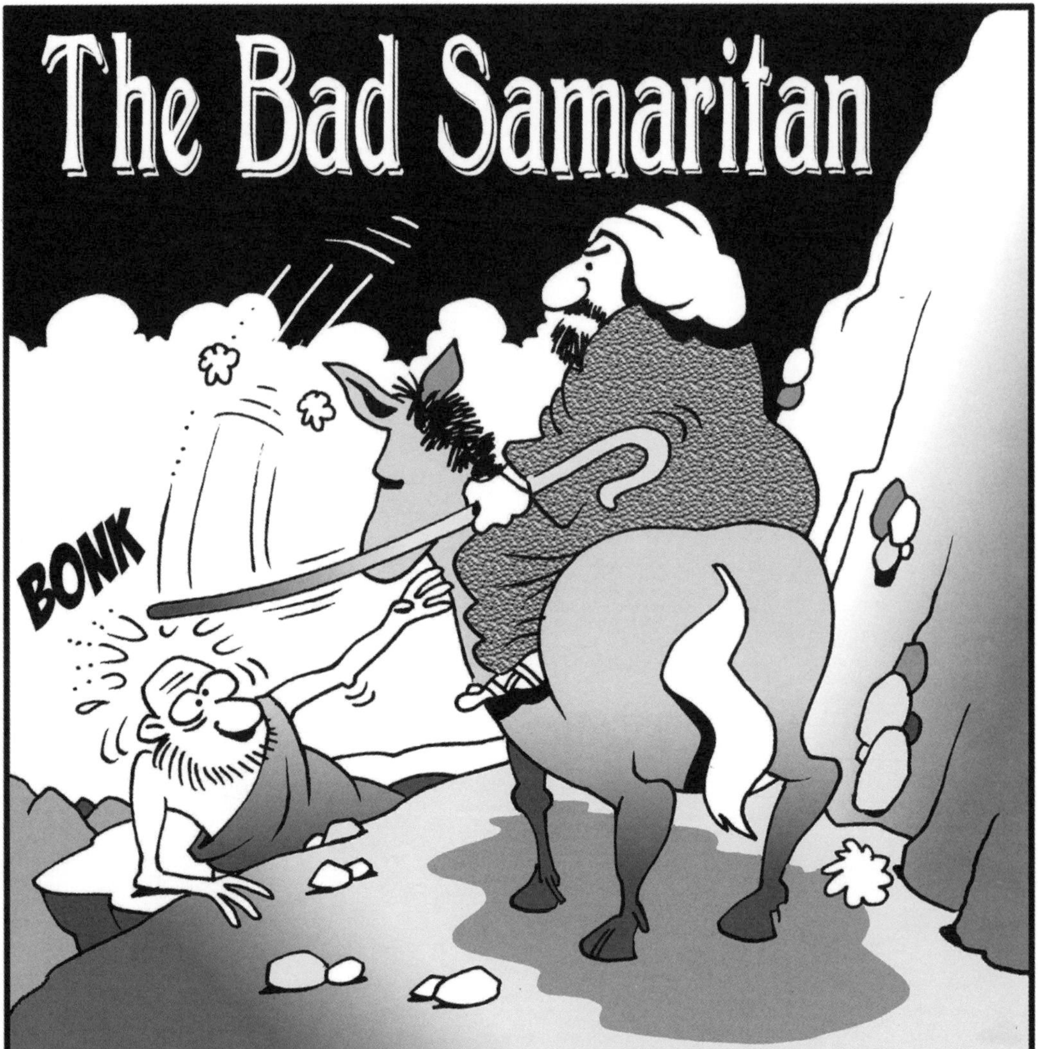
The Bad Samaritan
BONK

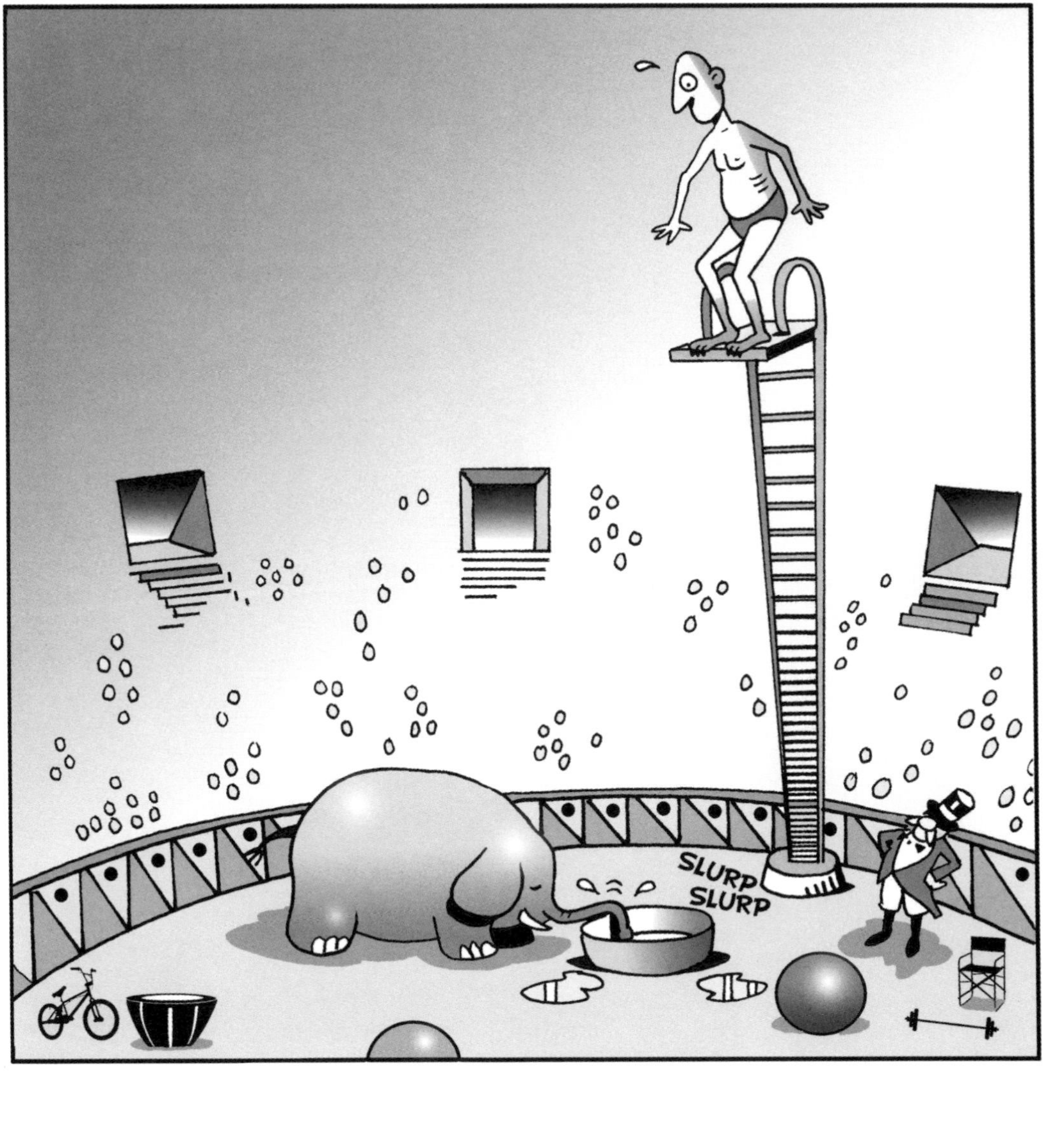
SLURP
SLURP

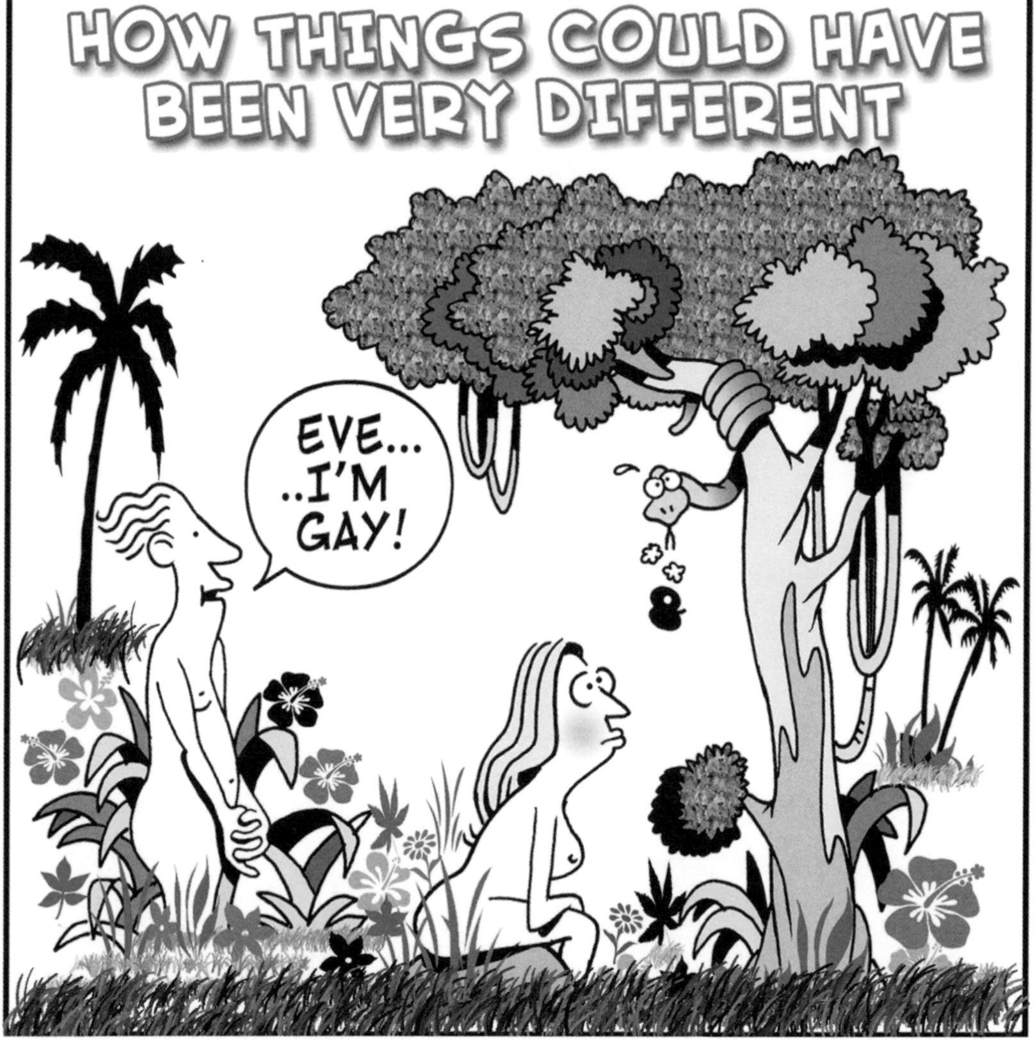
HOW THINGS COULD HAVE BEEN VERY DIFFERENT
EVE... ..I'M GAY!

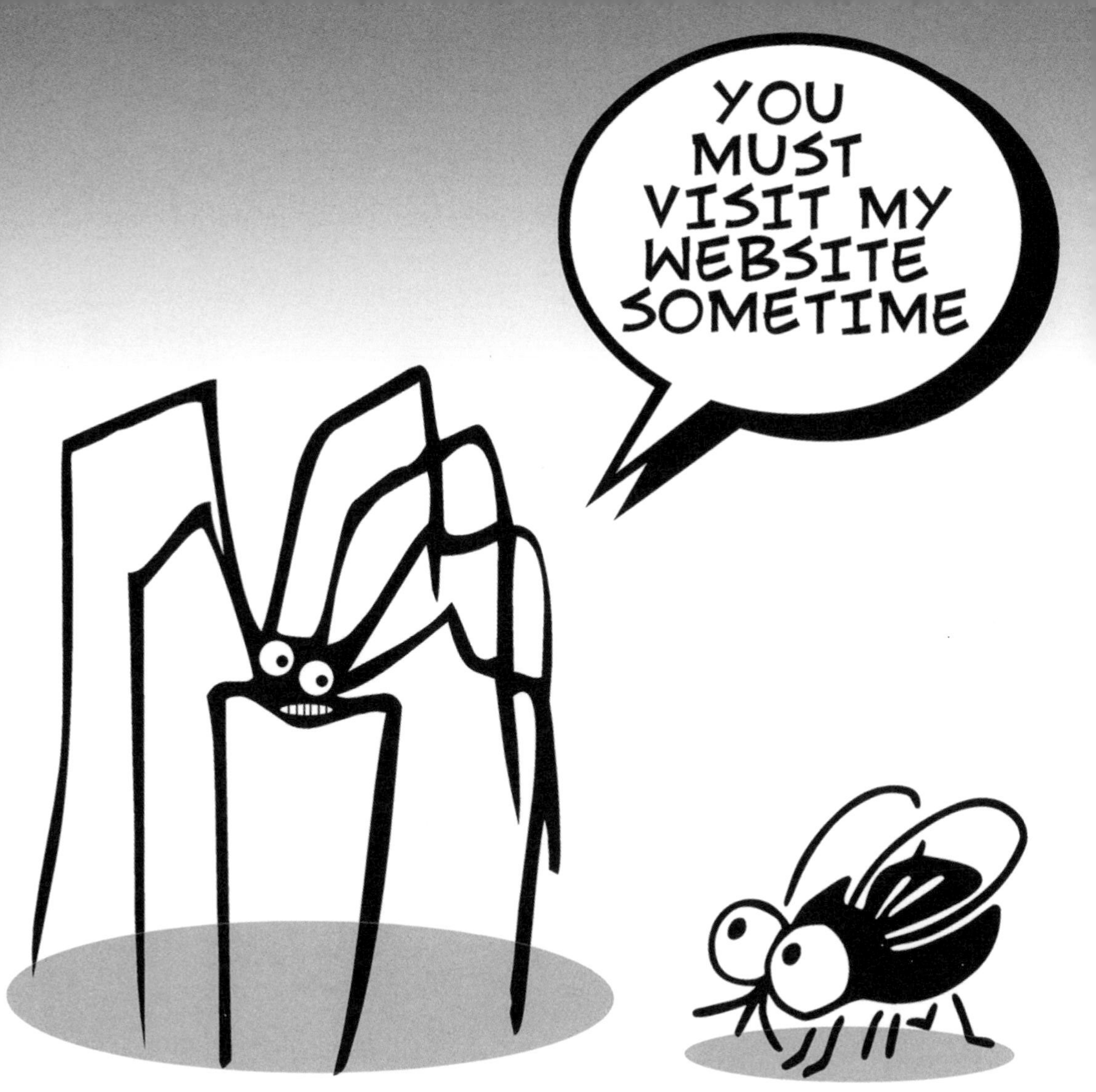
YOU MUST VISIT MY WEBSITE SOMETIME

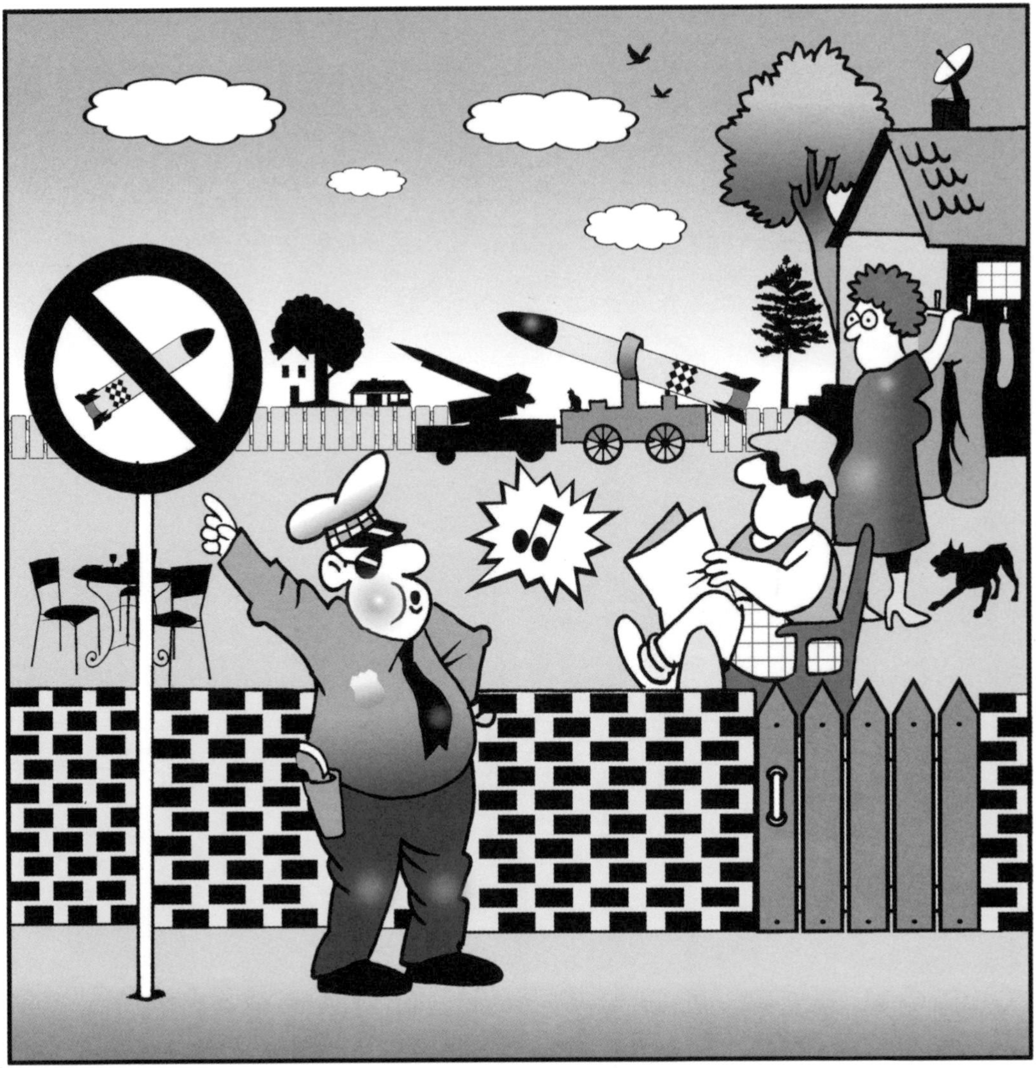

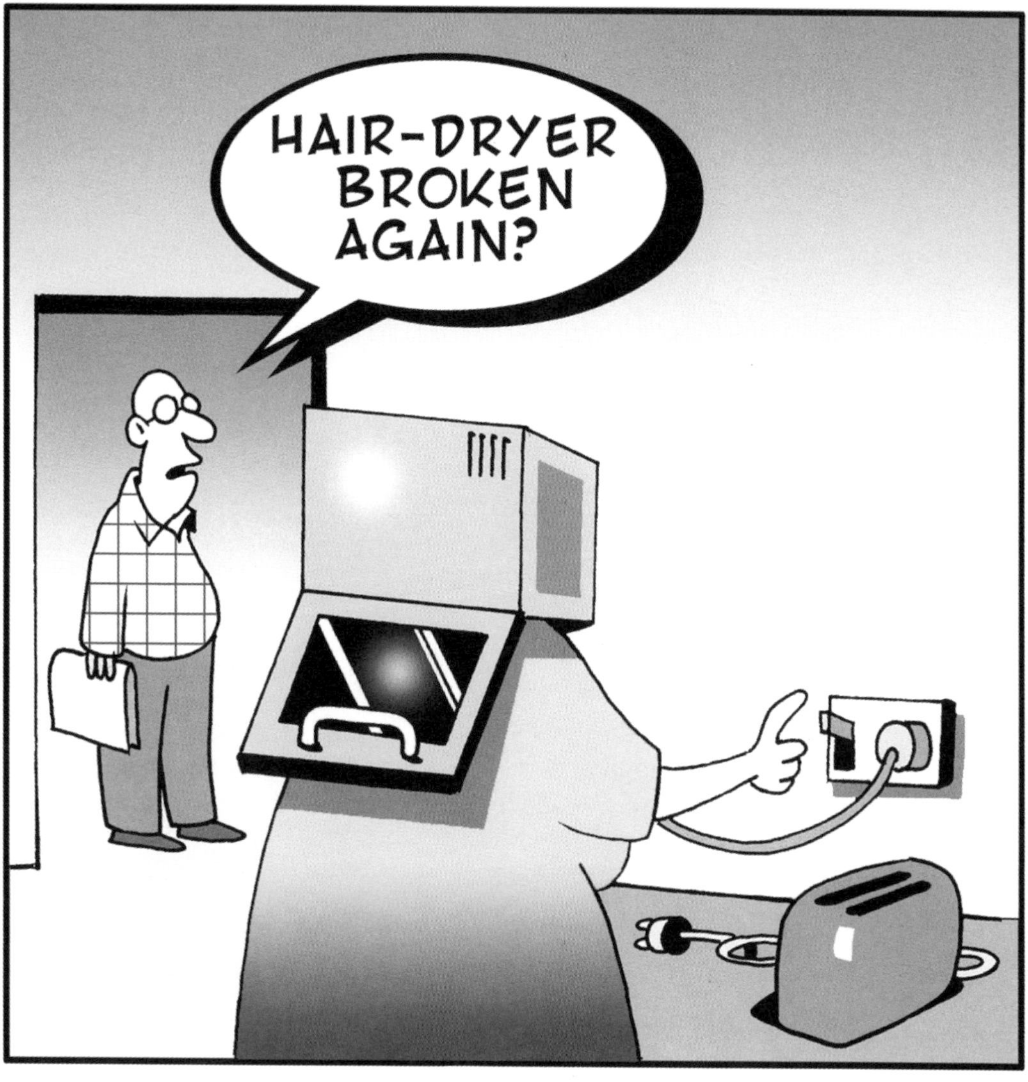
HAIR-DRYER BROKEN AGAIN?

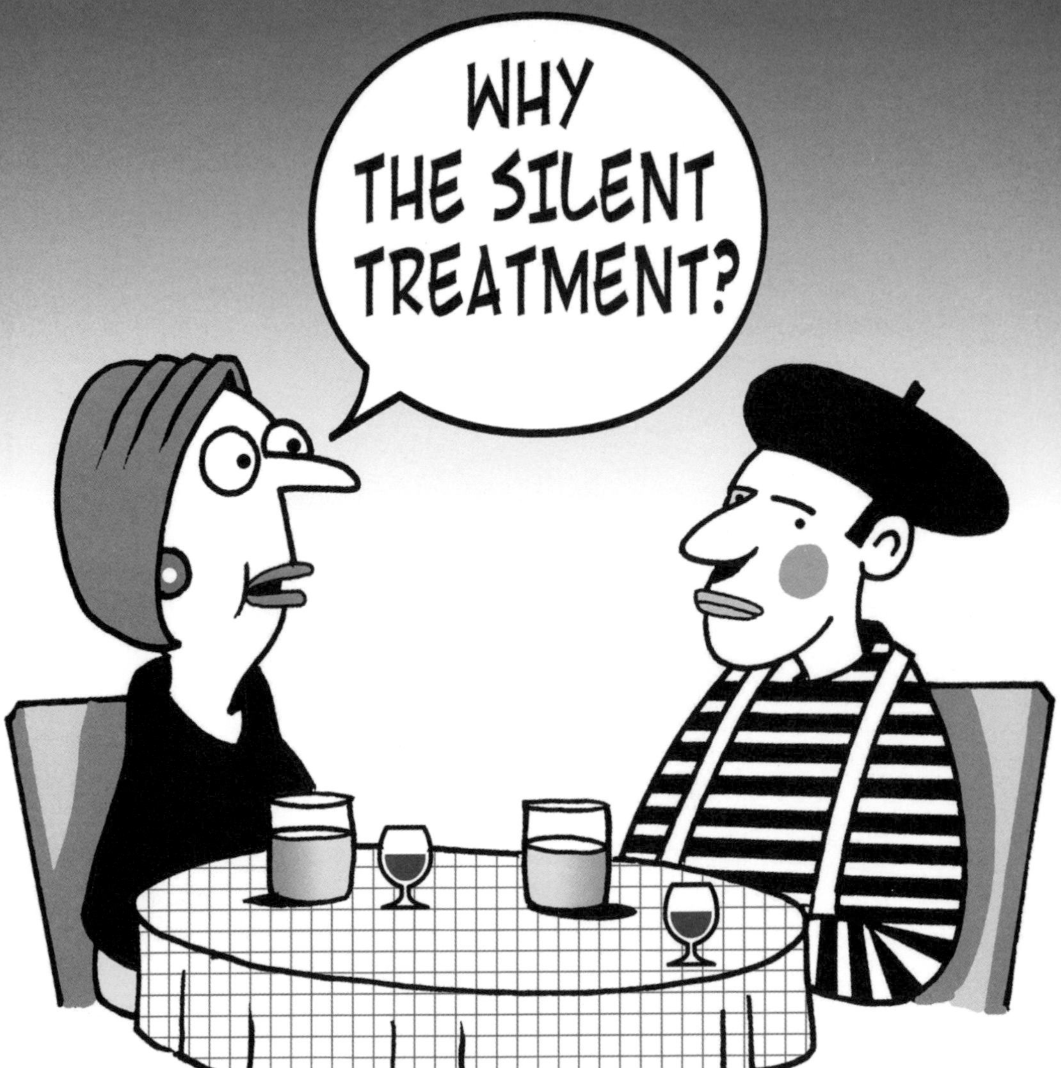
WHY THE SILENT TREATMENT?

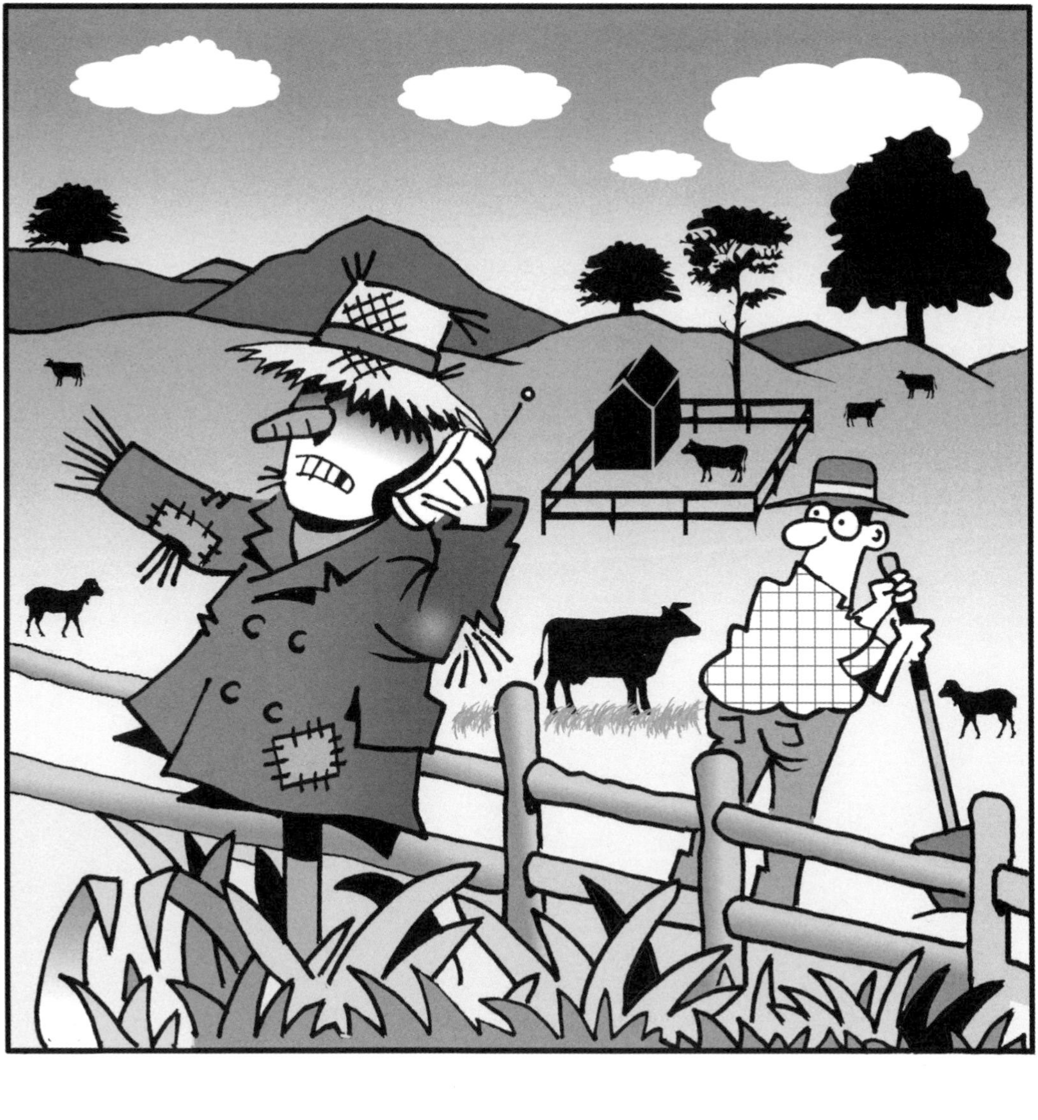

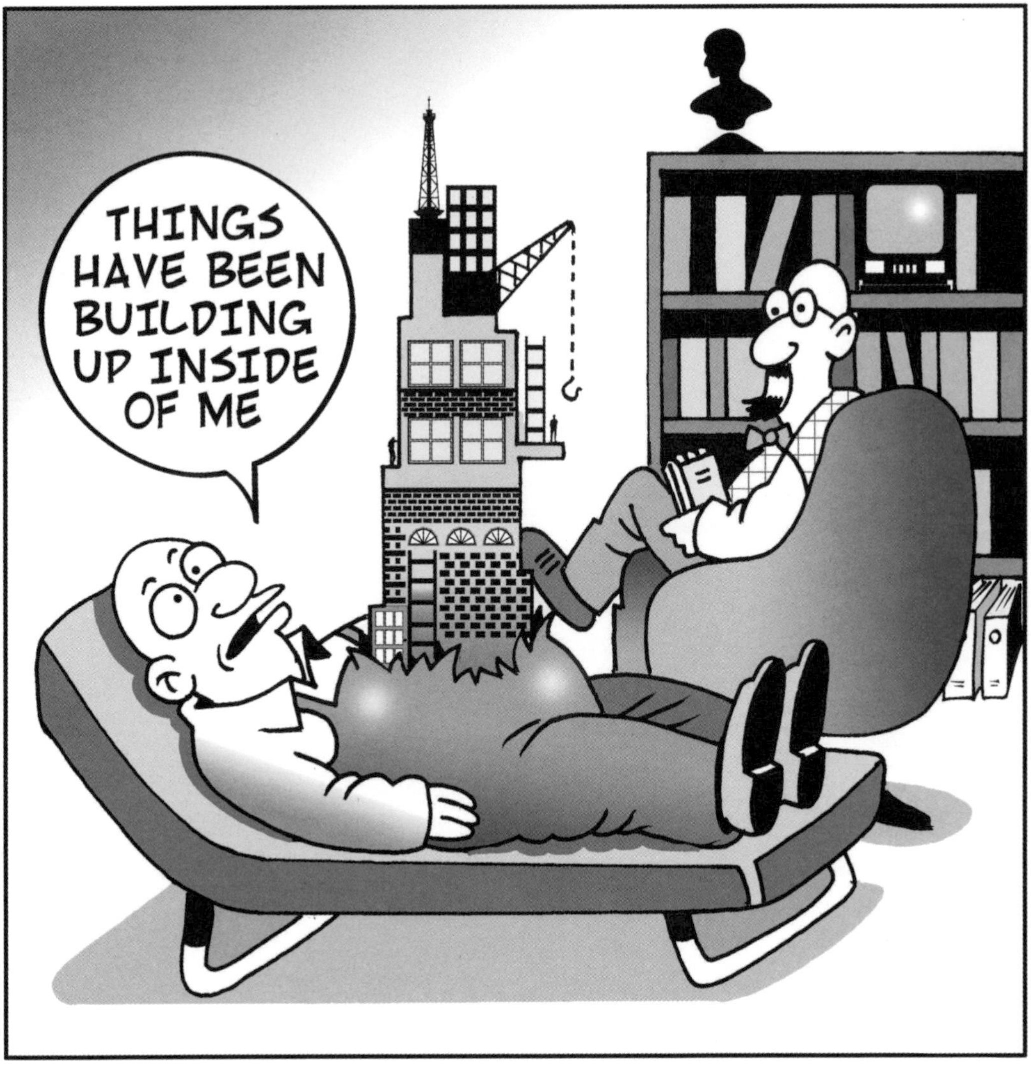
THINGS HAVE BEEN BUILDING UP INSIDE OF ME

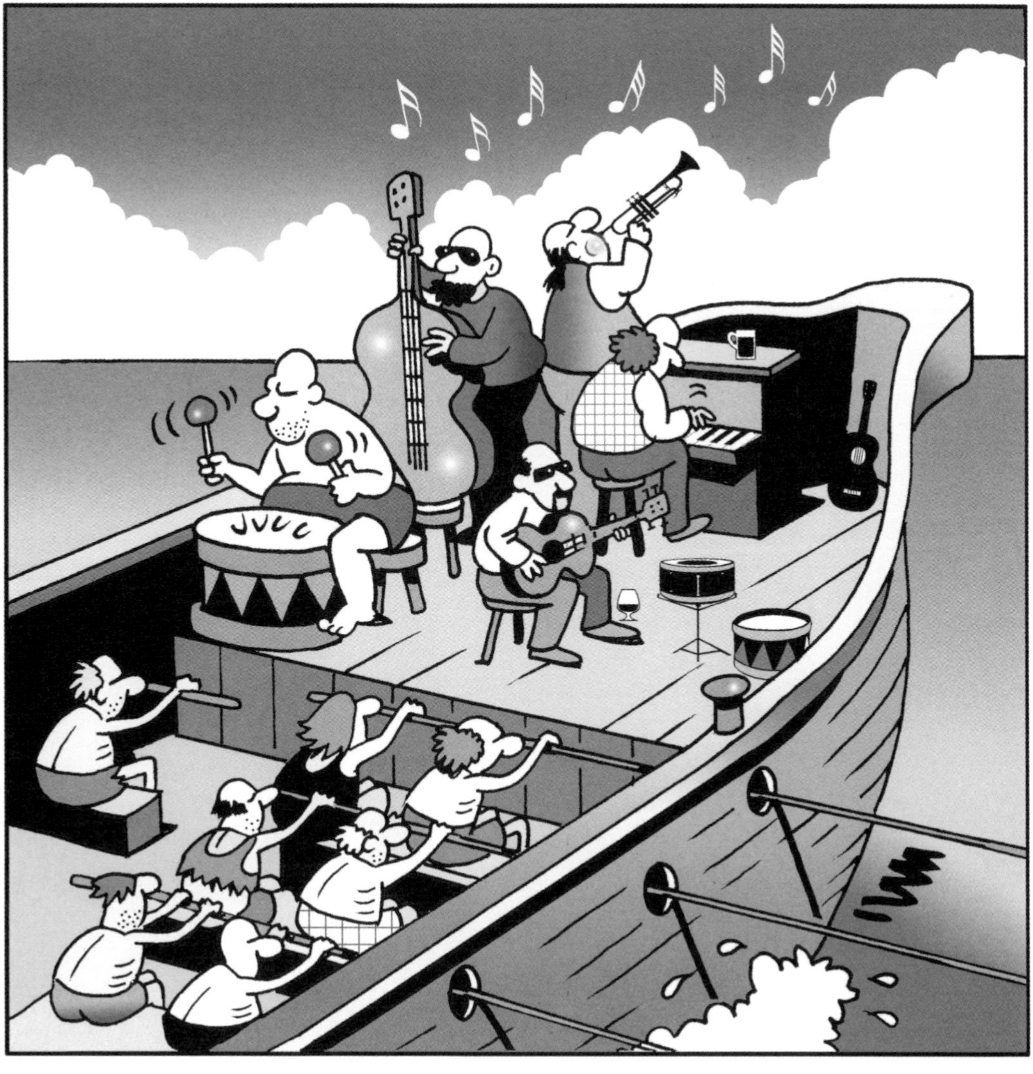

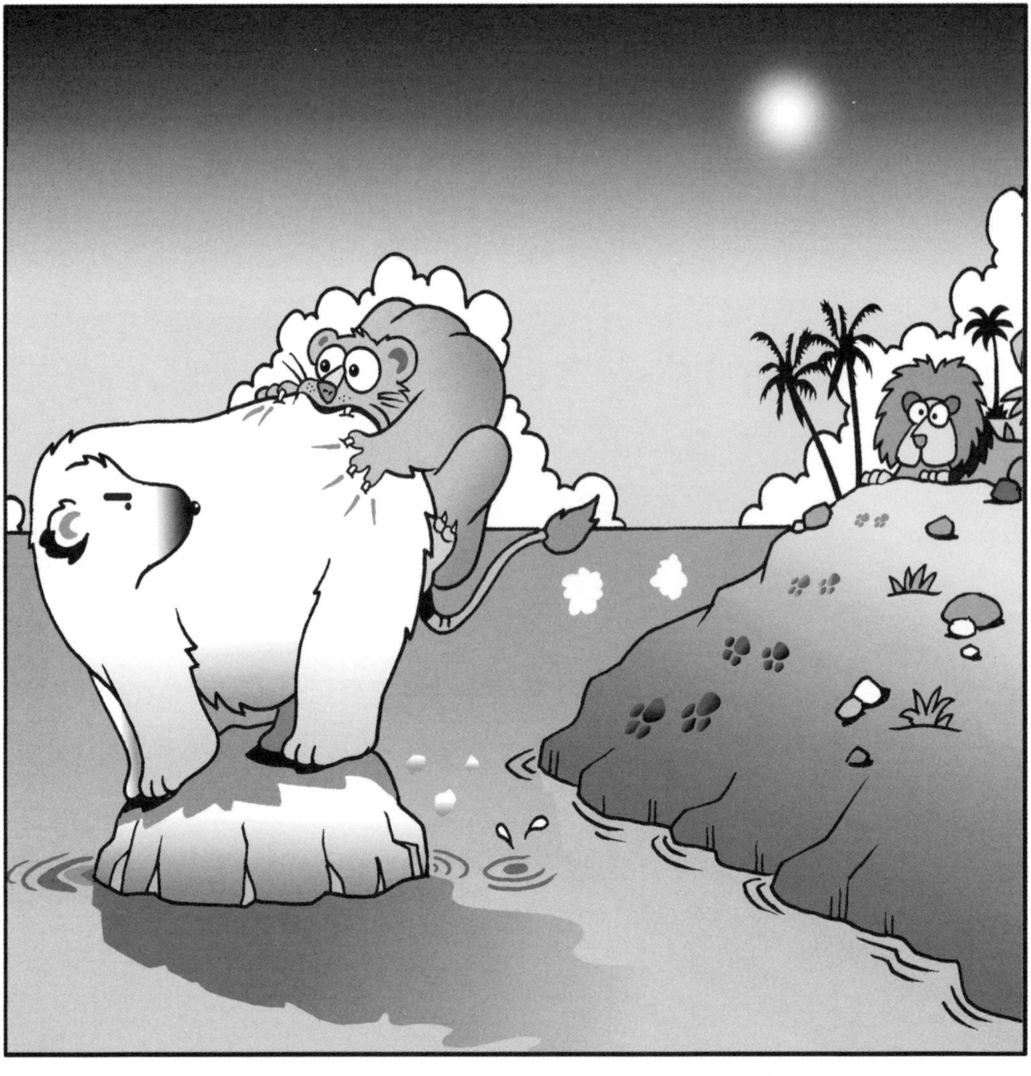

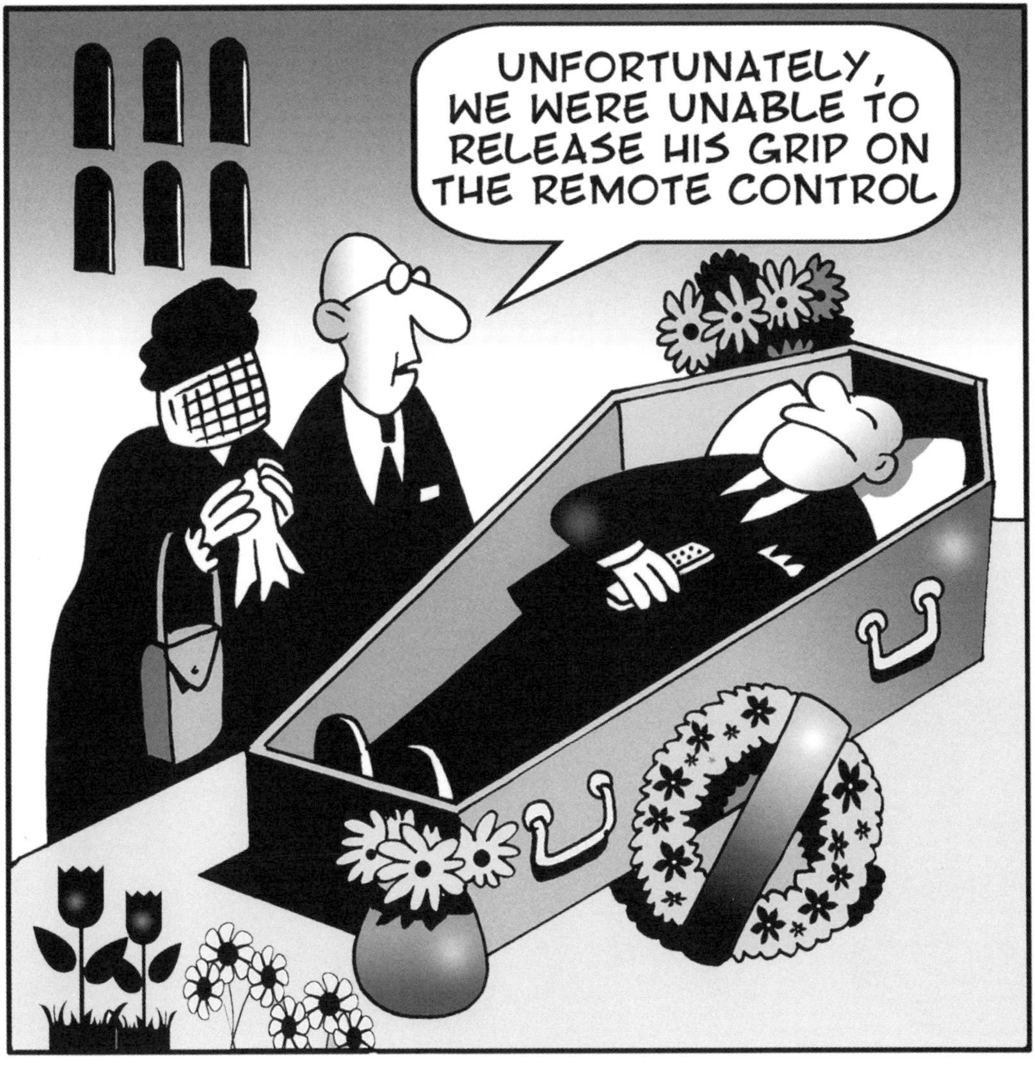
UNFORTUNATELY, WE WERE UNABLE TO RELEASE HIS GRIP ON THE REMOTE CONTROL

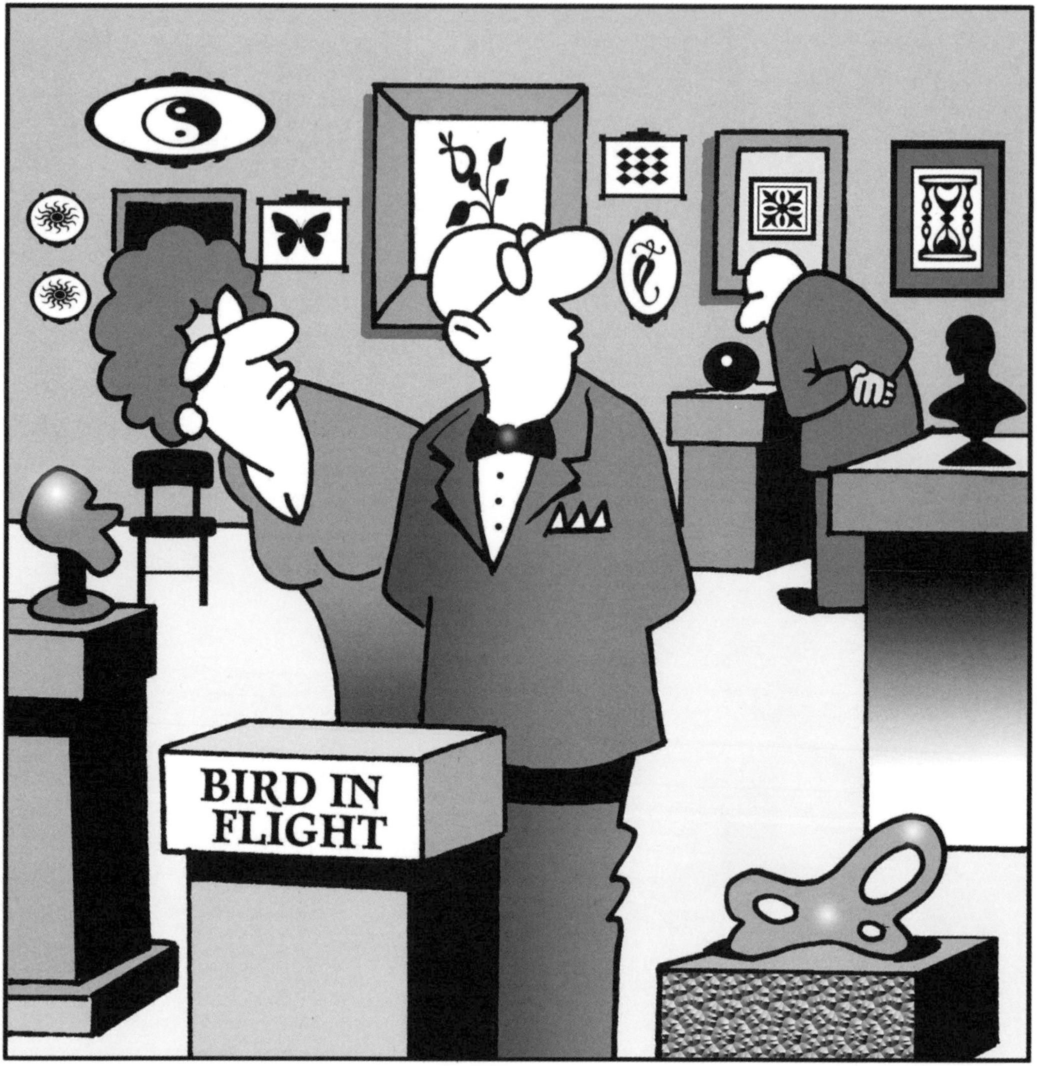
BIRD IN
FLIGHT

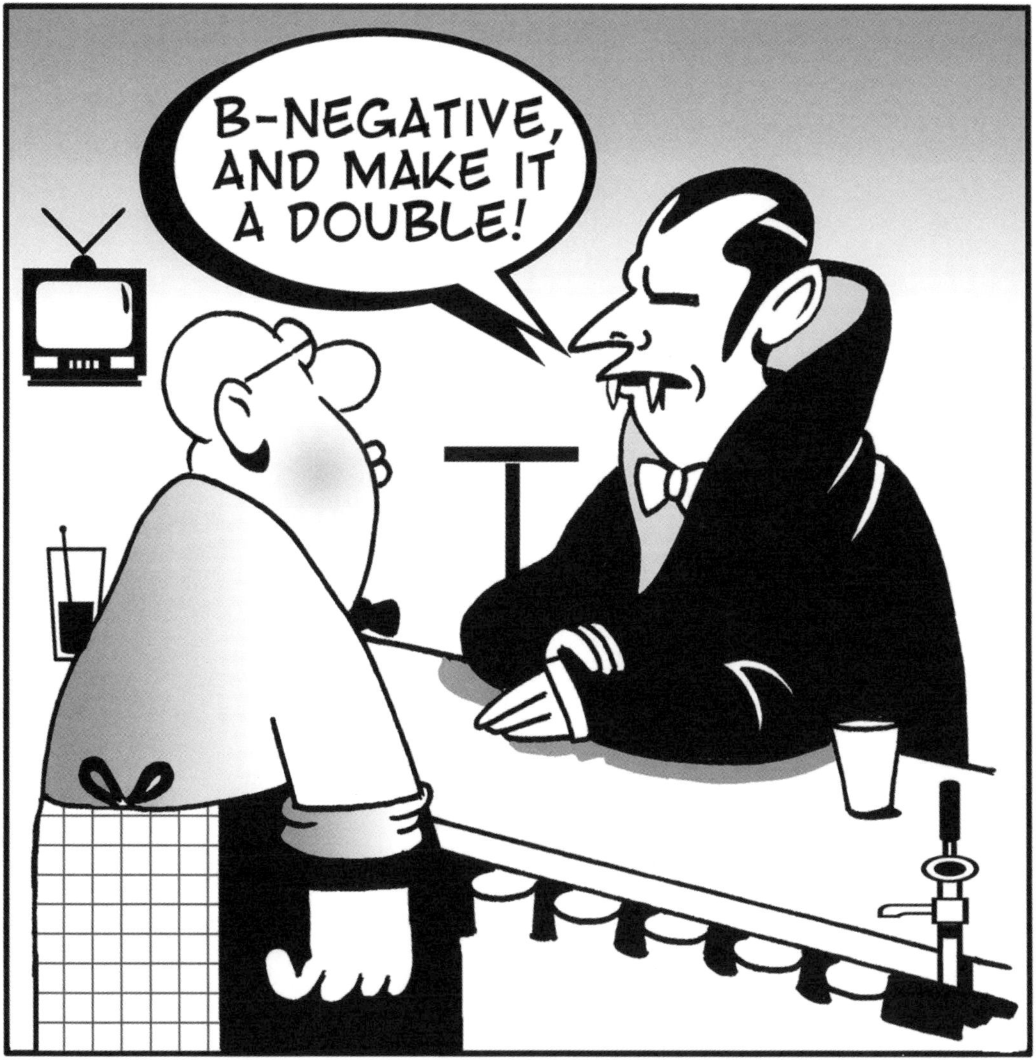
B-NEGATIVE, AND MAKE IT A DOUBLE!

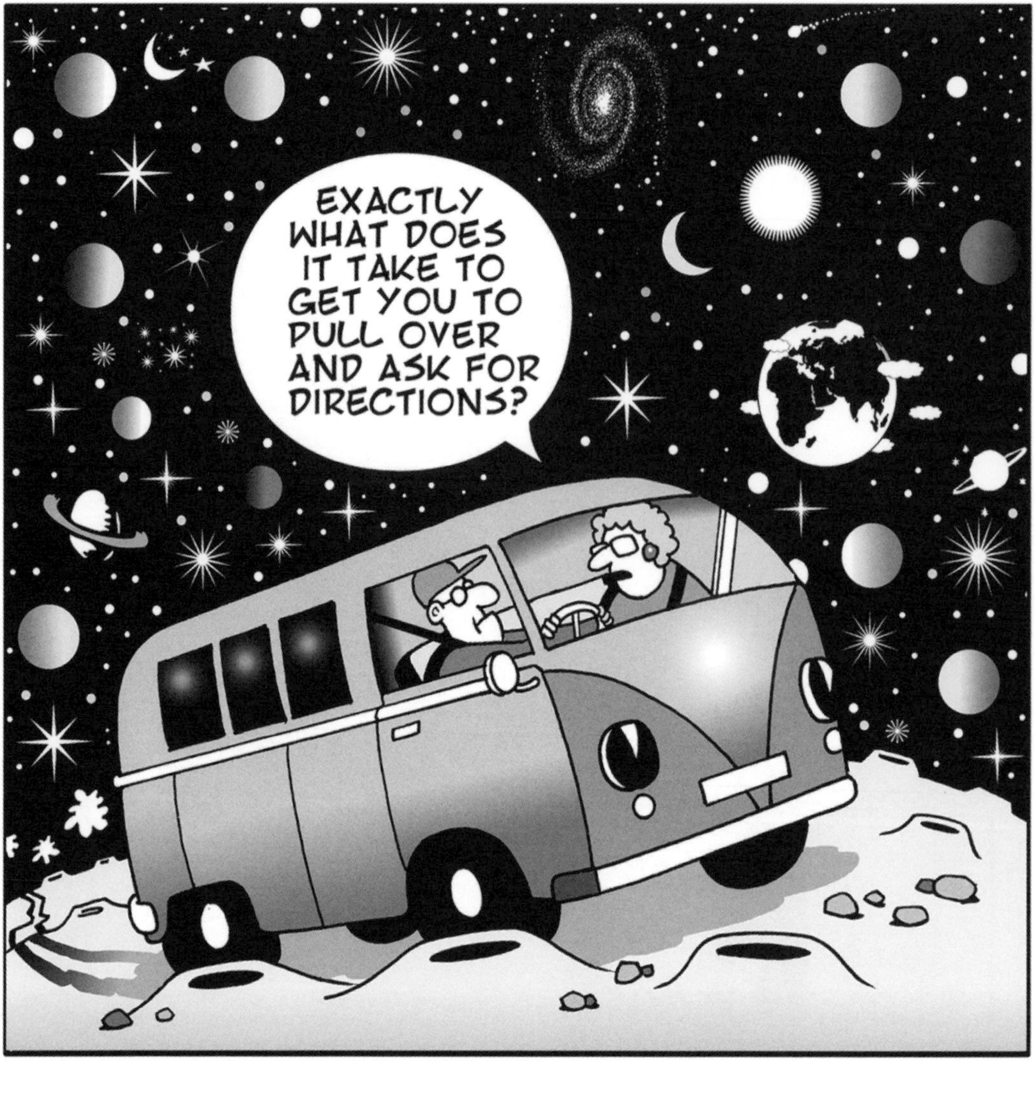
EXACTLY WHAT DOES IT TAKE TO GET YOU TO PULL OVER AND ASK FOR DIRECTIONS?

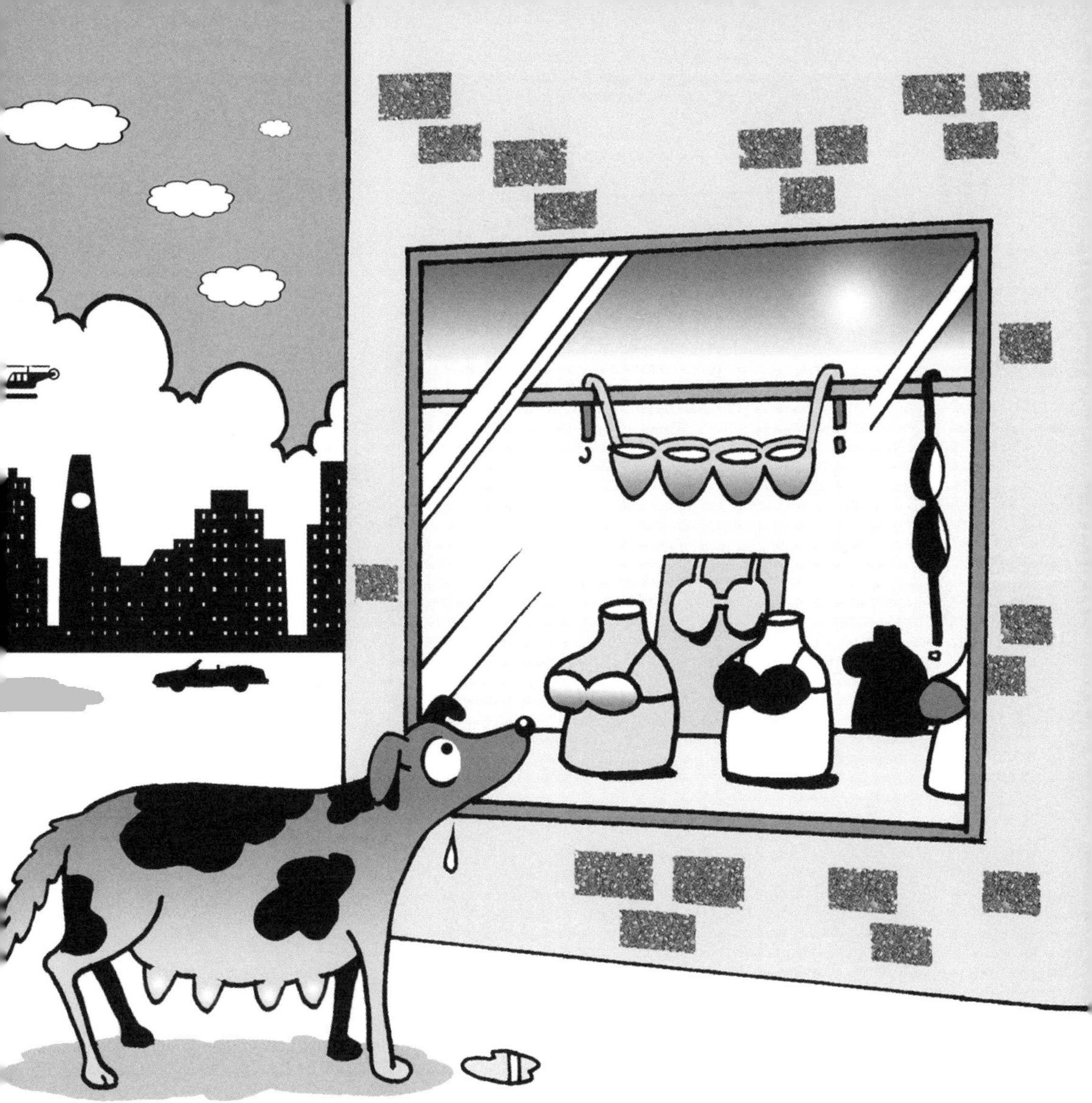

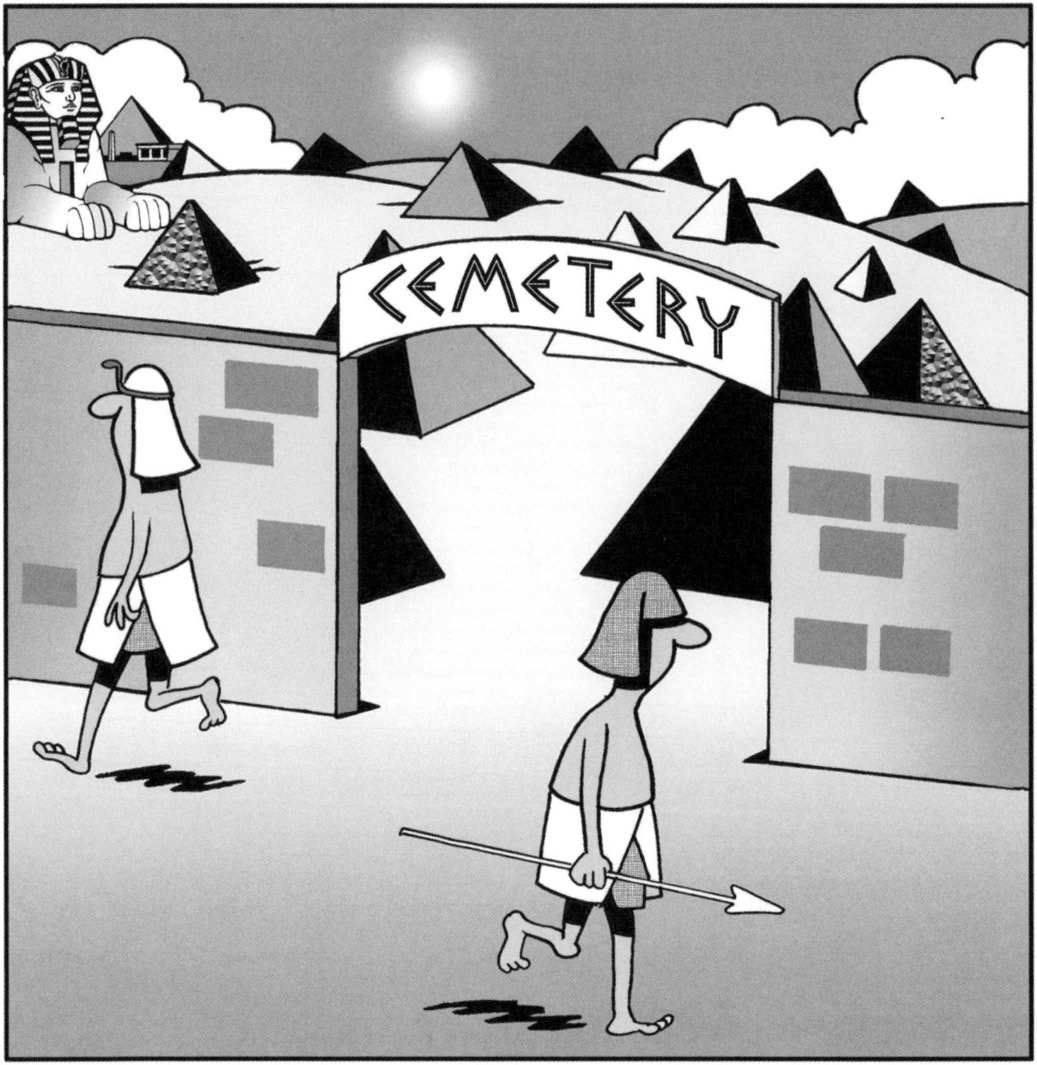
CEMETERY

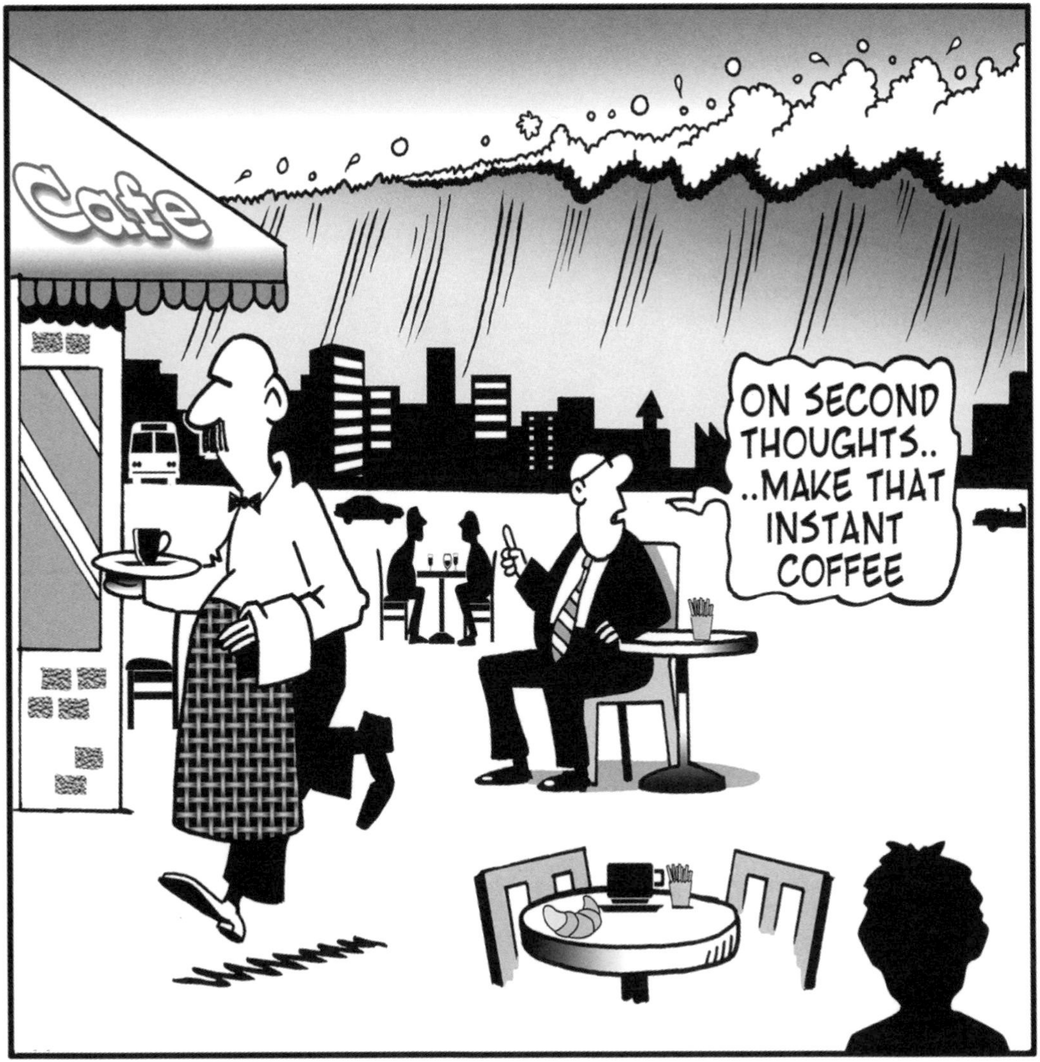
Cafe
ON SECOND THOUGHTS.. ..MAKE THAT INSTANT COFFEE

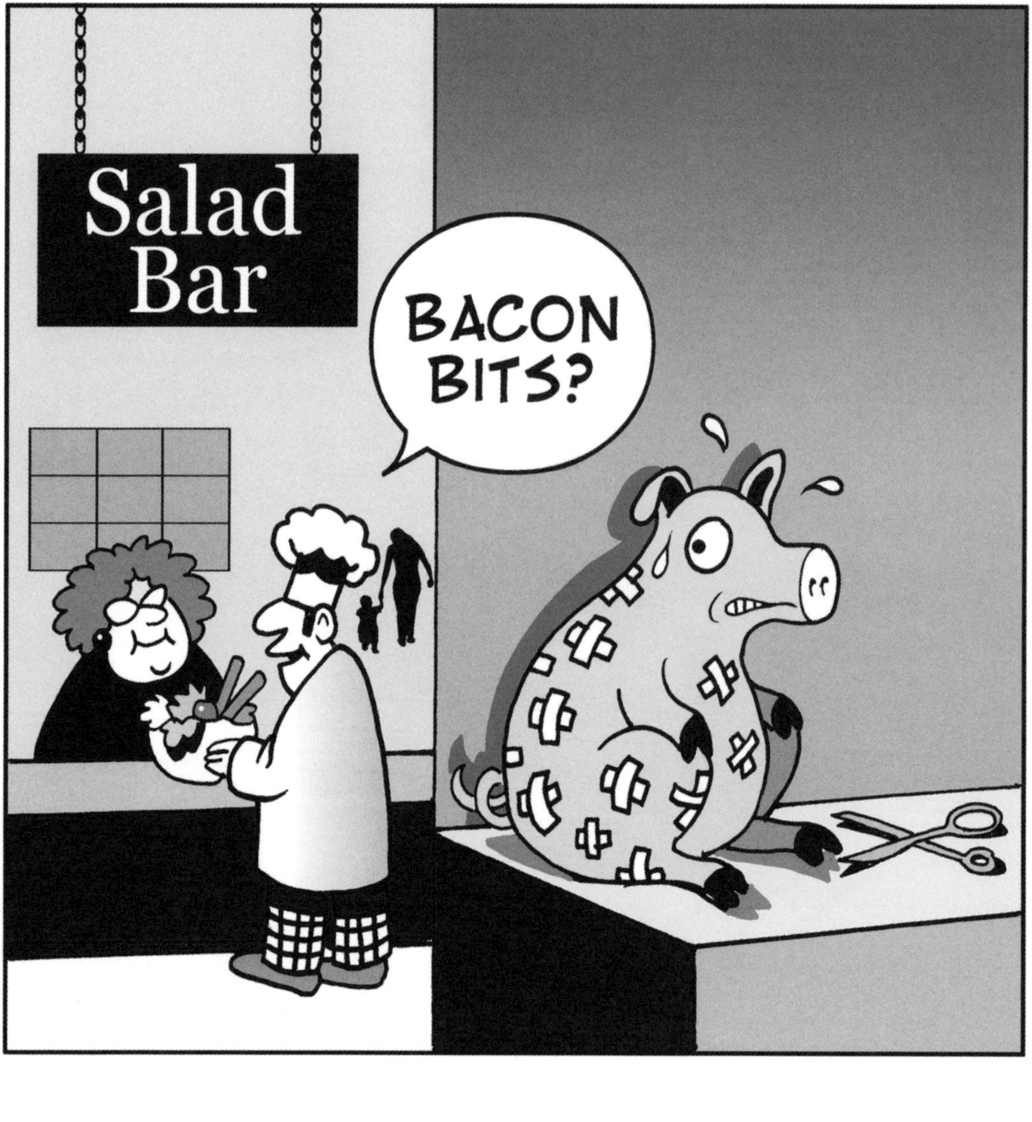
Salad Bar
BACON BITS?

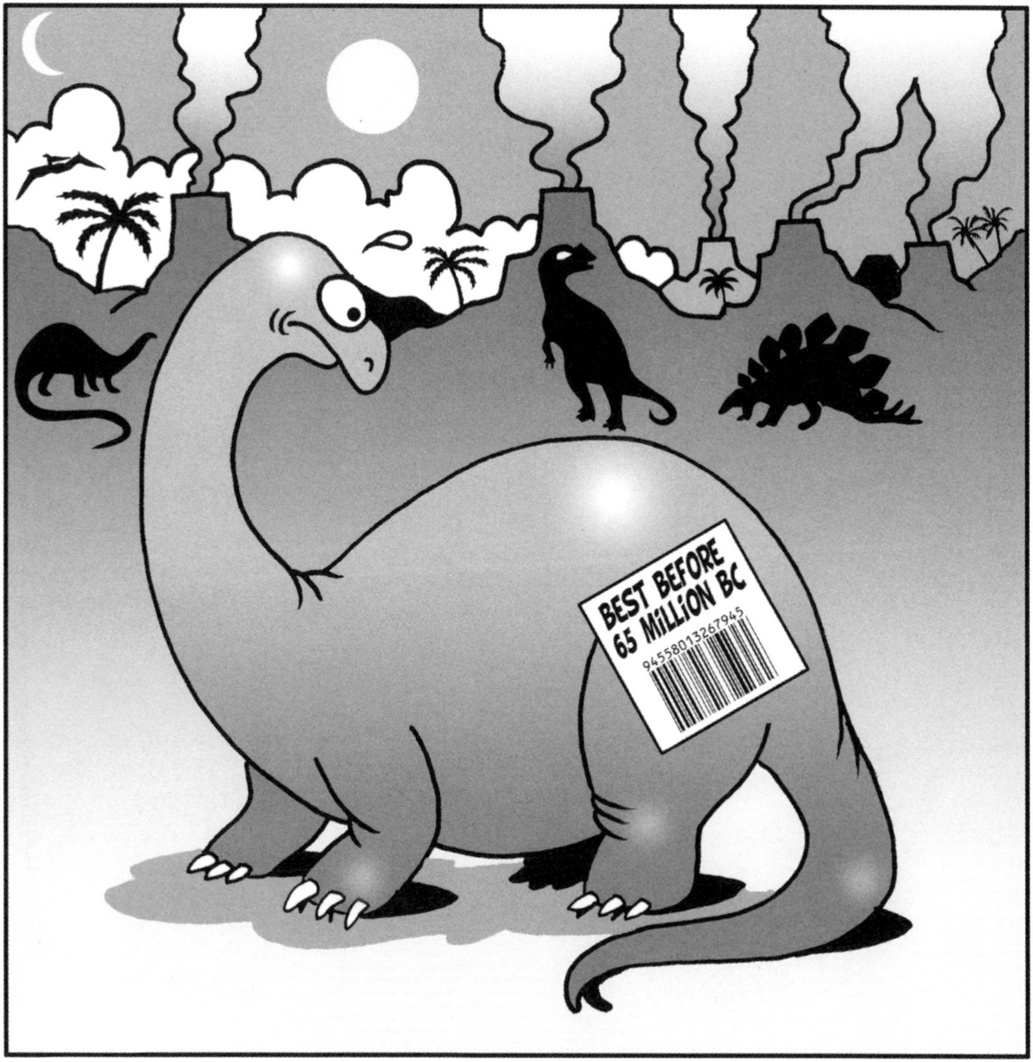
BEST BEFORE
65 MILLiON BC
94558013267945

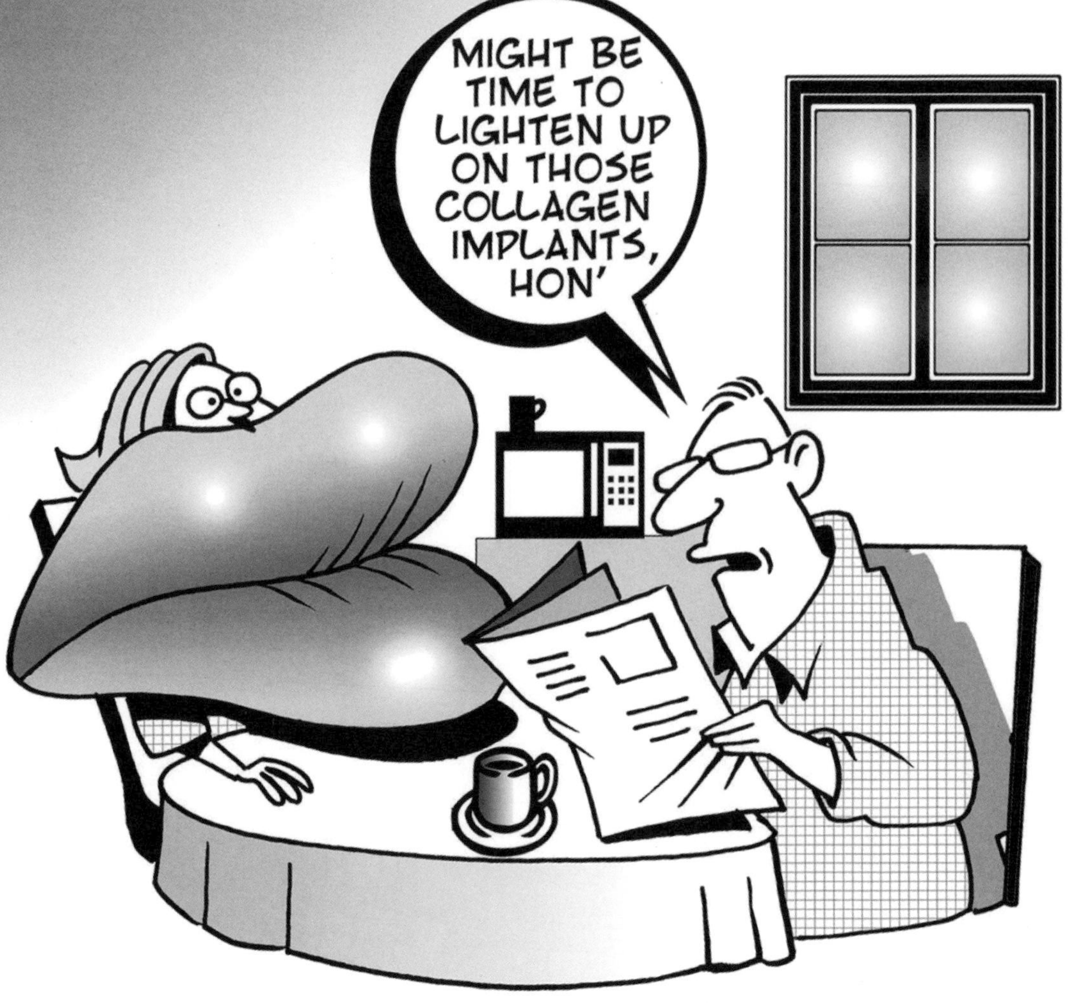
MIGHT BE TIME TO LIGHTEN UP ON THOSE COLLAGEN IMPLANTS, HON'

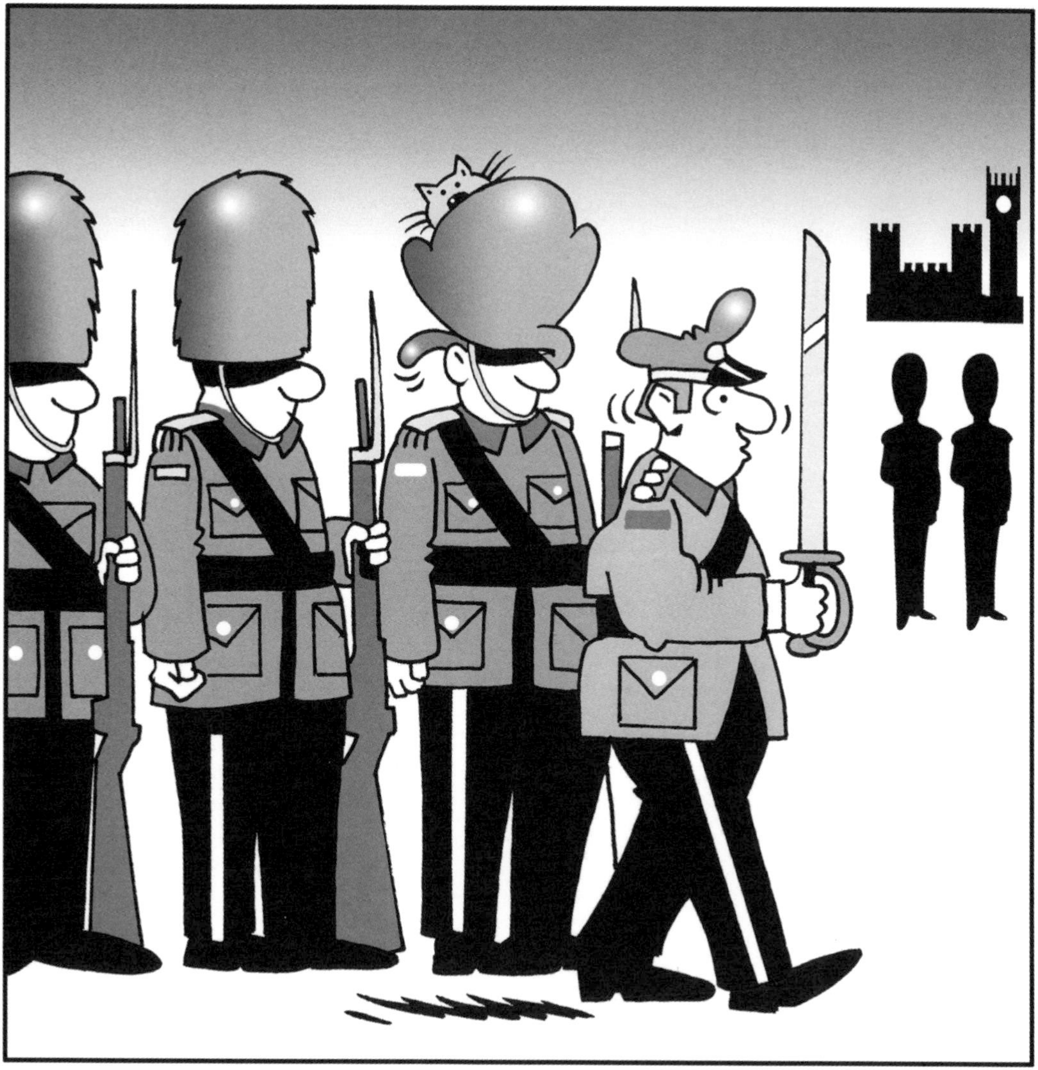

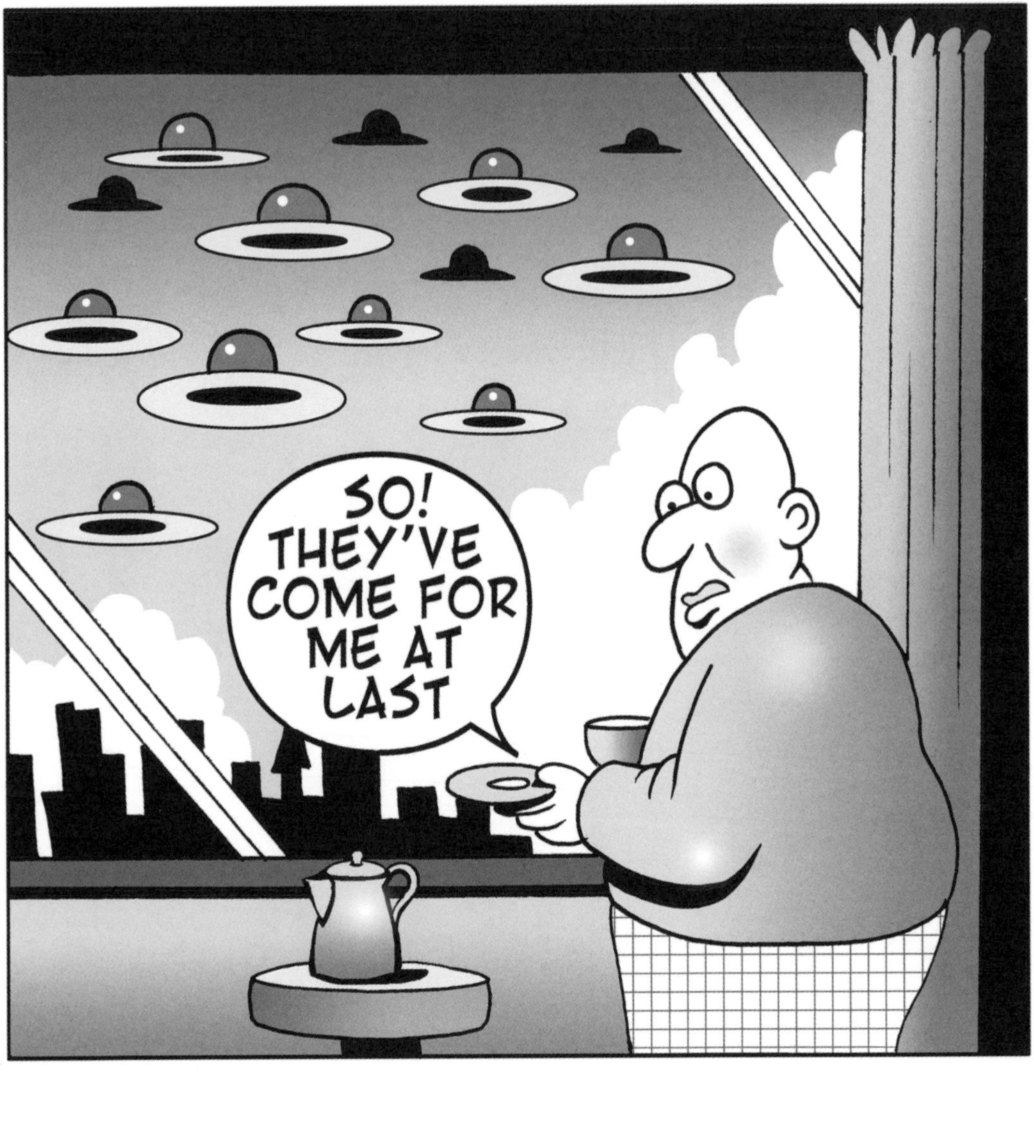
SO! THEY'VE COME FOR ME AT LAST

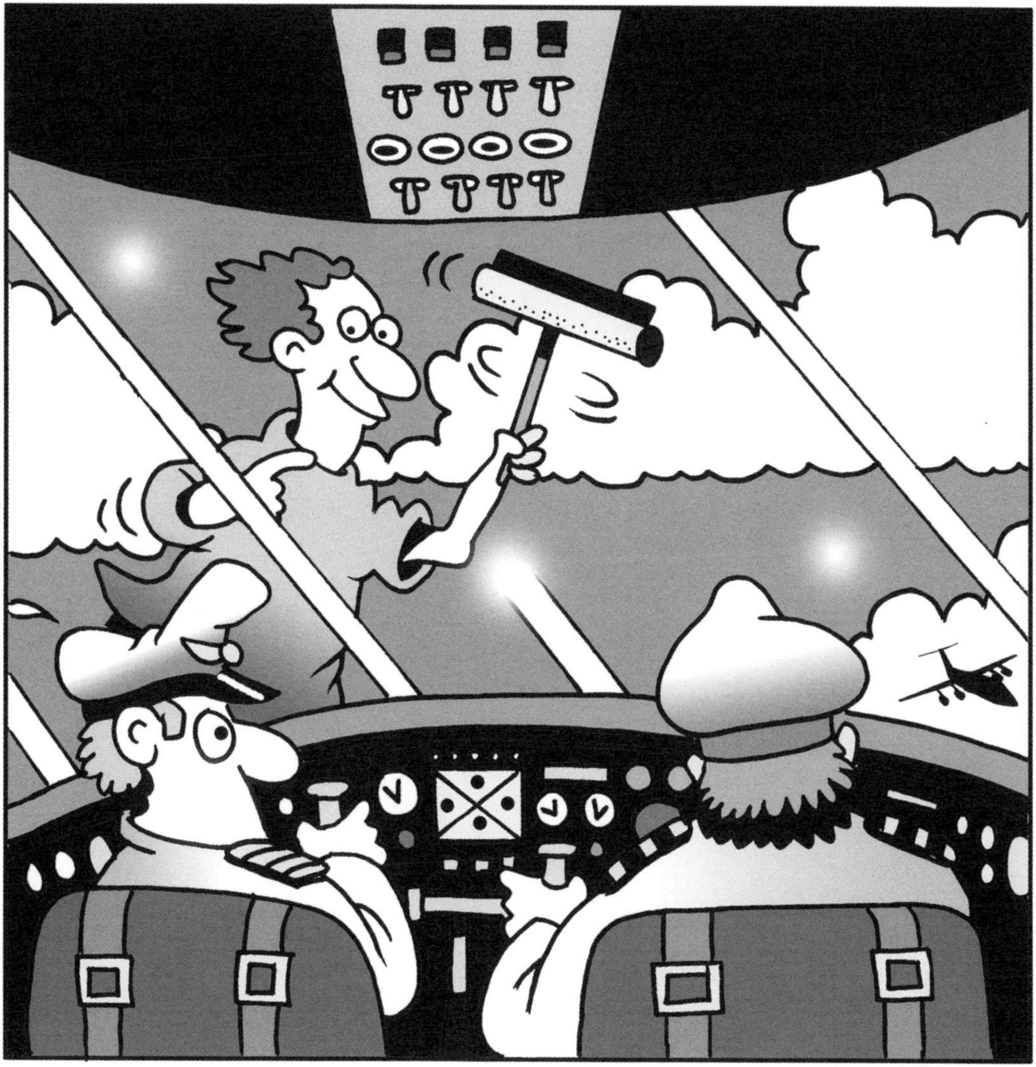

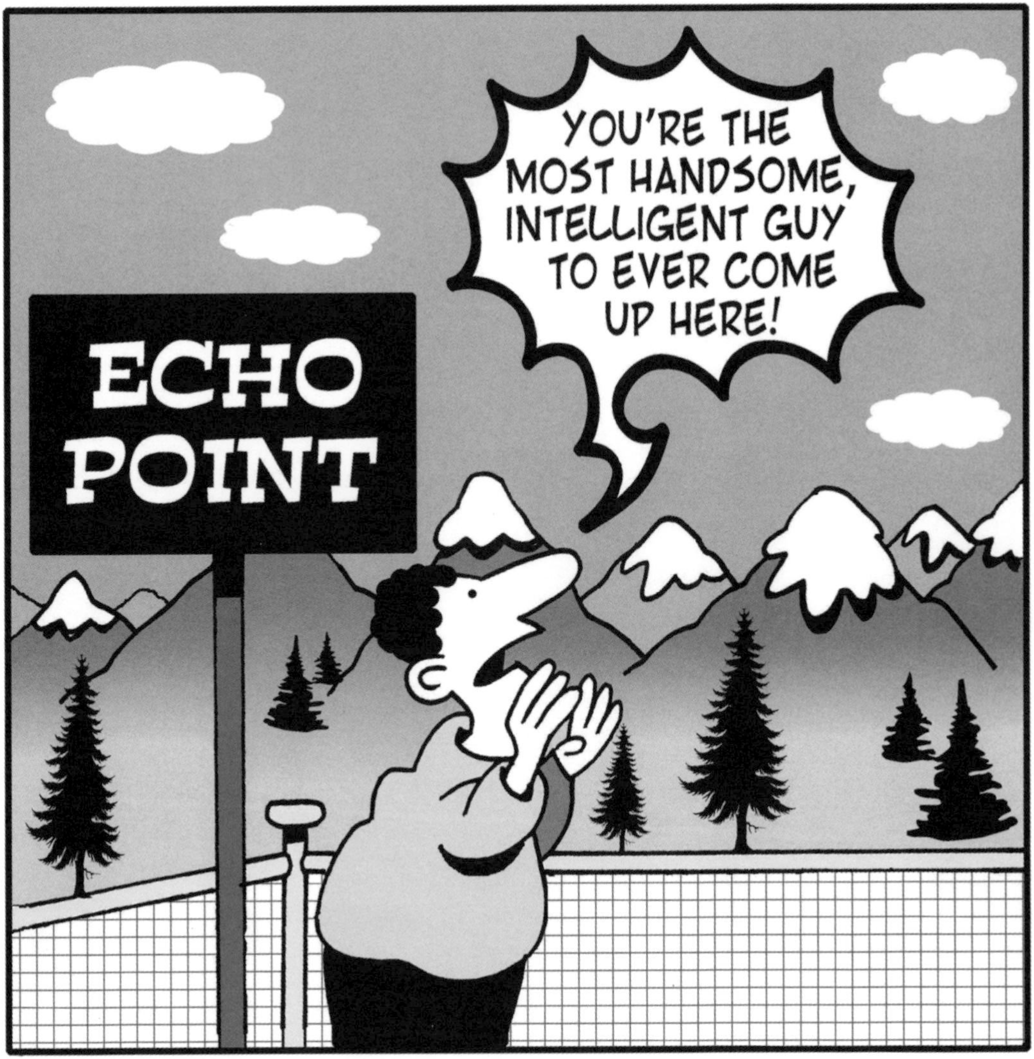
ECHO POINT
YOU'RE THE MOST HANDSOME, INTELLIGENT GUY TO EVER COME UP HERE!

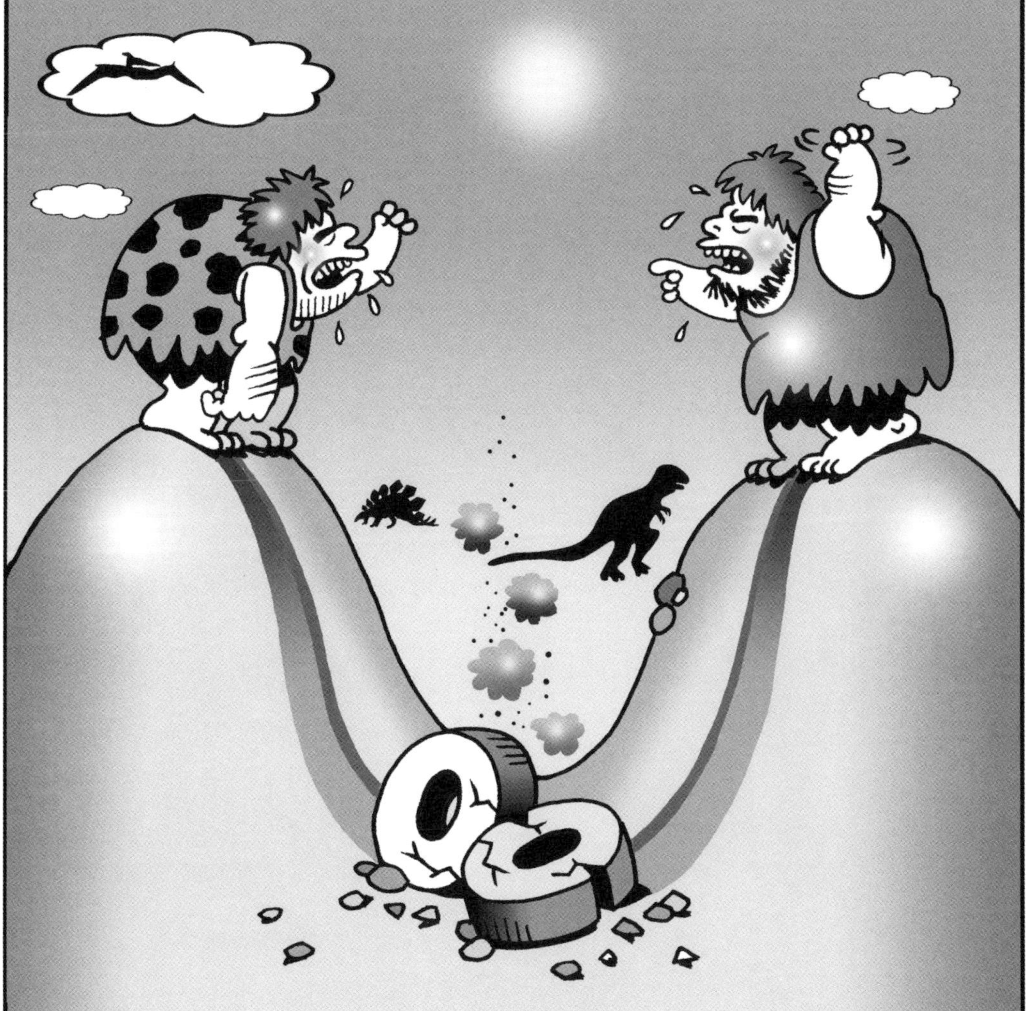

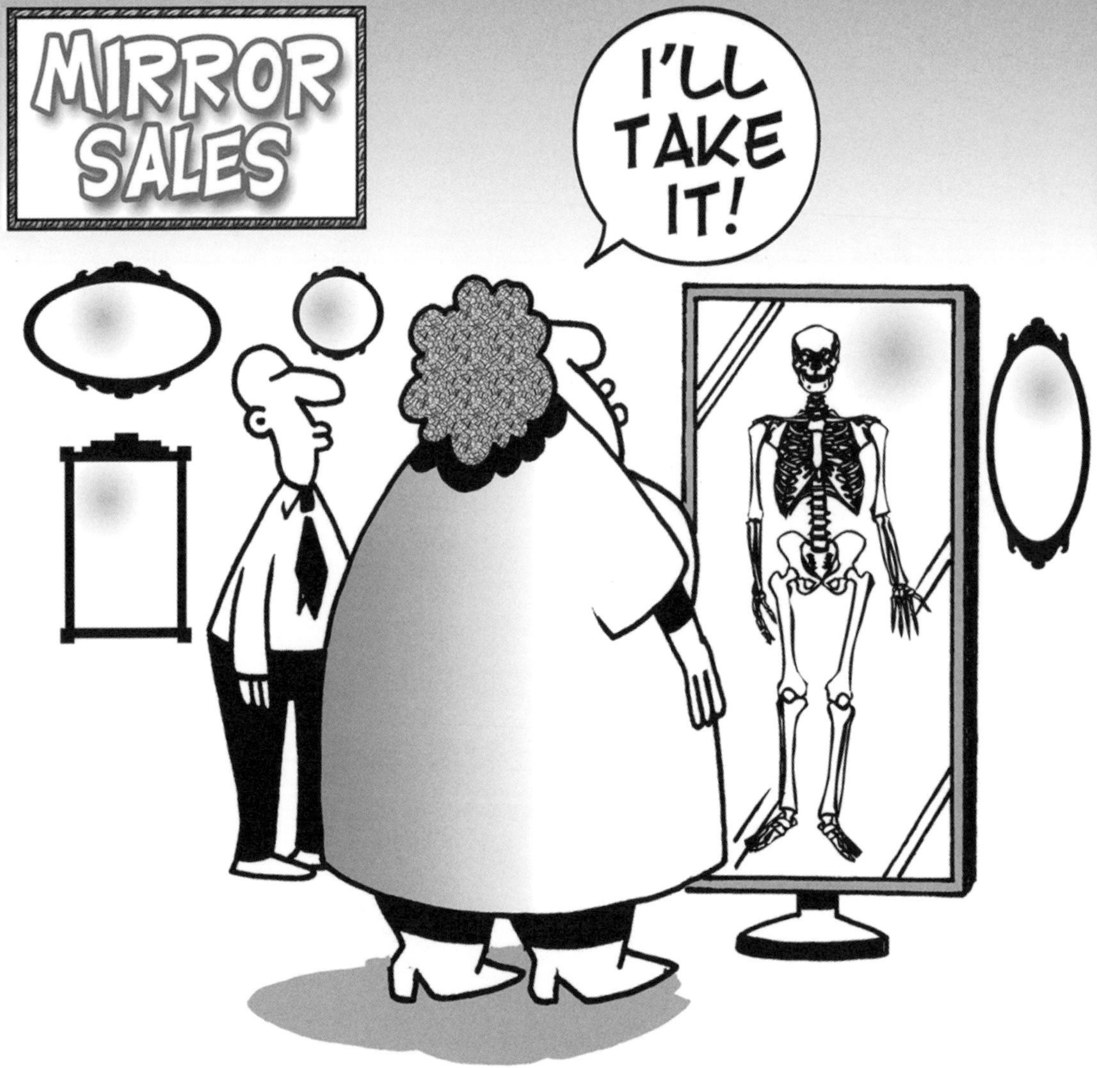
MIRROR SALES
I'LL TAKE IT!

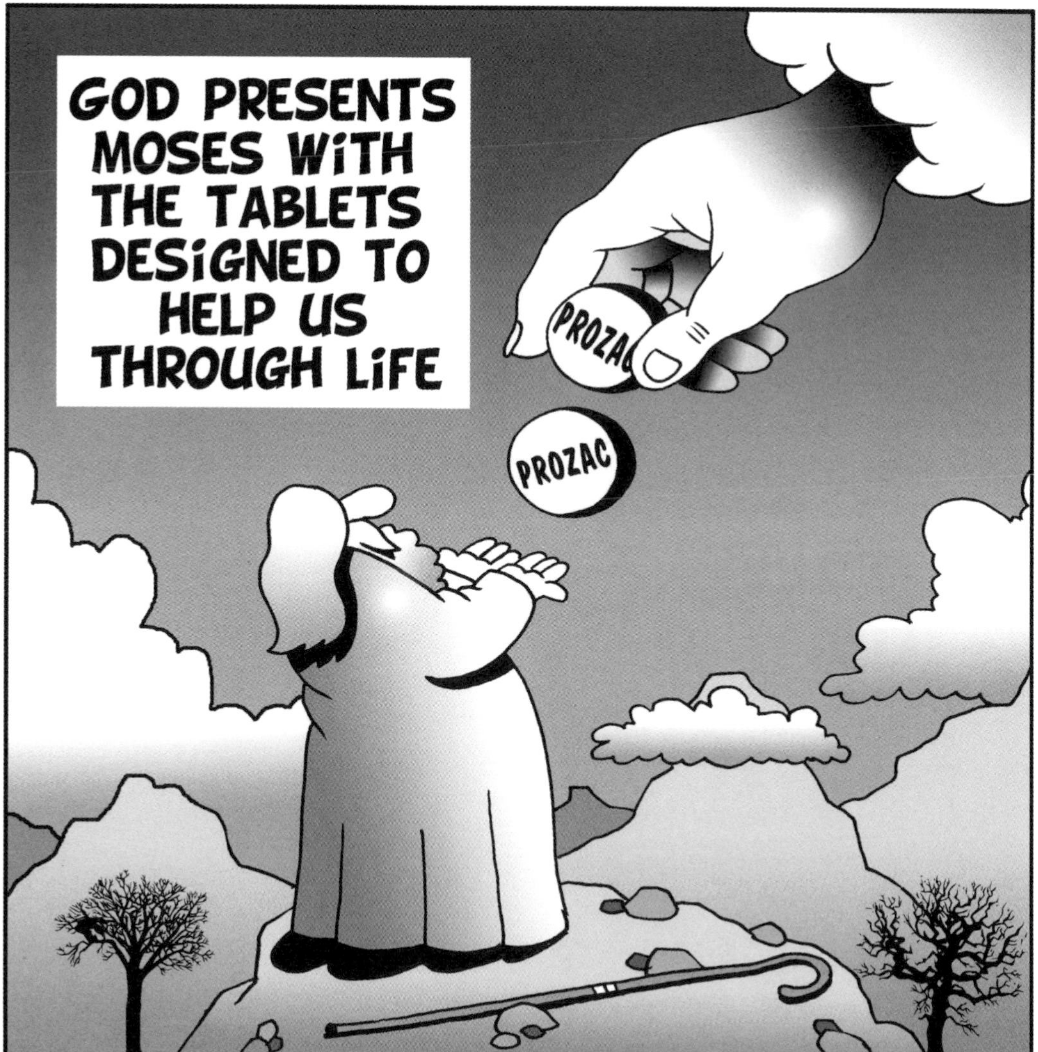
GOD PRESENTS MOSES WiTH THE TABLETS DESiGNED TO HELP US THROUGH LiFE
PROZAC
PROZAC

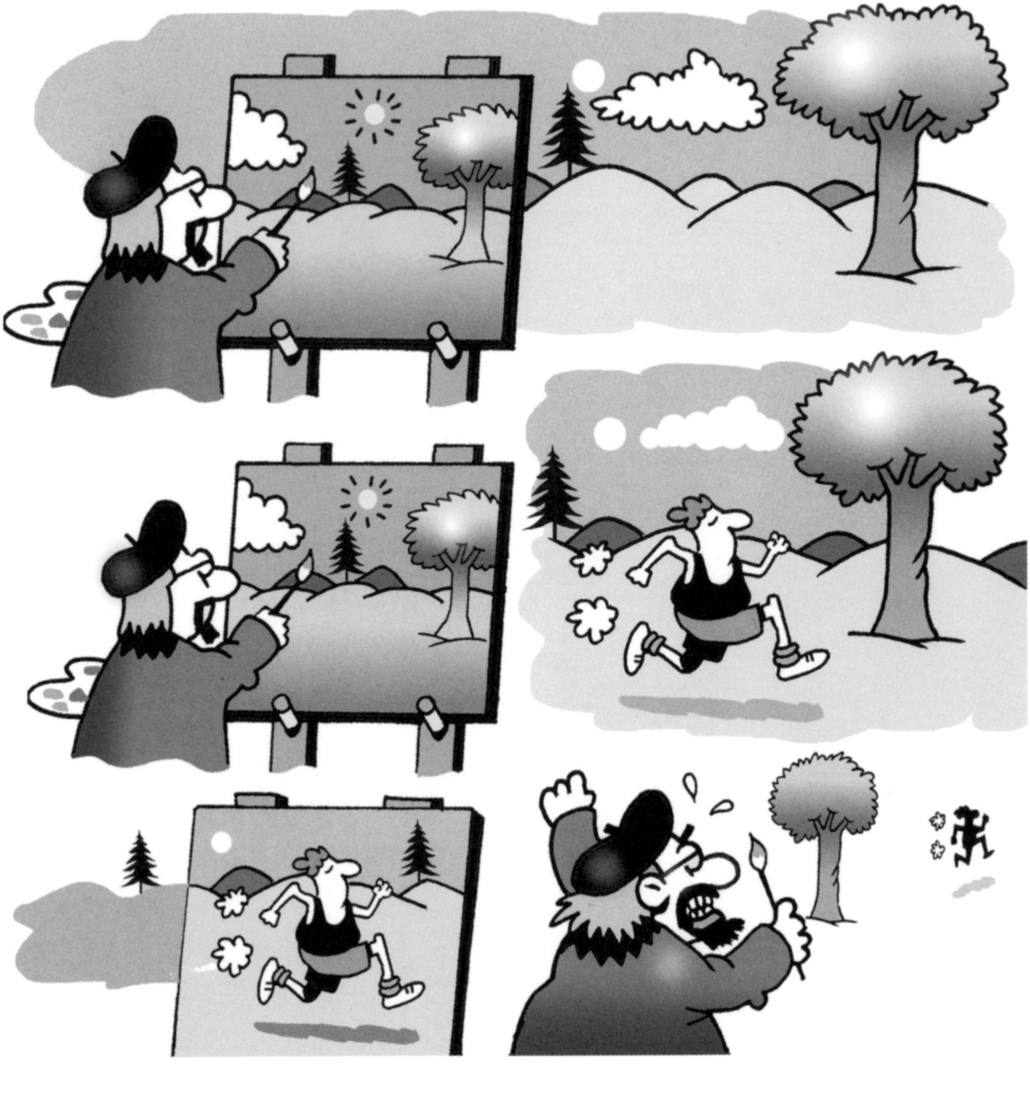

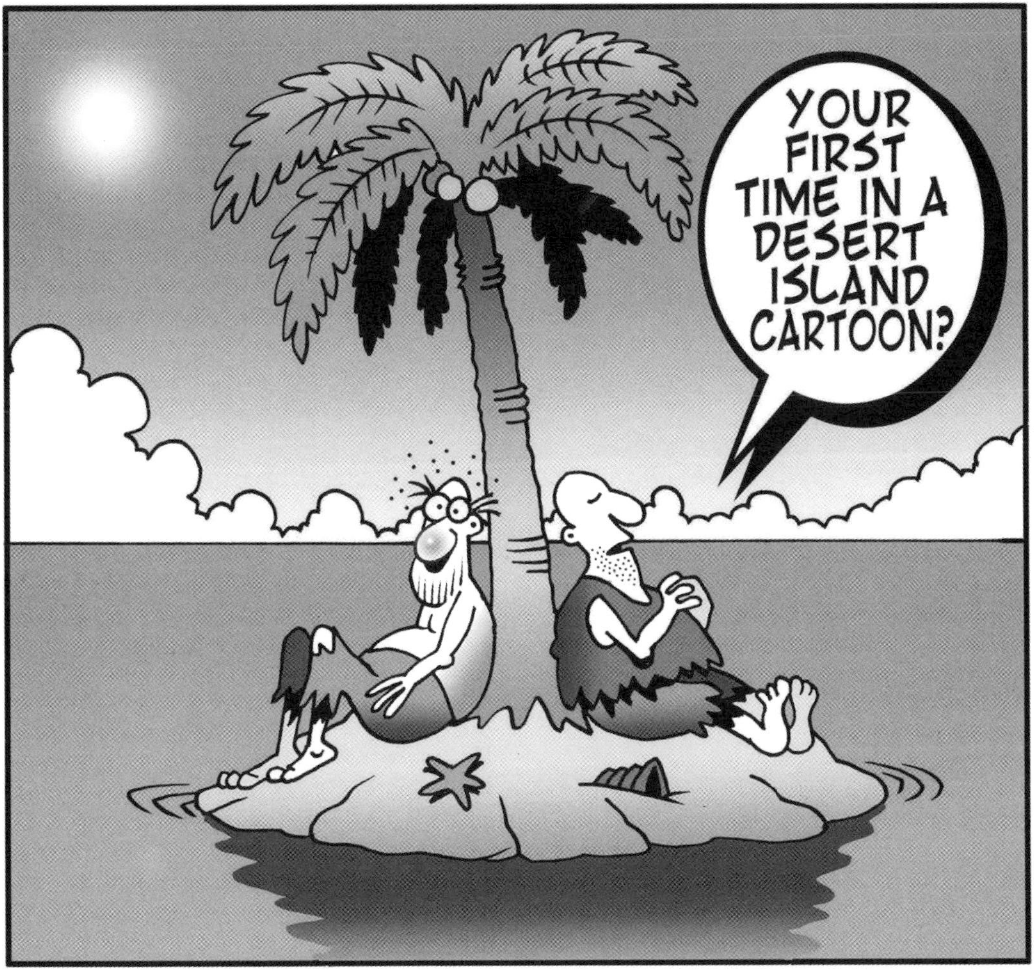
YOUR FIRST TIME IN A DESERT ISLAND CARTOON?

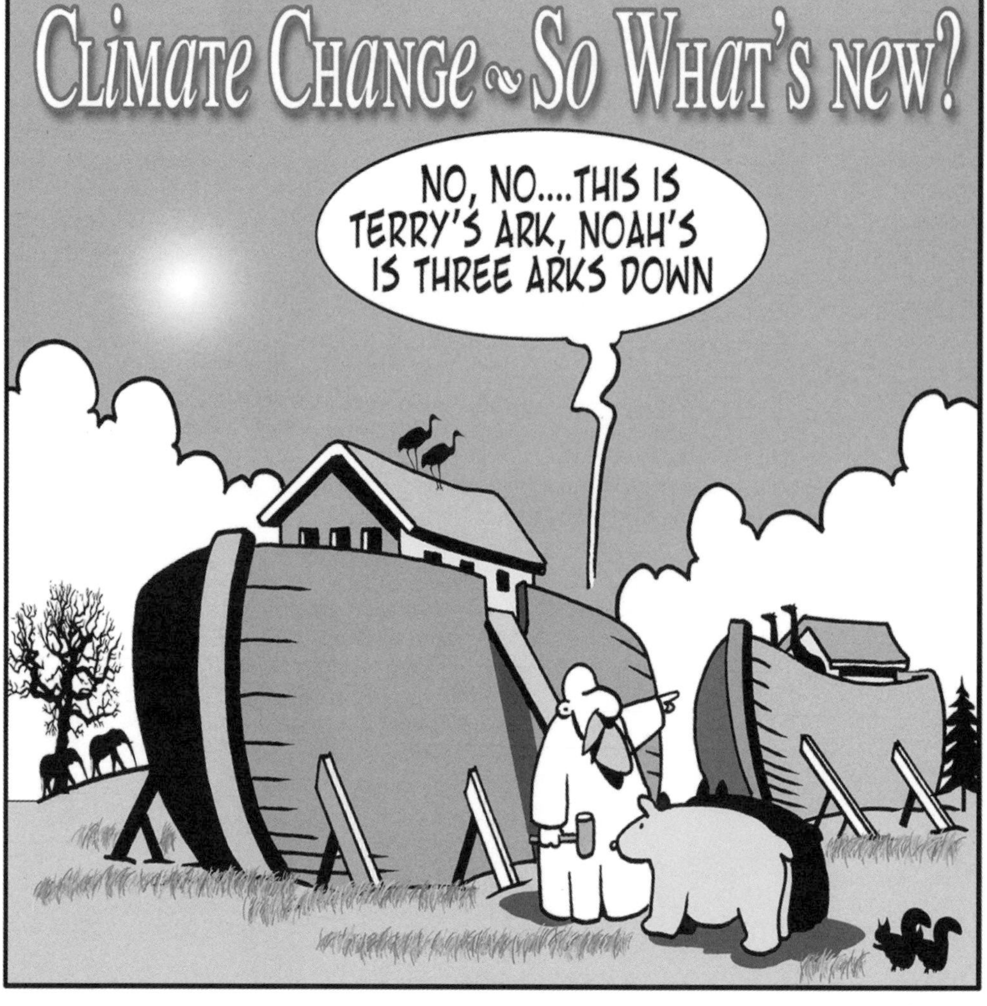
CLIMATE CHANGE ~ SO WHAT'S NEW?
NO, NO....THIS IS TERRY'S ARK, NOAH'S IS THREE ARKS DOWN

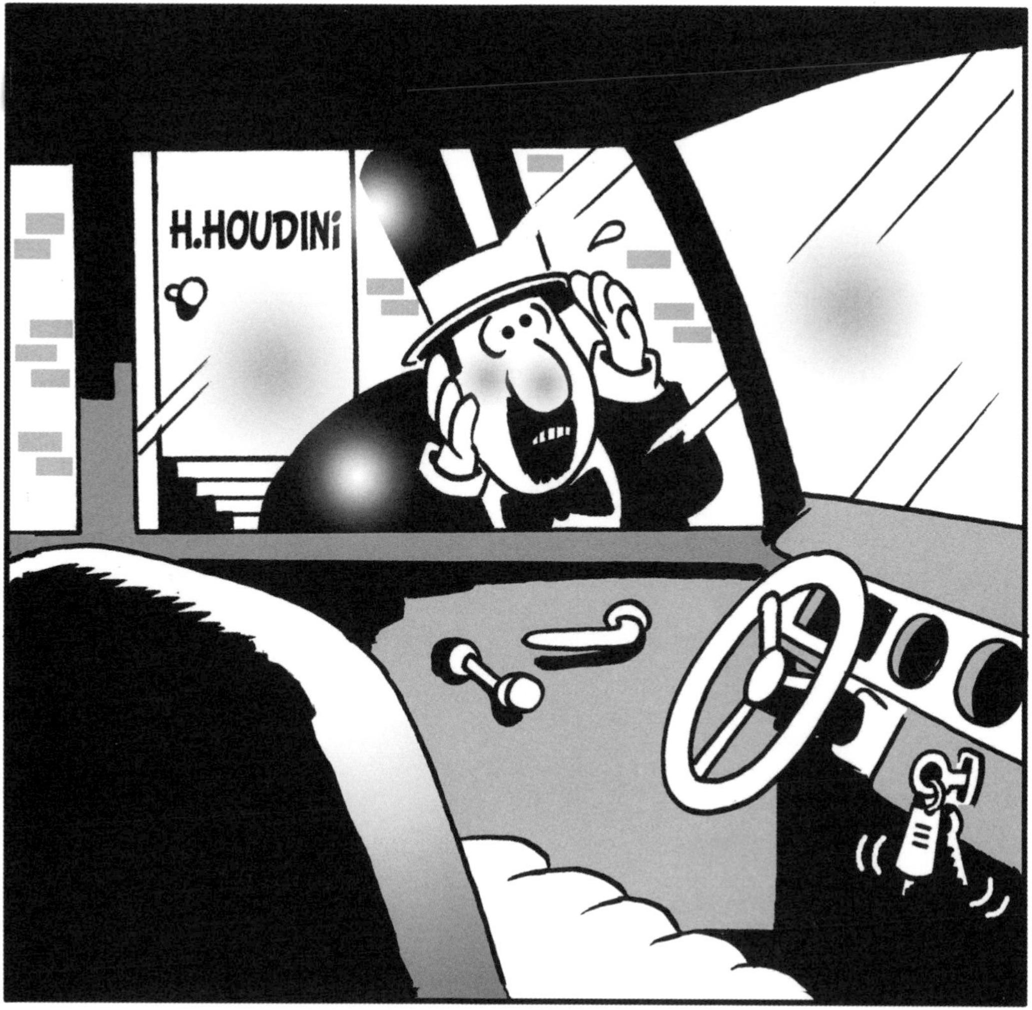
H.HOUDINI

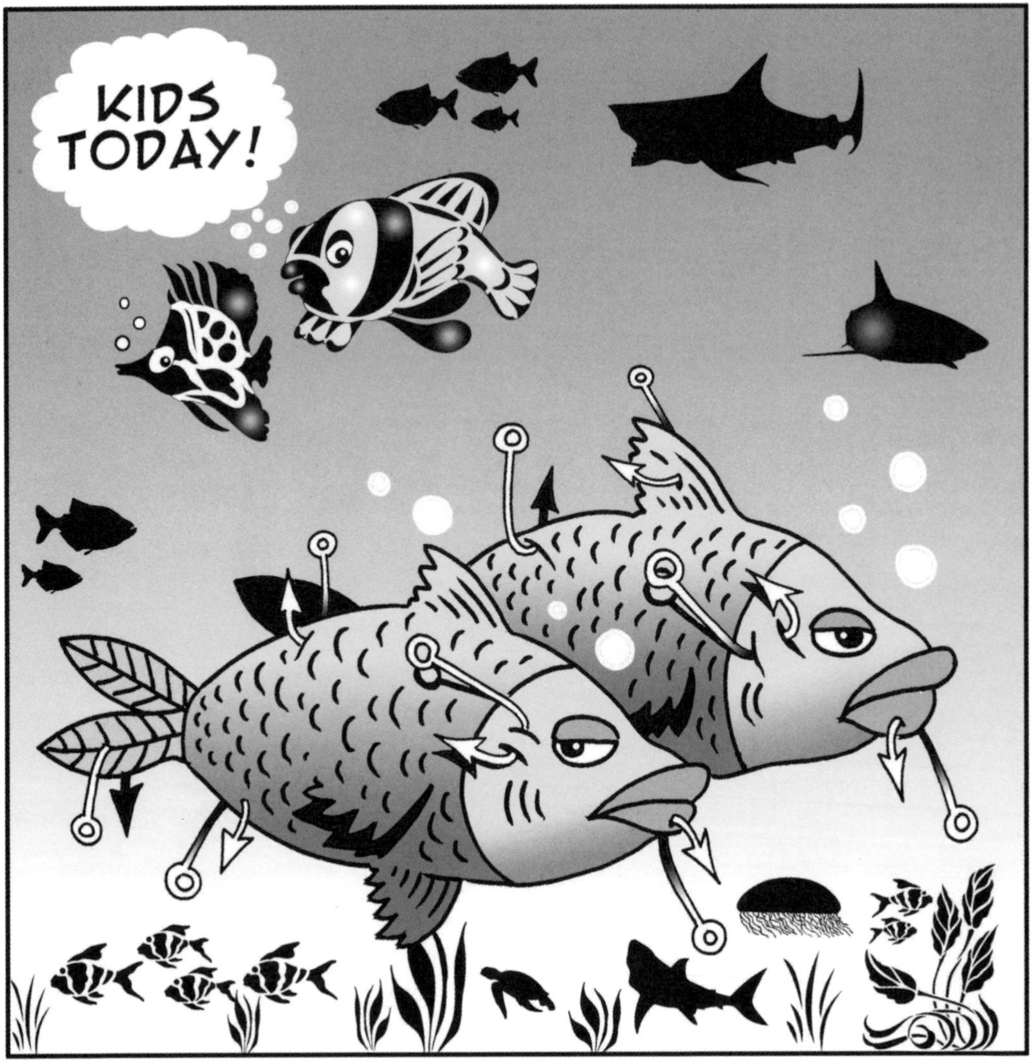
KIDS TODAY!

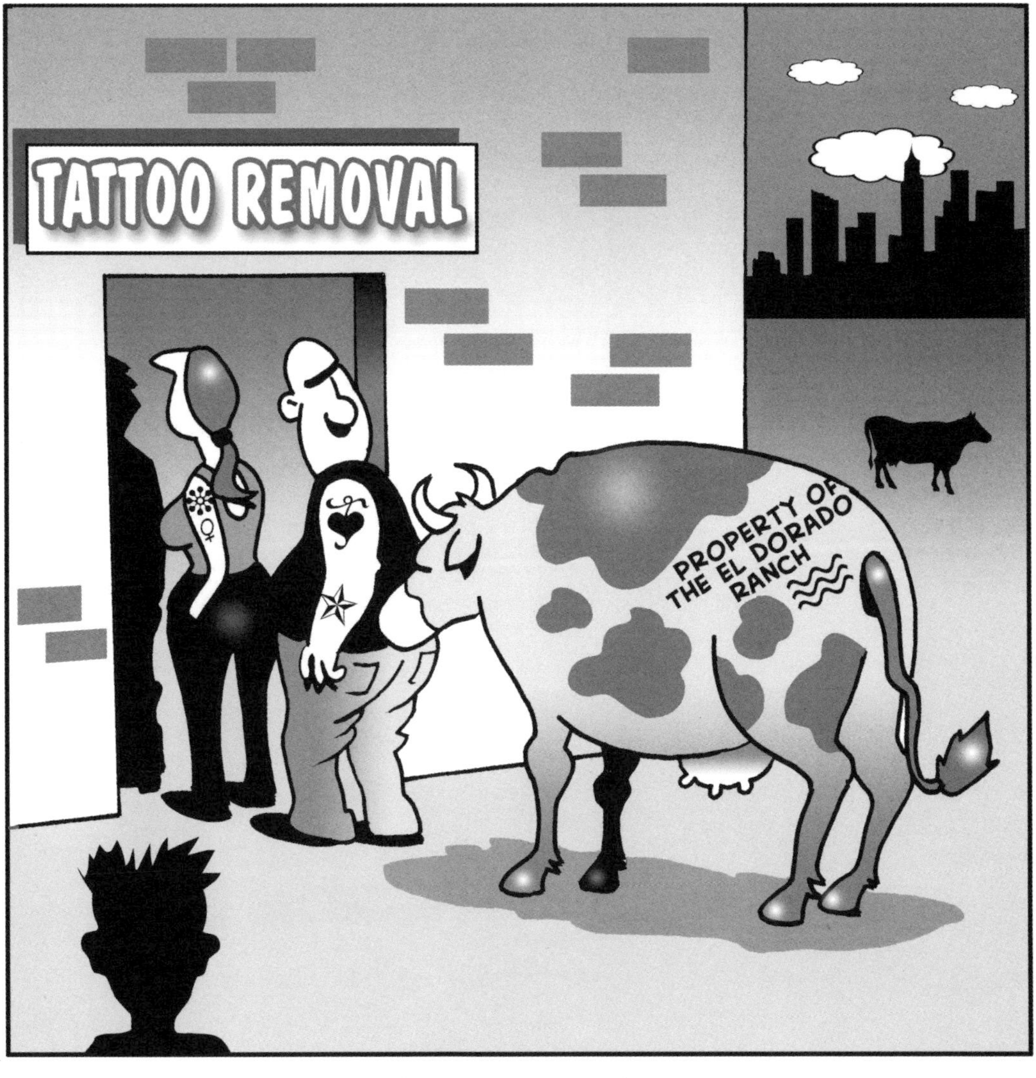
TATTOO REMOVAL
PROPERTY OF THE EL DORADO RANCH

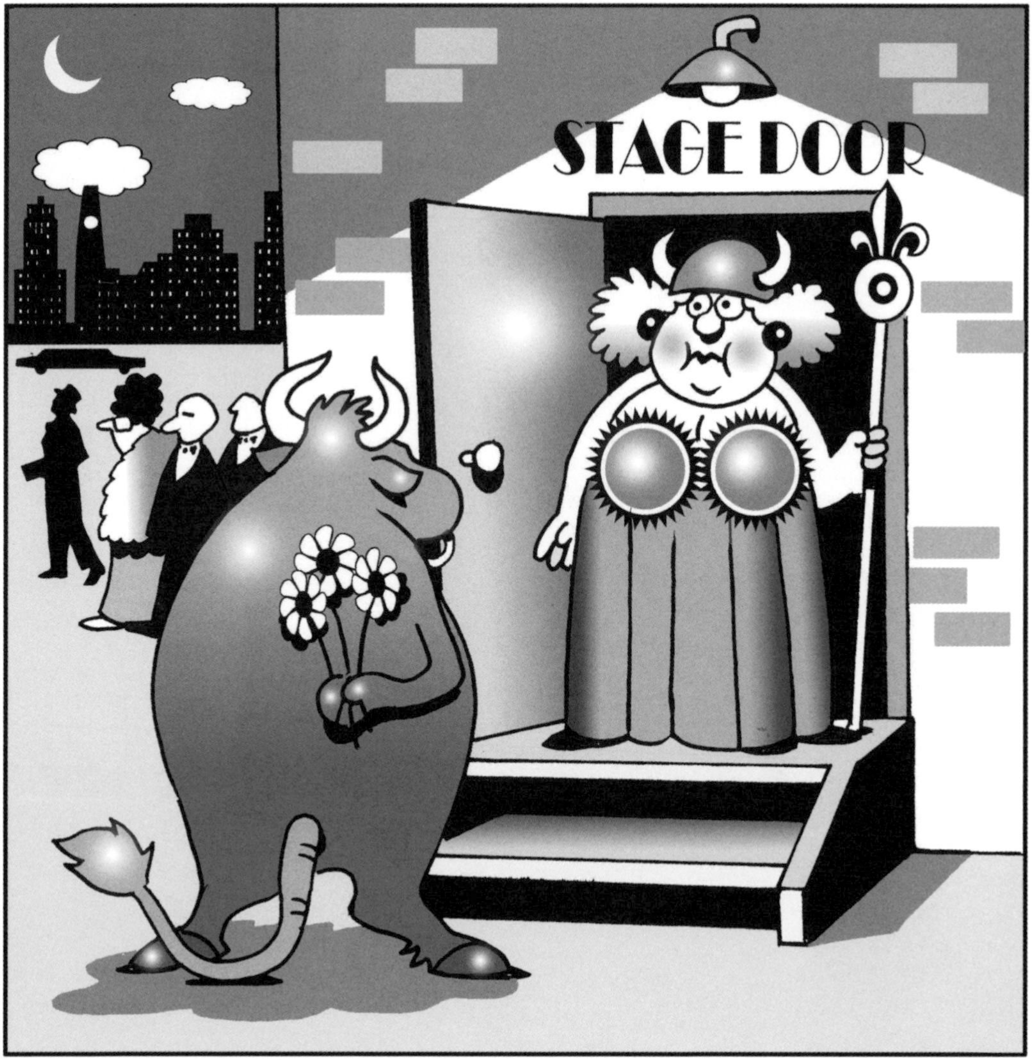
STAGE DOOR

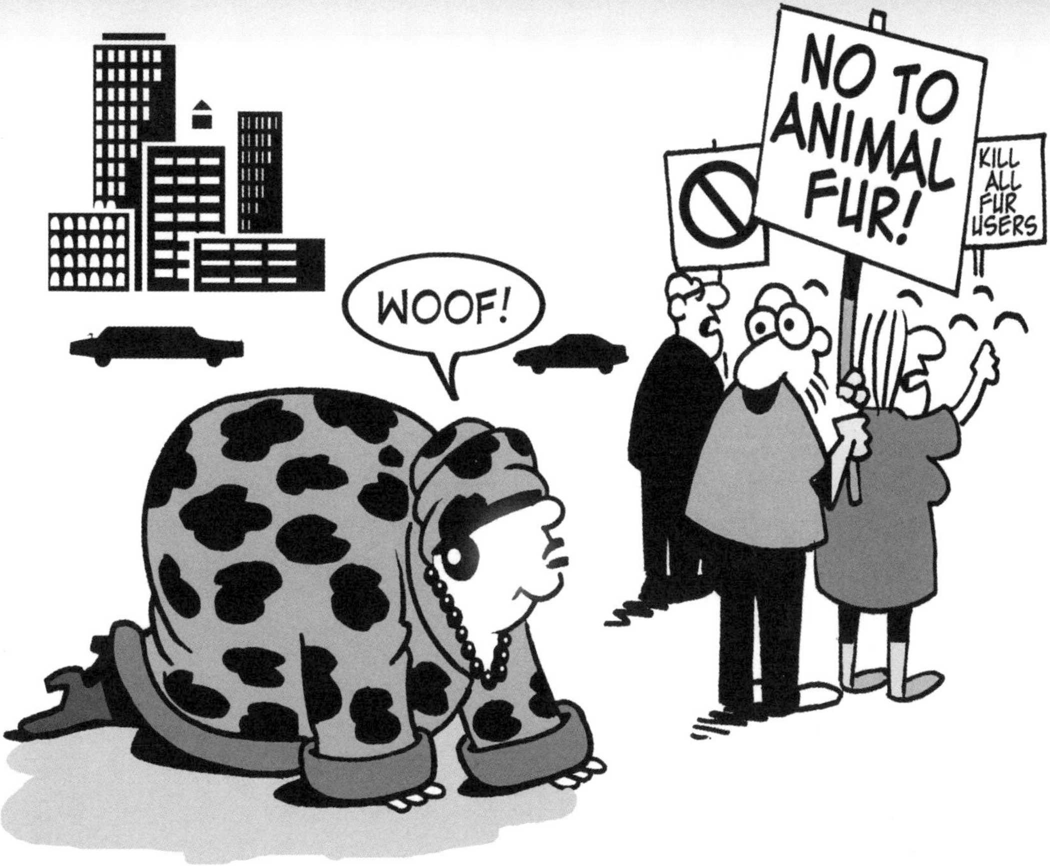
WOOF!
NO TO ANIMAL FUR!
KILL ALL FUR USERS

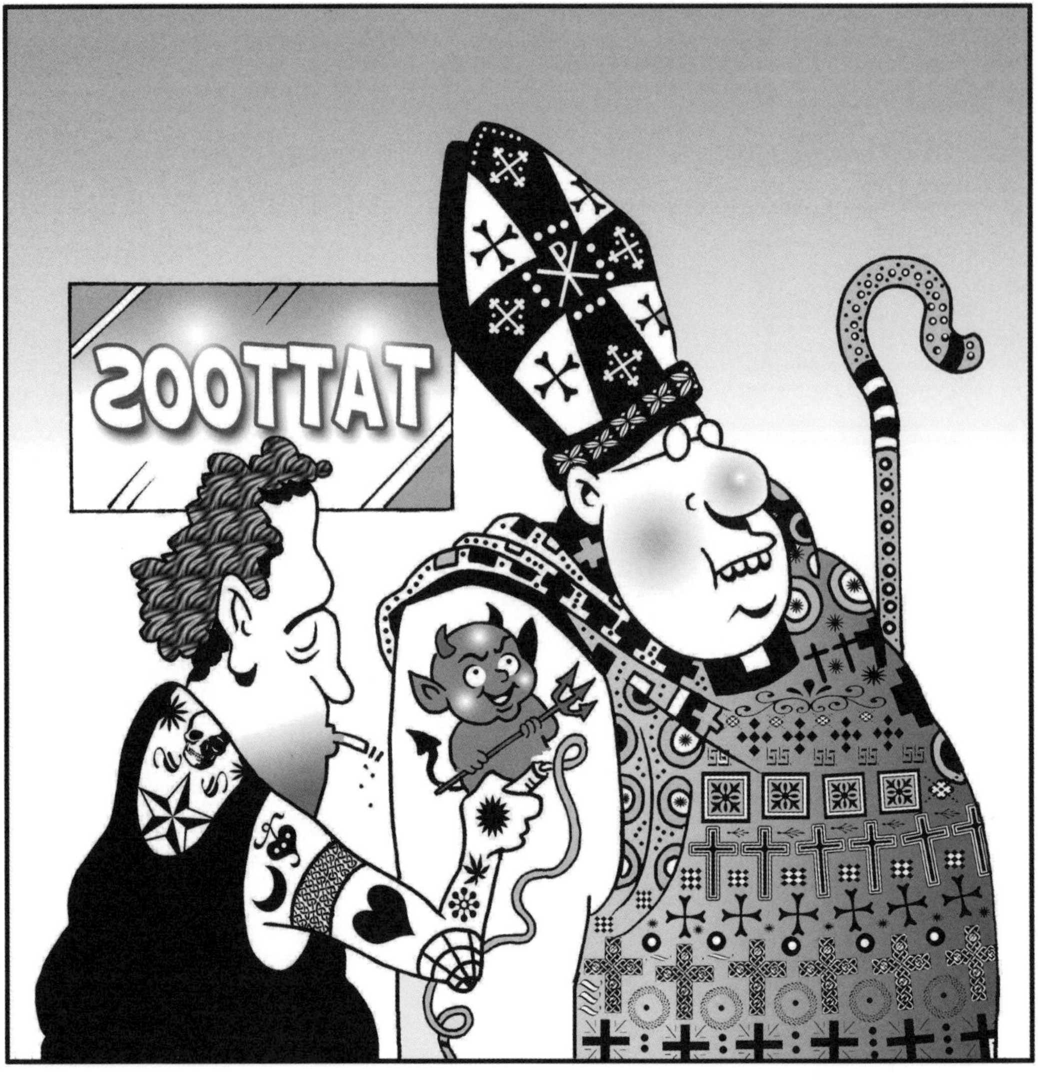
TATTOOS

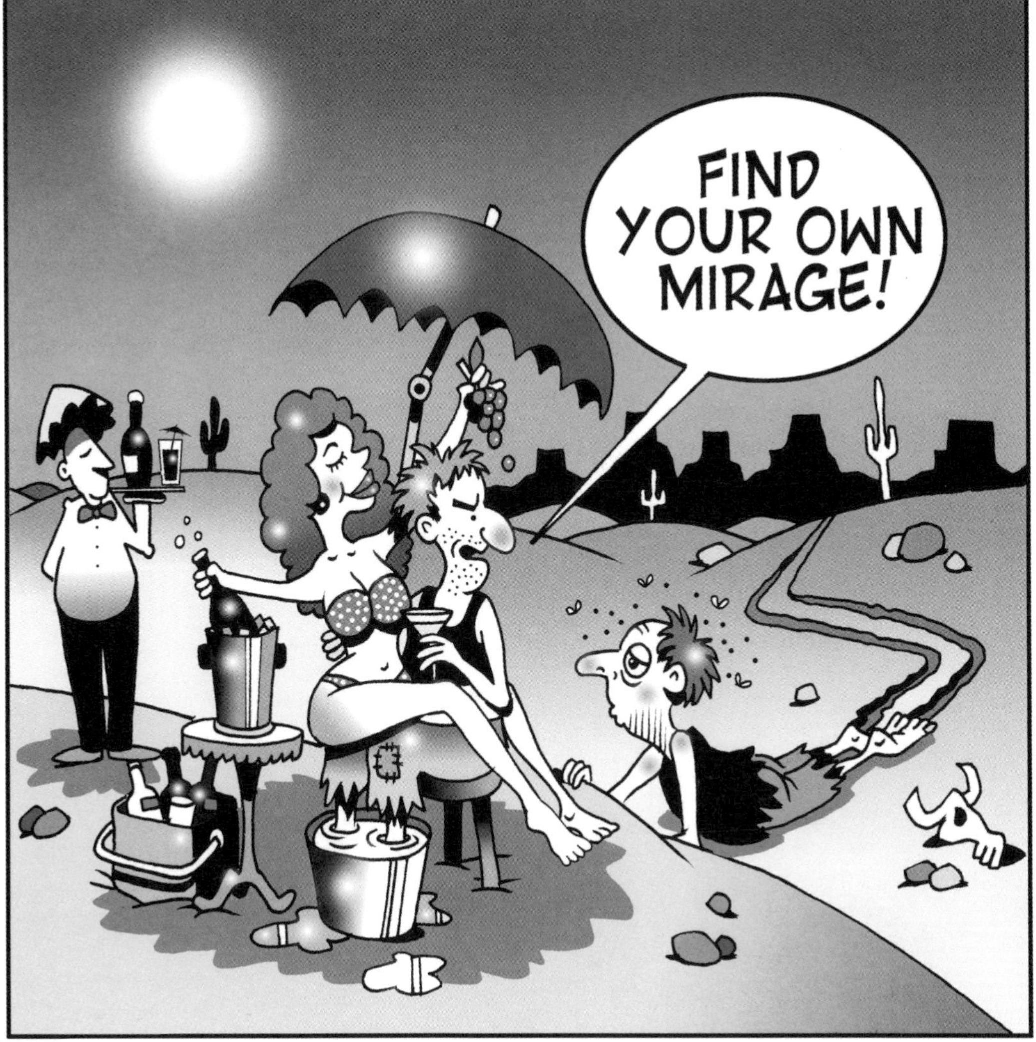
FIND YOUR OWN MIRAGE!

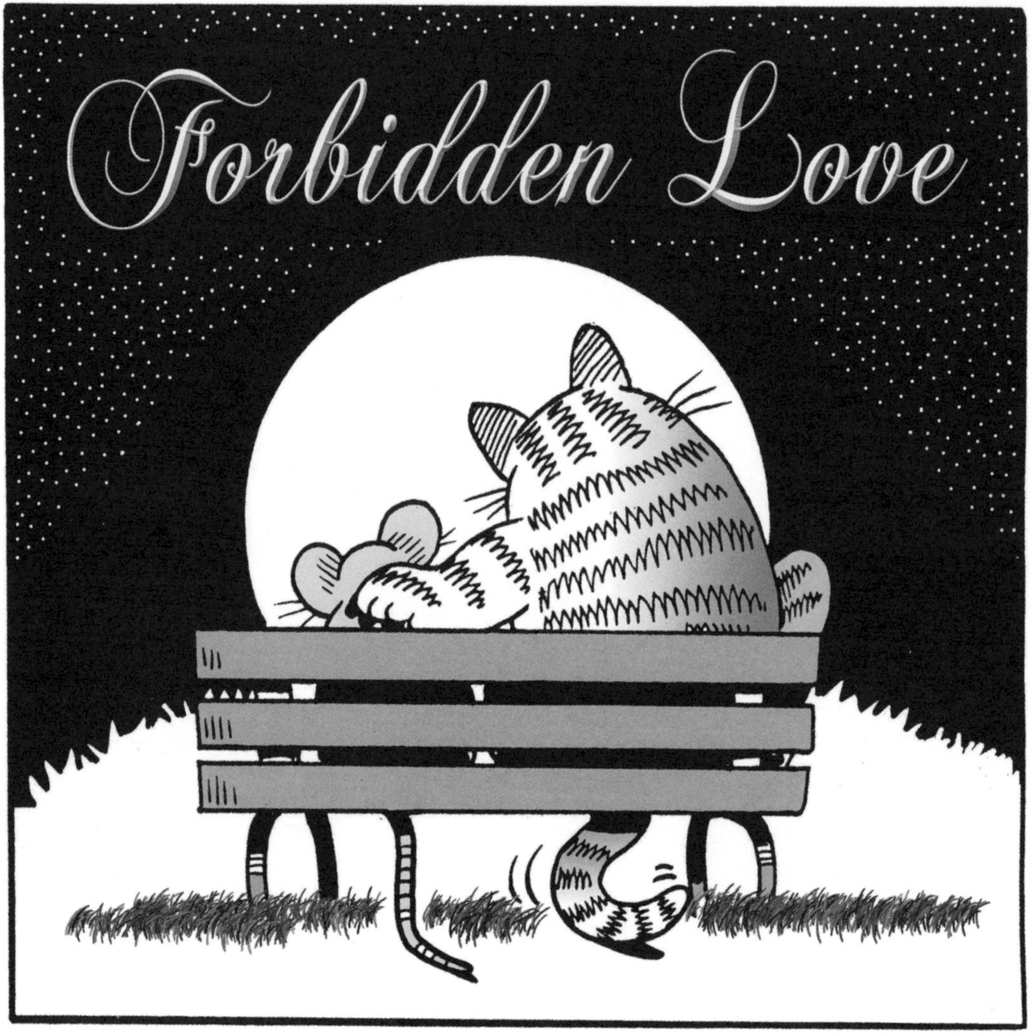
Forbidden Love

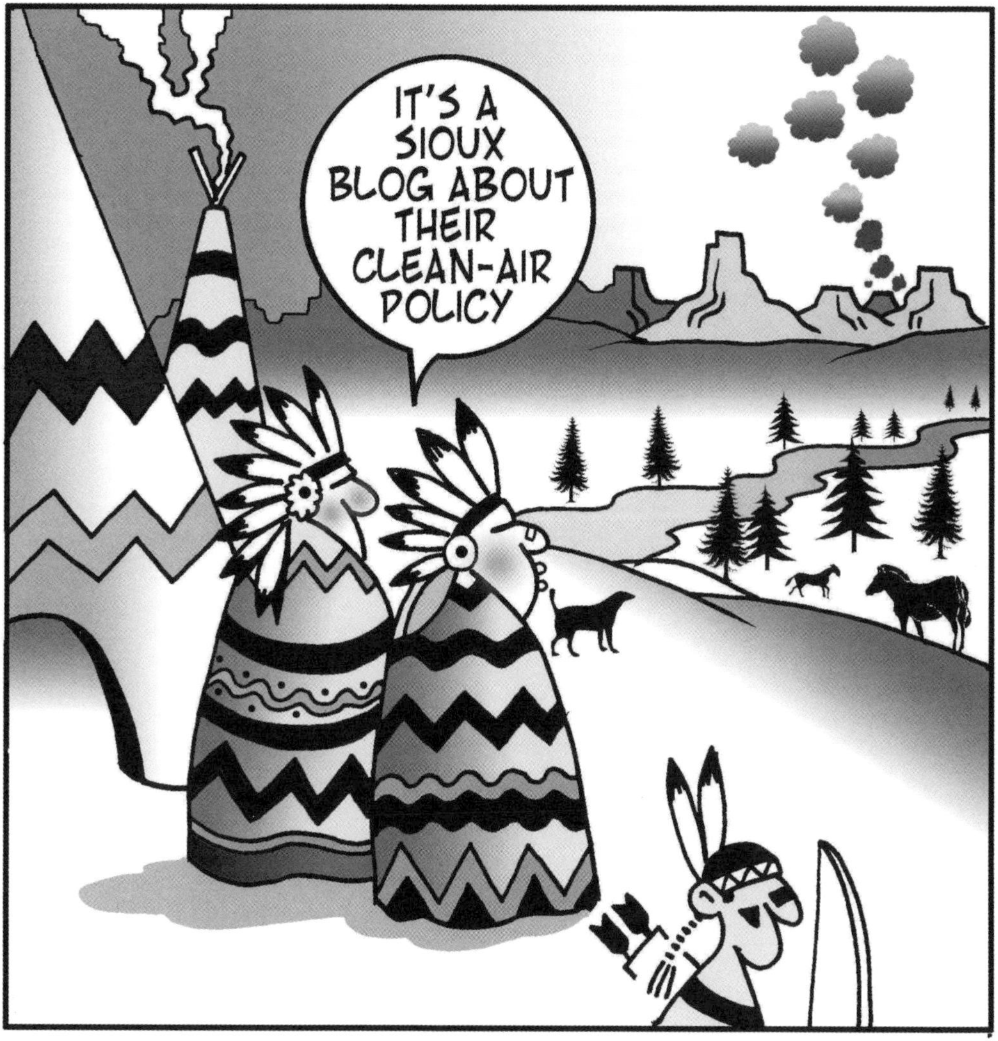
IT'S A SIOUX BLOG ABOUT THEIR CLEAN-AIR POLICY

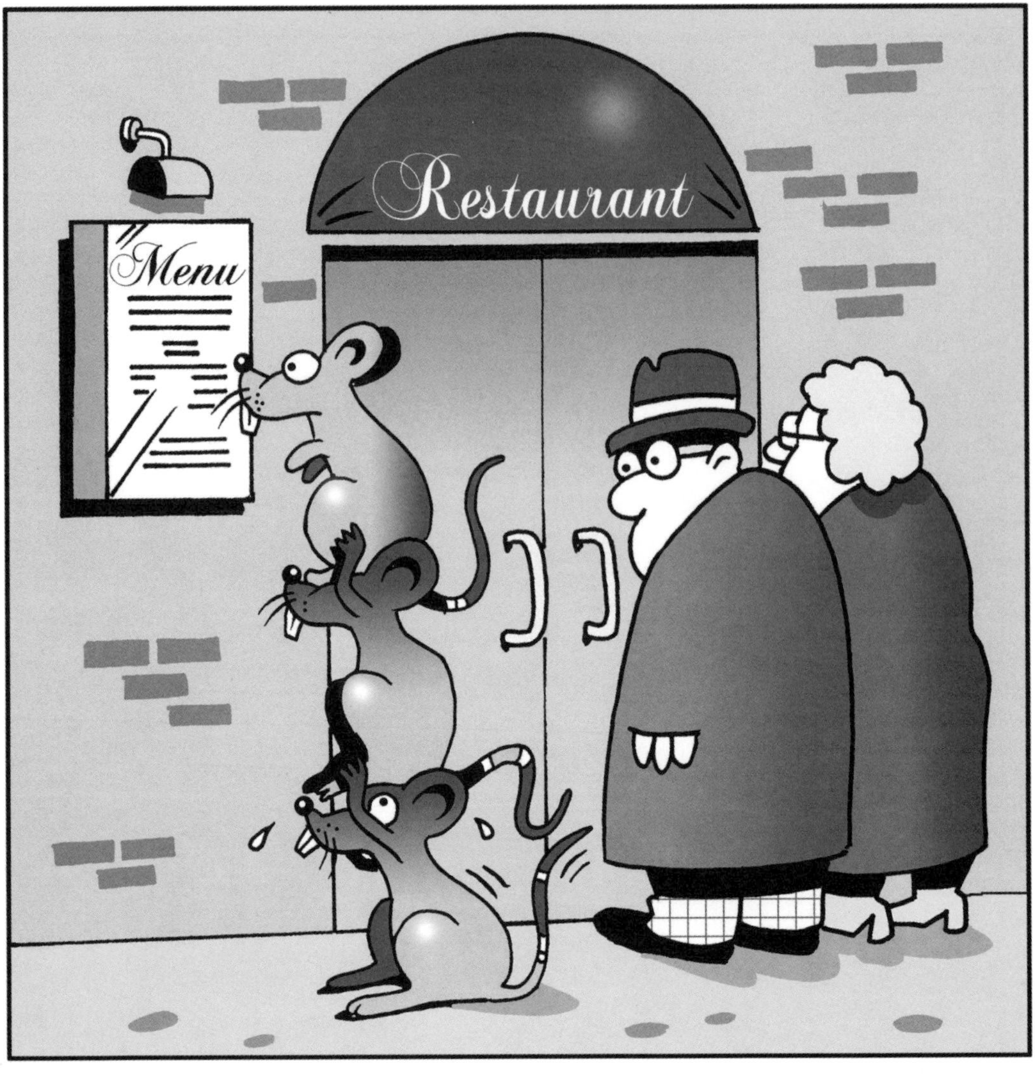
Restaurant
Menu

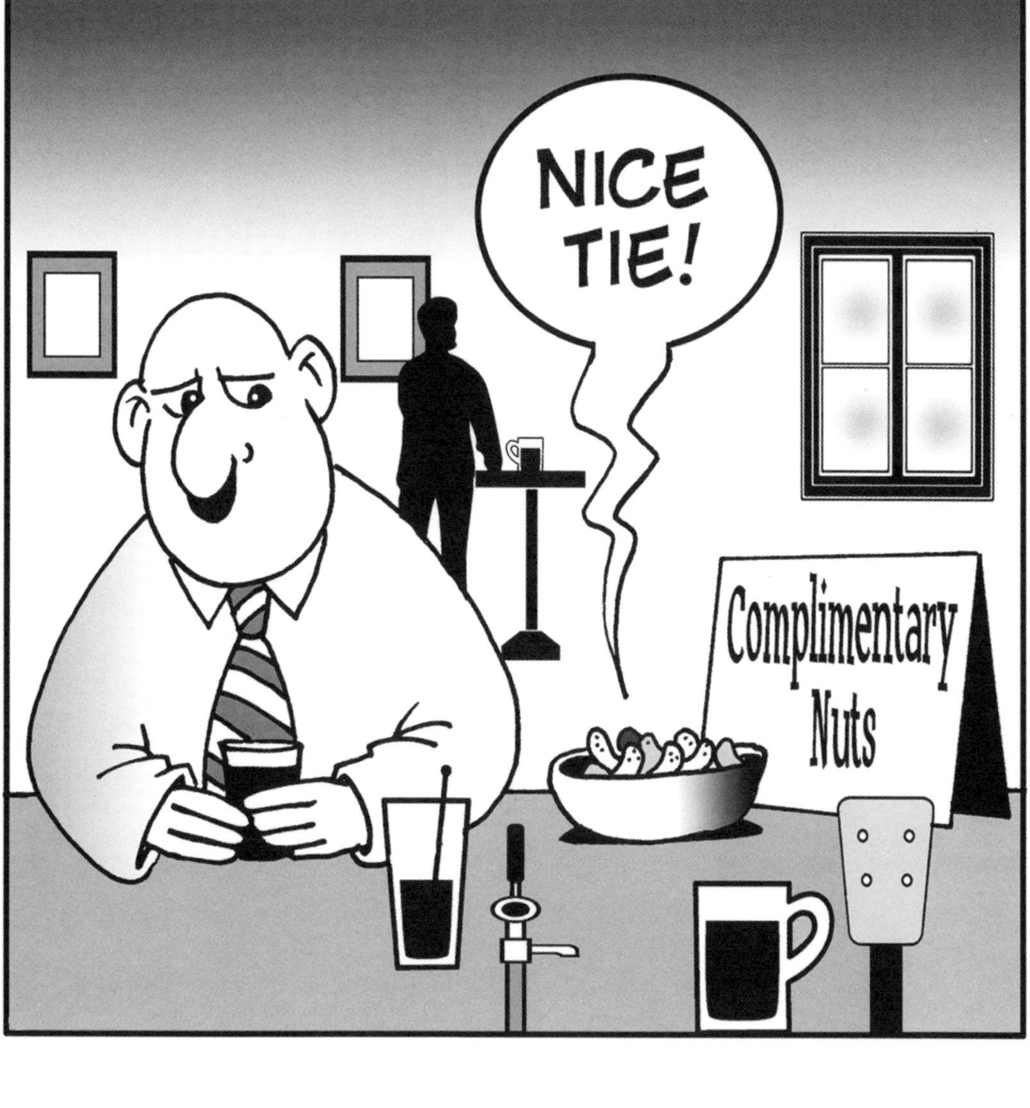
NICE TIE!
Complimentary Nuts

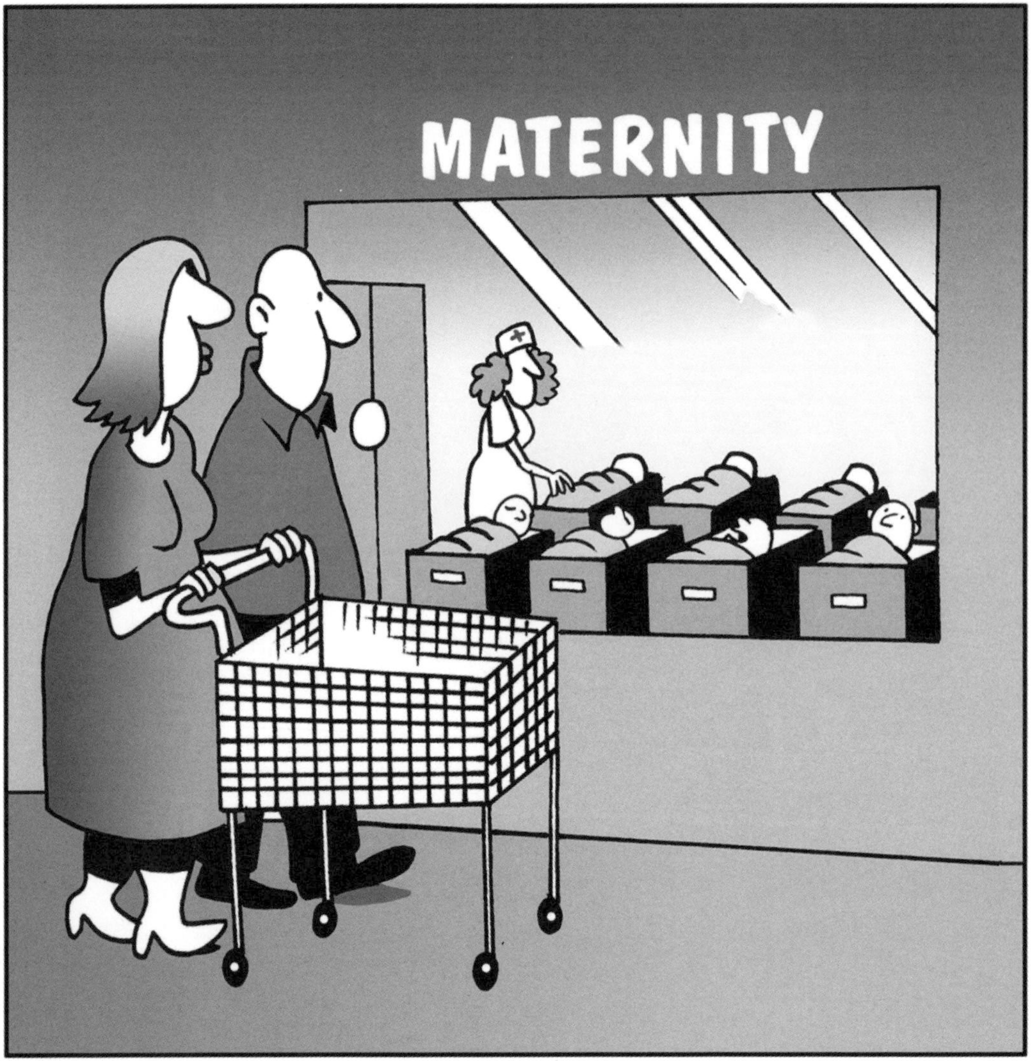
MATERNITY

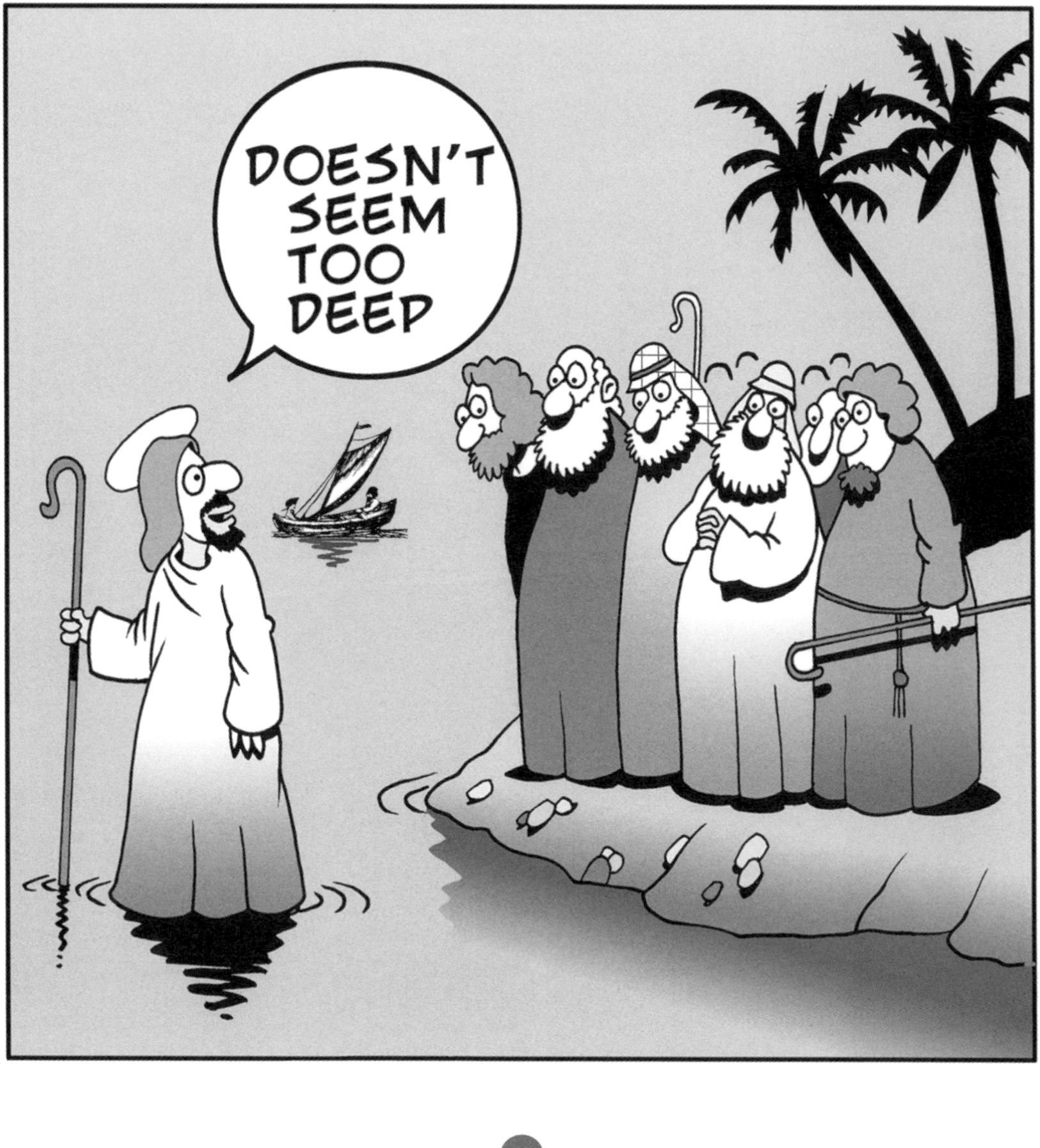
DOESN'T SEEM TOO DEEP

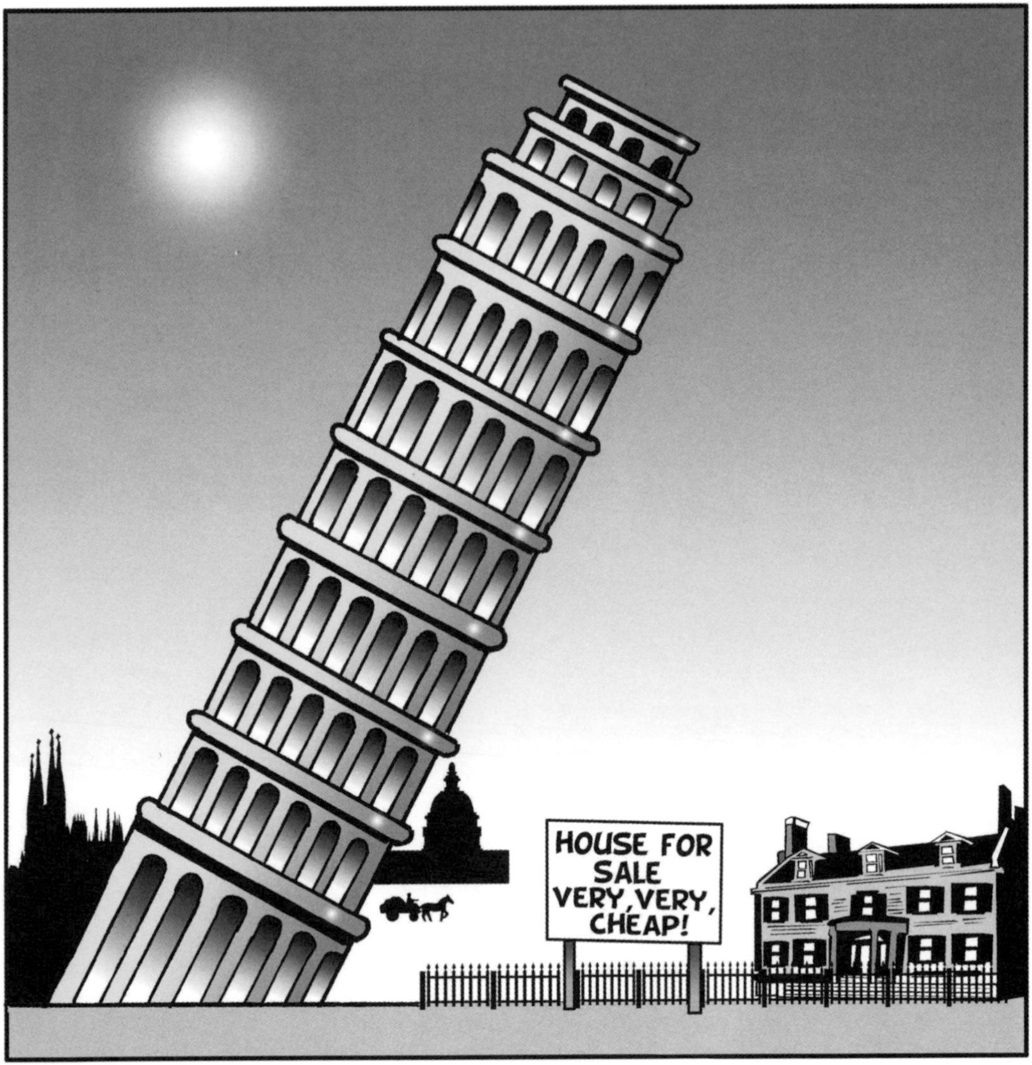
HOUSE FOR SALE VERY, VERY, CHEAP!

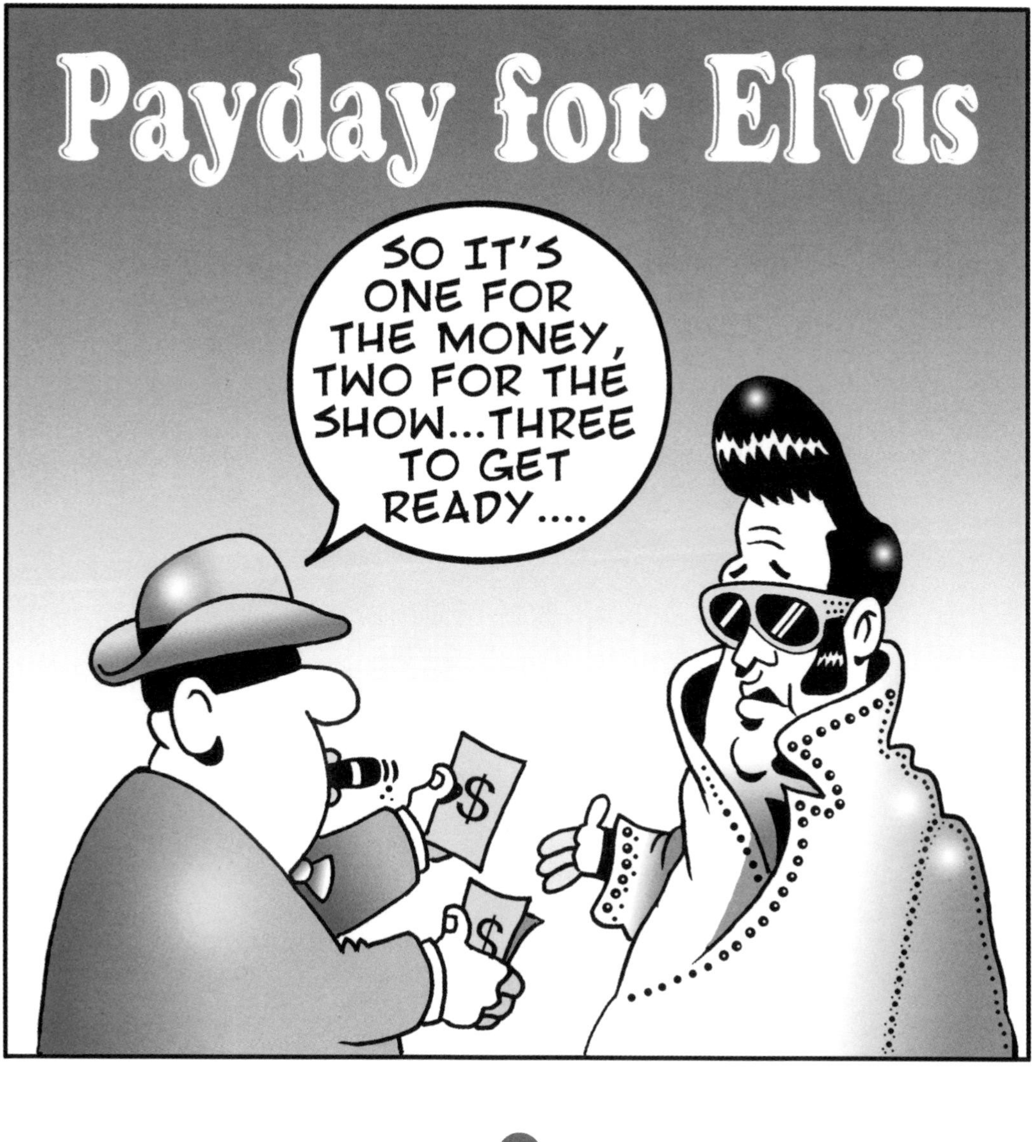
Payday for Elvis
SO IT'S ONE FOR THE MONEY, TWO FOR THE SHOW...THREE TO GET READY....

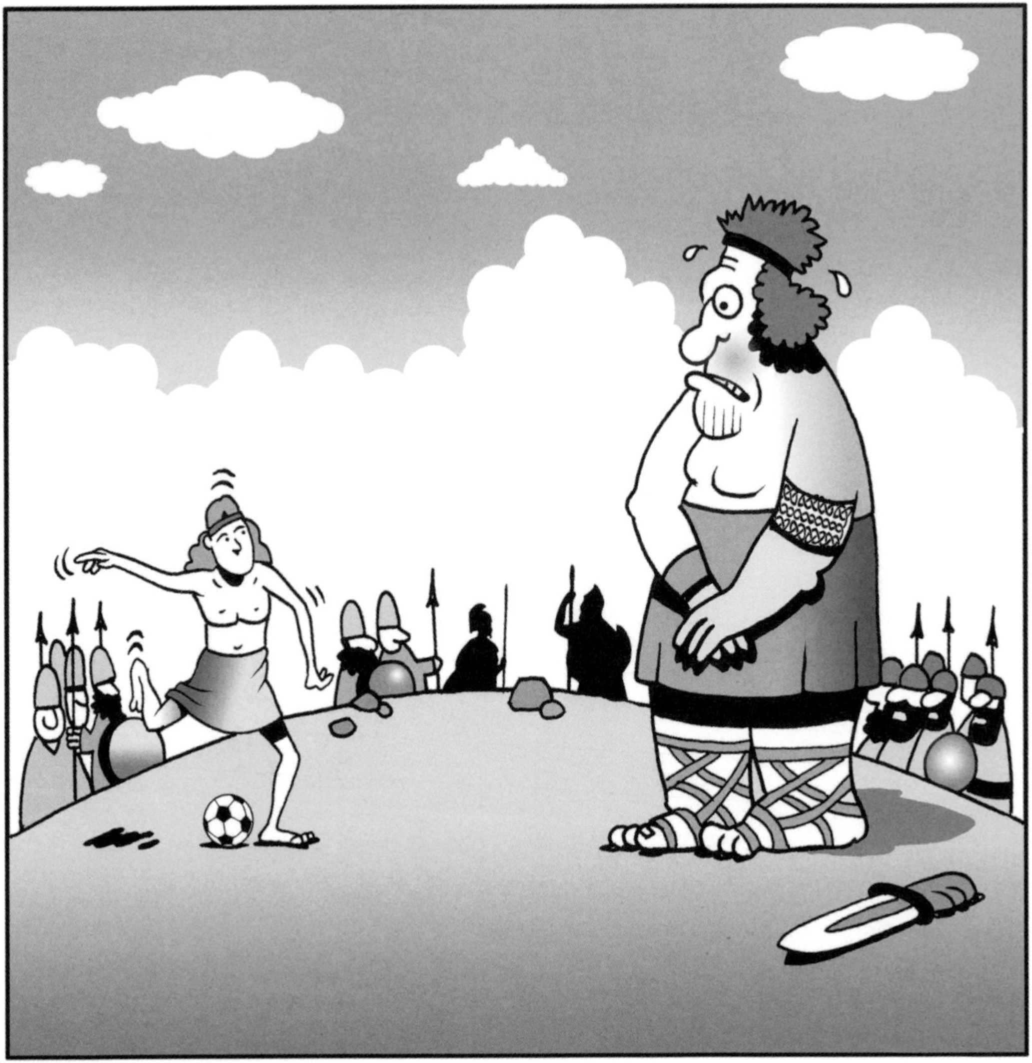

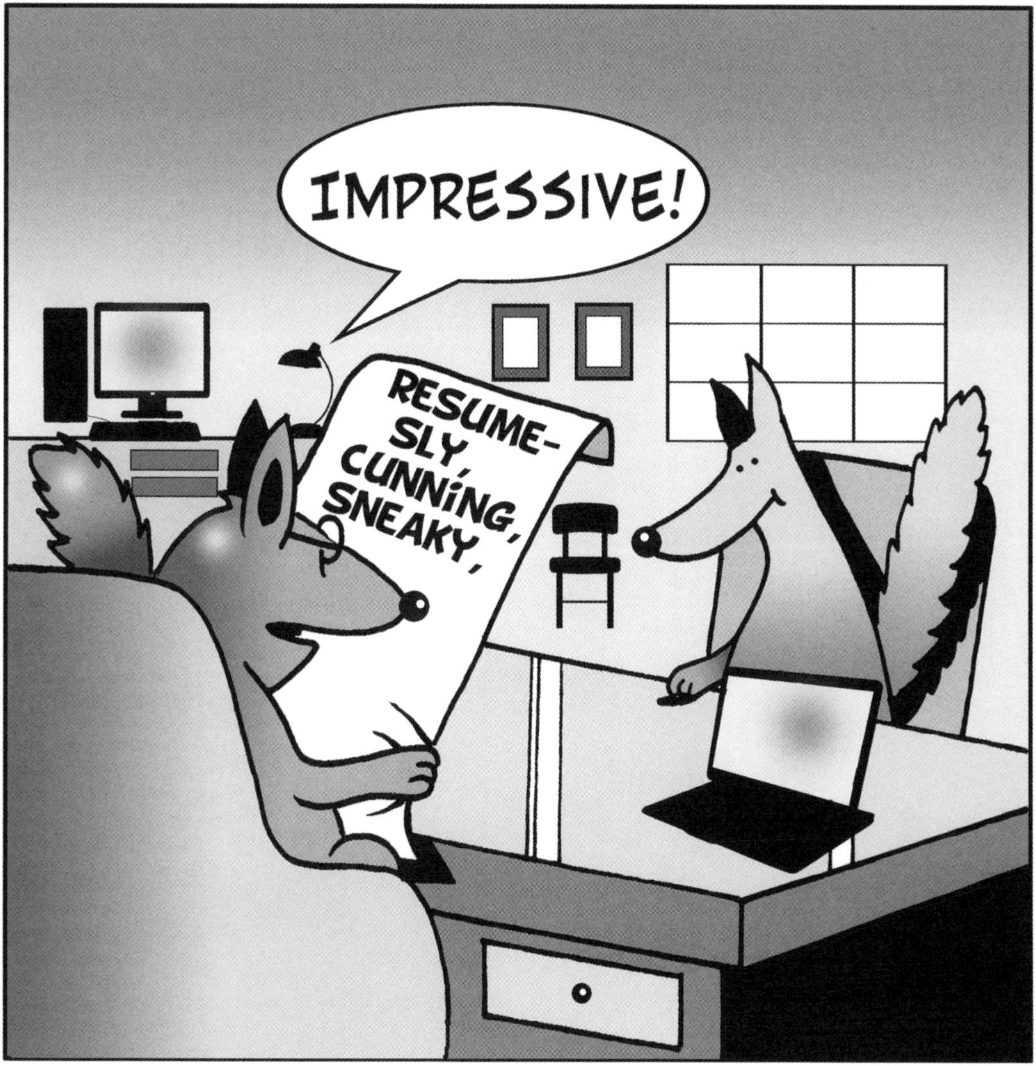
IMPRESSIVE!
RESUME-
SLY,
CUNNING,
SNEAKY,

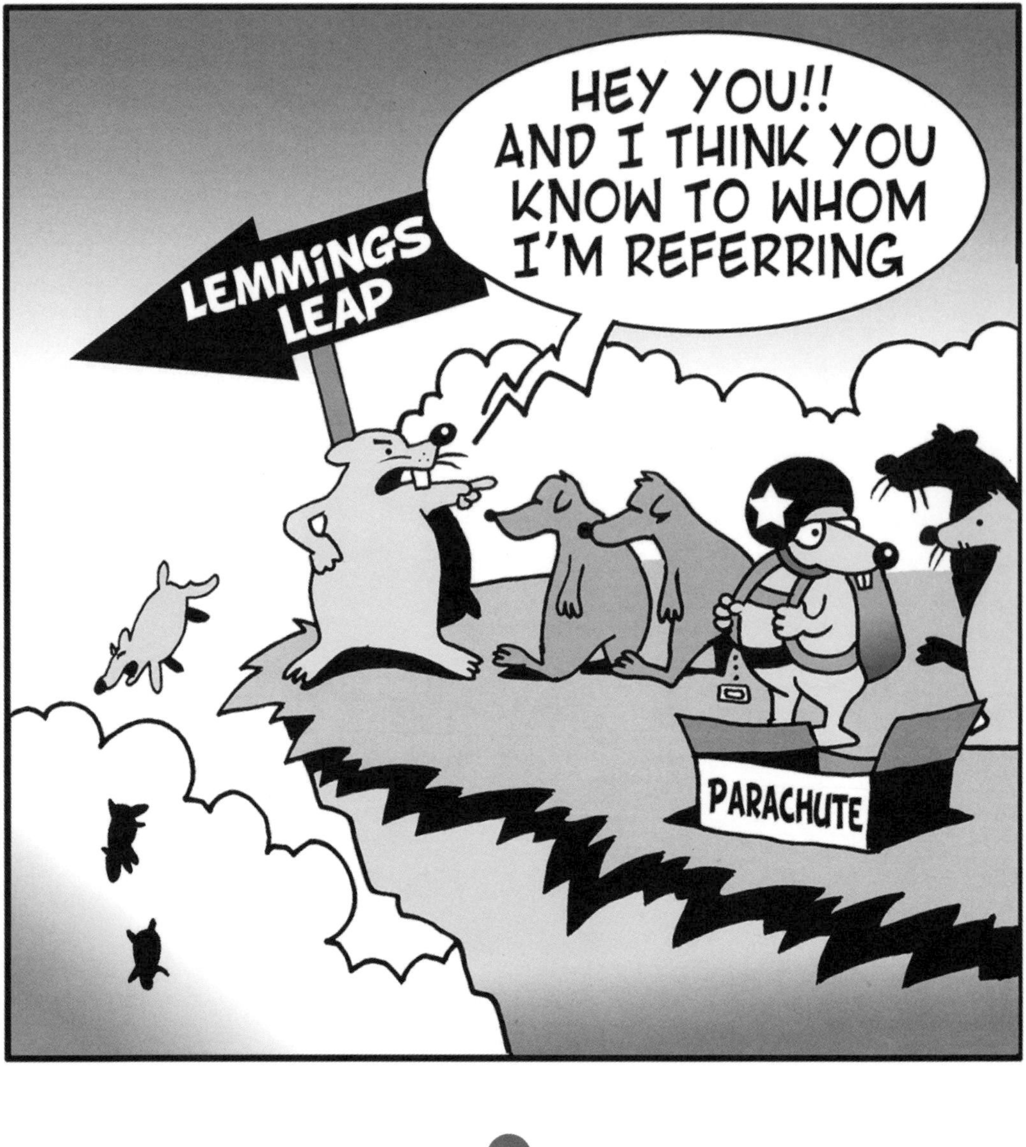
LEMMINGS LEAP
HEY YOU!! AND I THINK YOU KNOW TO WHOM I'M REFERRING
PARACHUTE

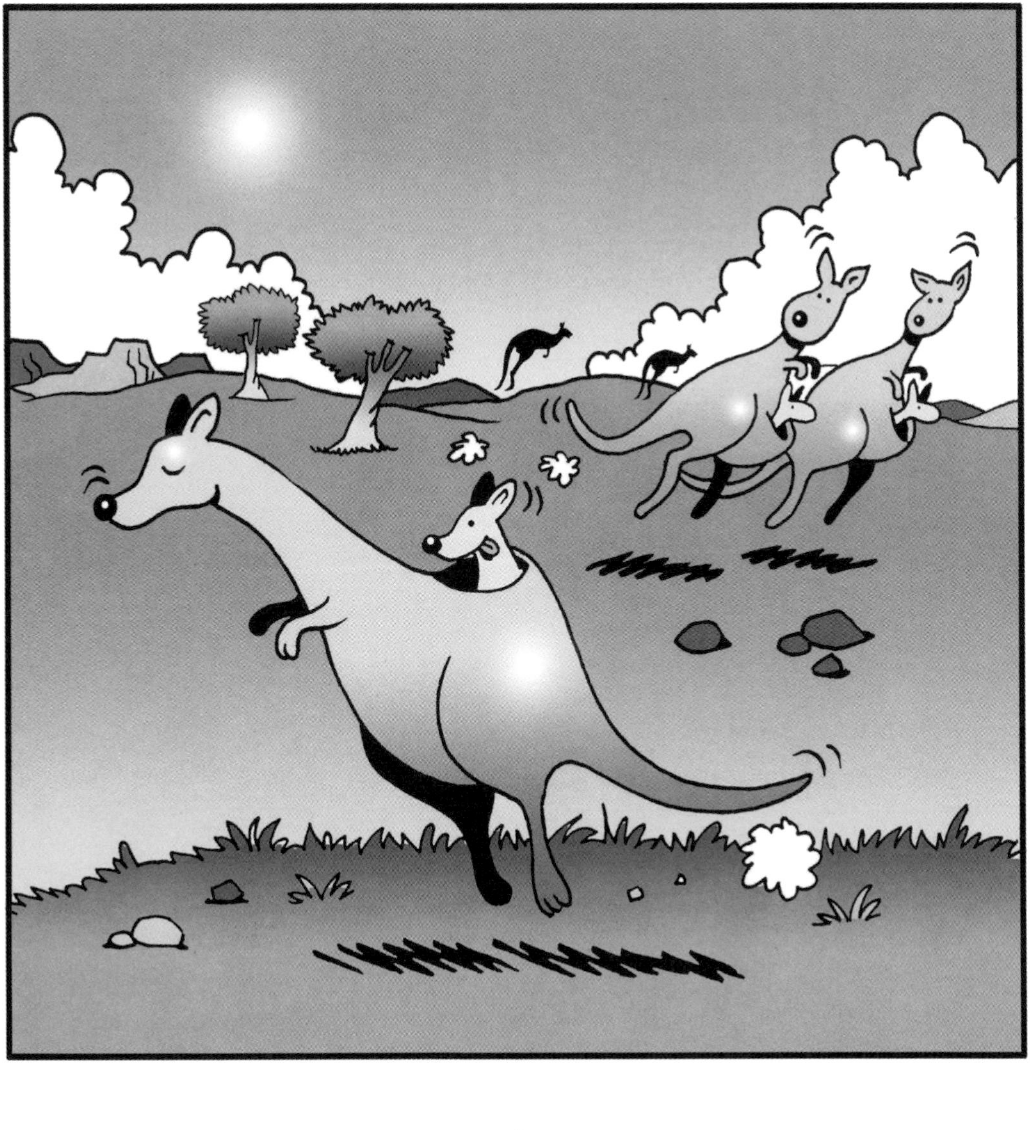

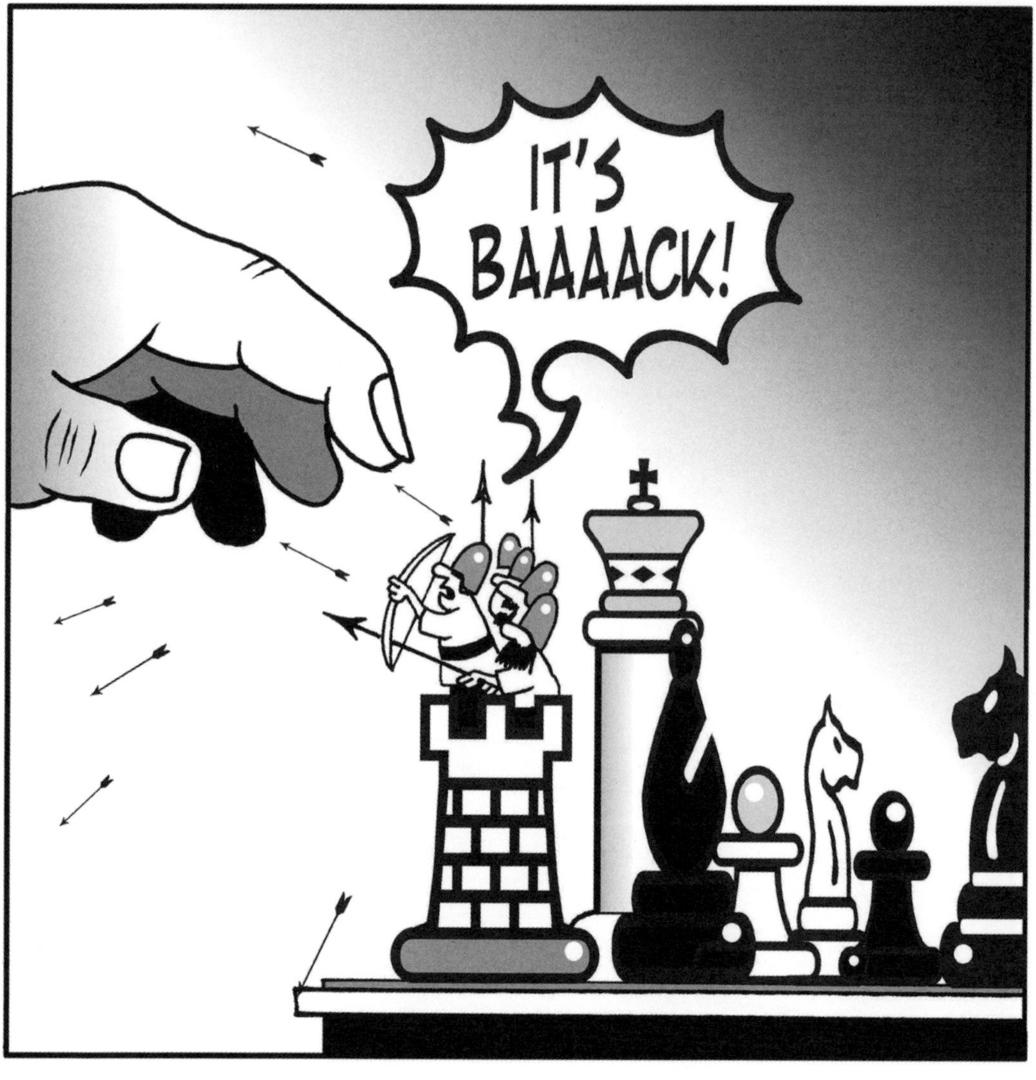
IT'S BAAAACK!

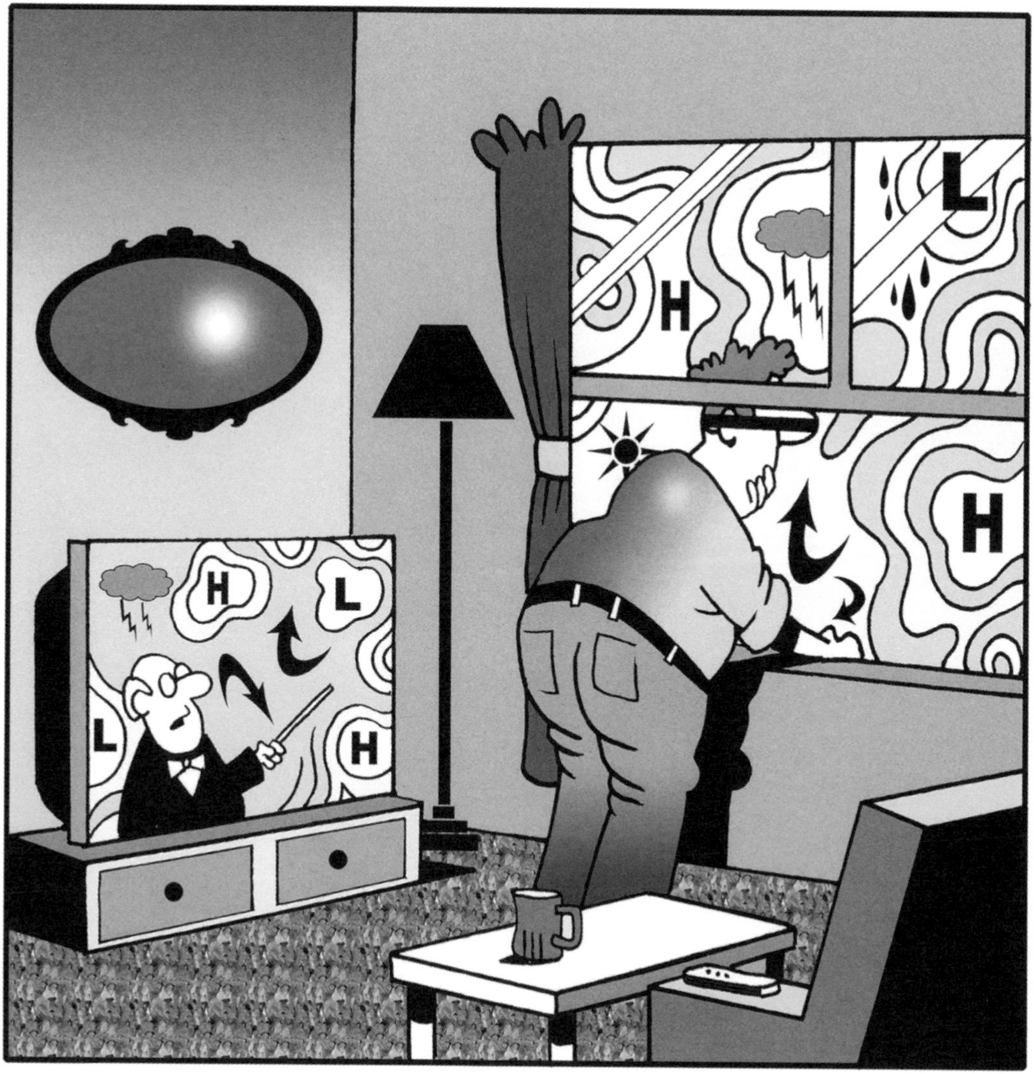
H
L
L
H
L
H
H

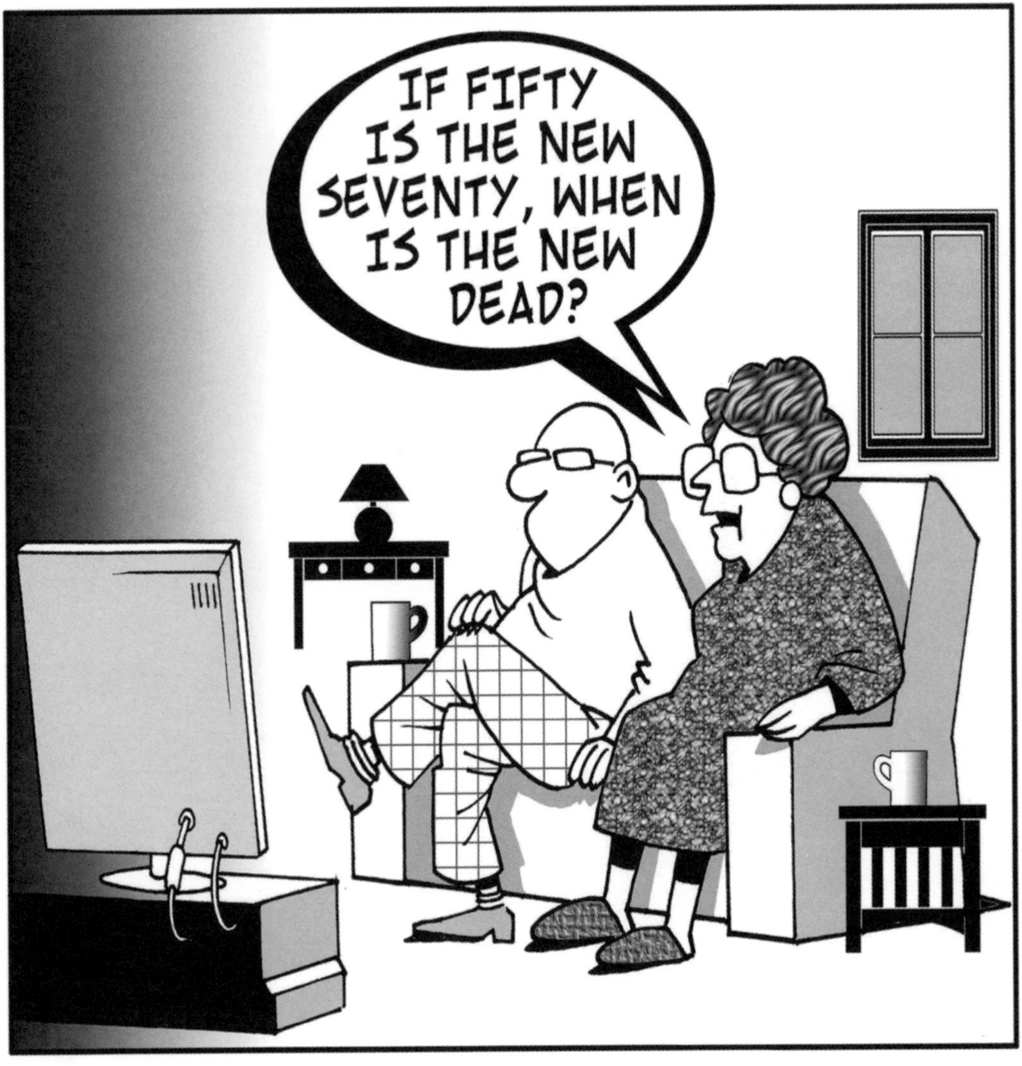
IF FIFTY IS THE NEW SEVENTY, WHEN IS THE NEW DEAD?

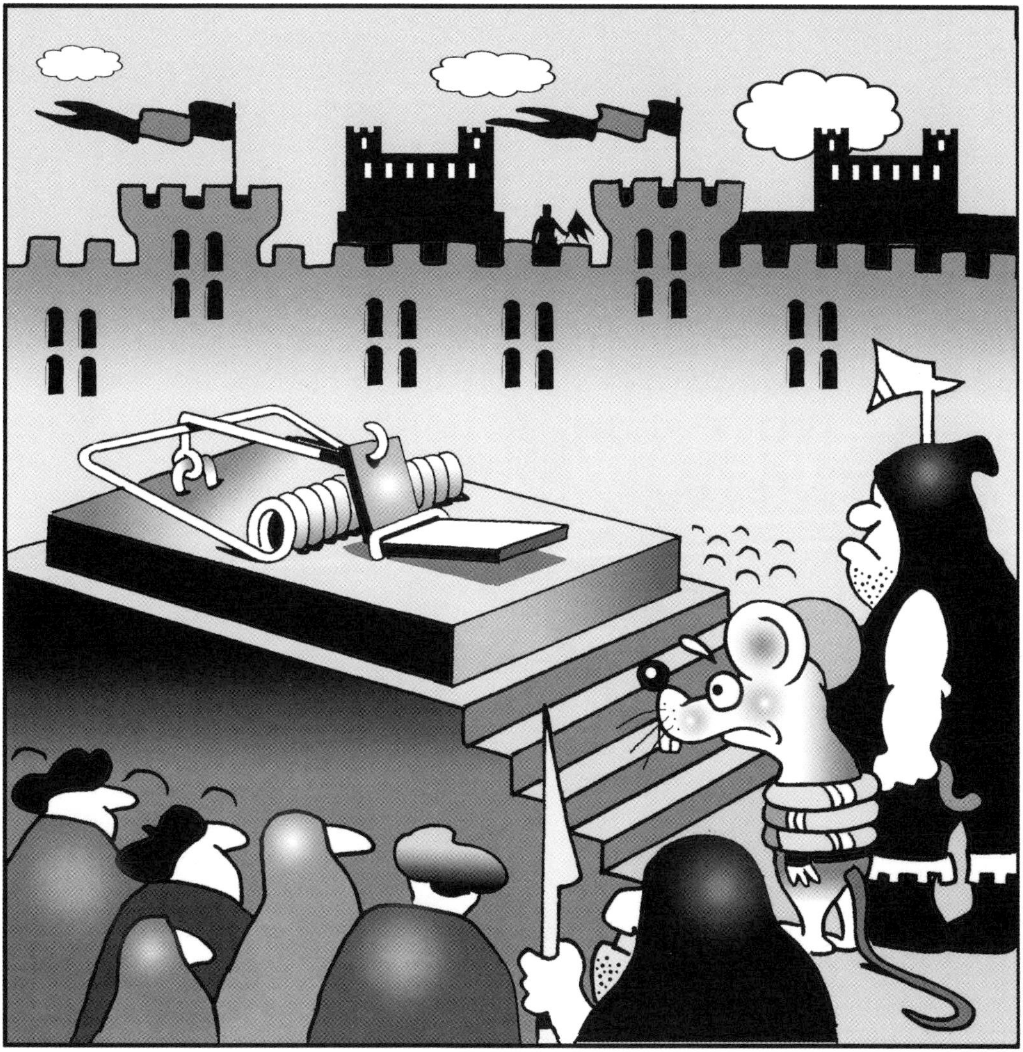

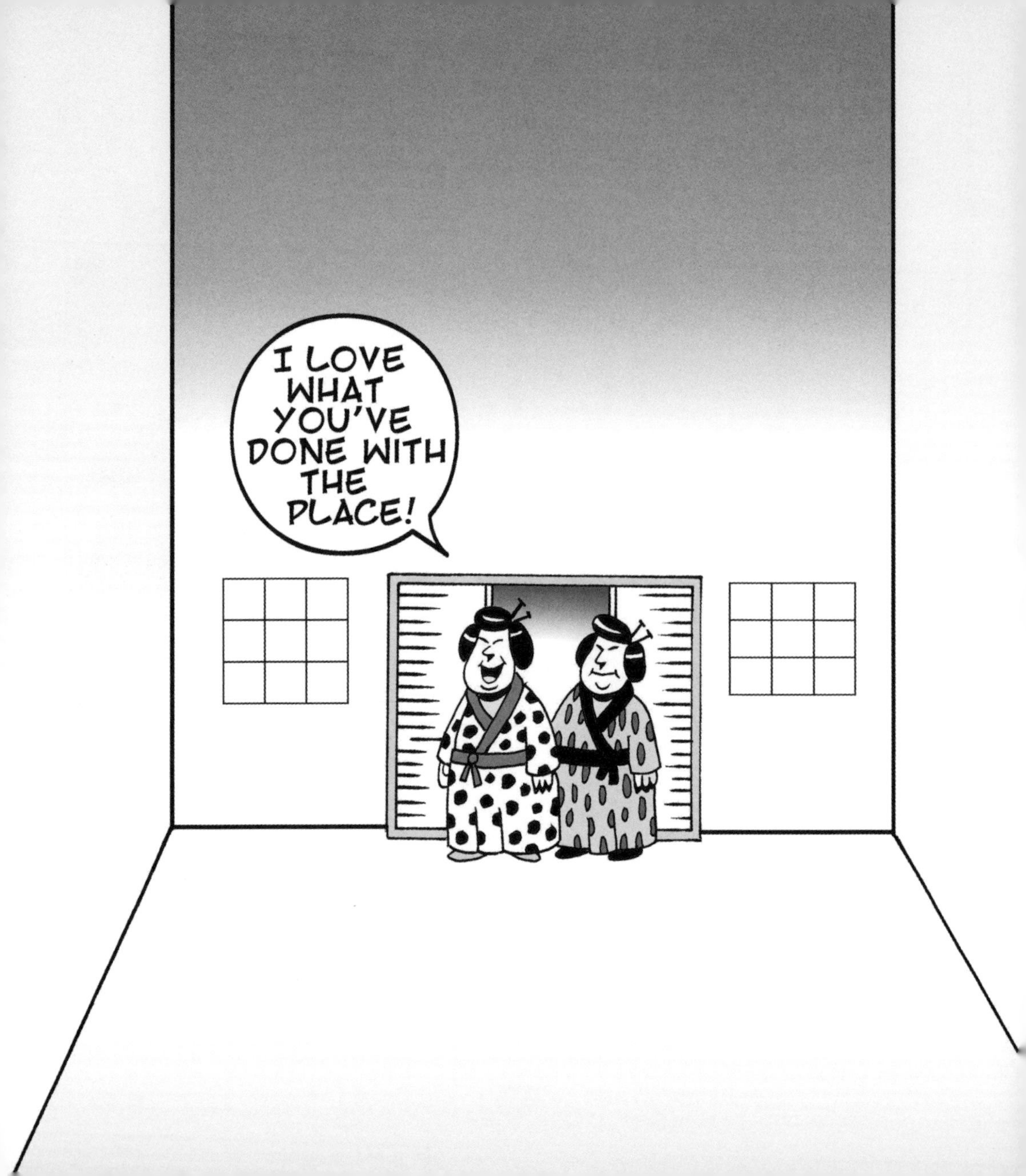
I LOVE WHAT YOU'VE DONE WITH THE PLACE!

William Tell's other three children

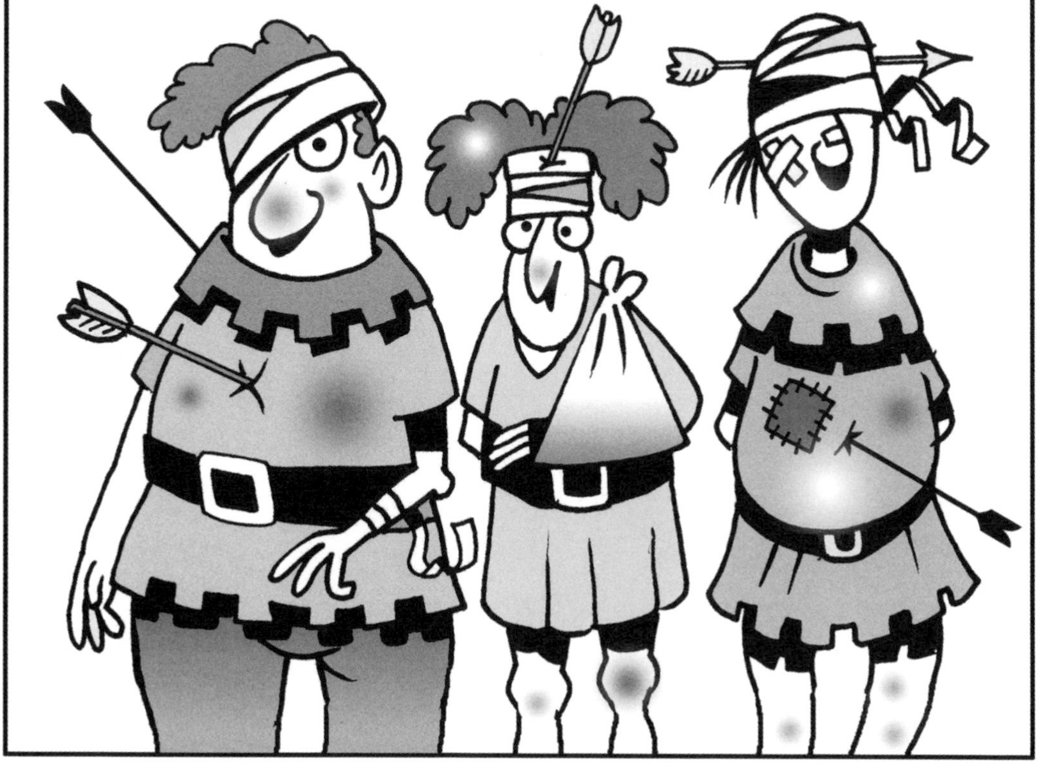

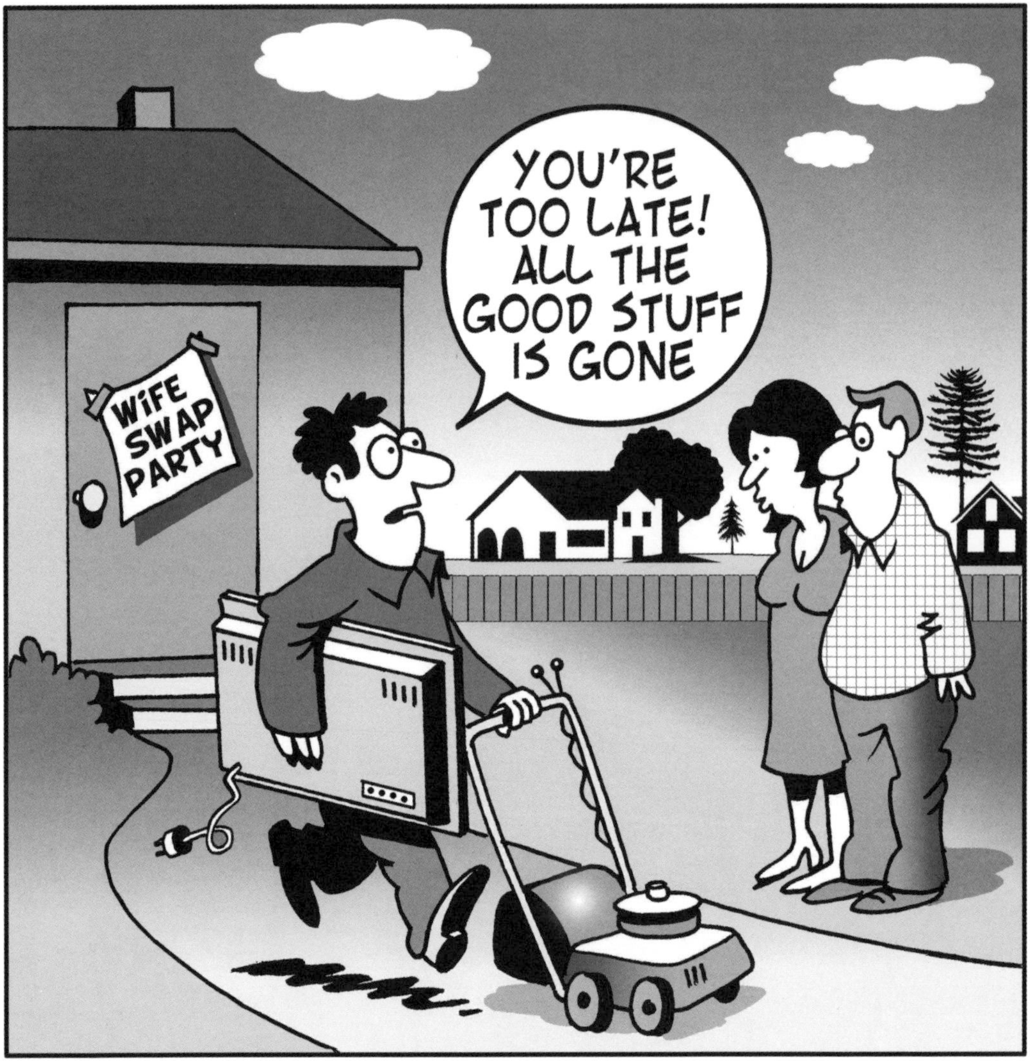
WiFE SWAP PARTY
YOU'RE TOO LATE! ALL THE GOOD STUFF IS GONE

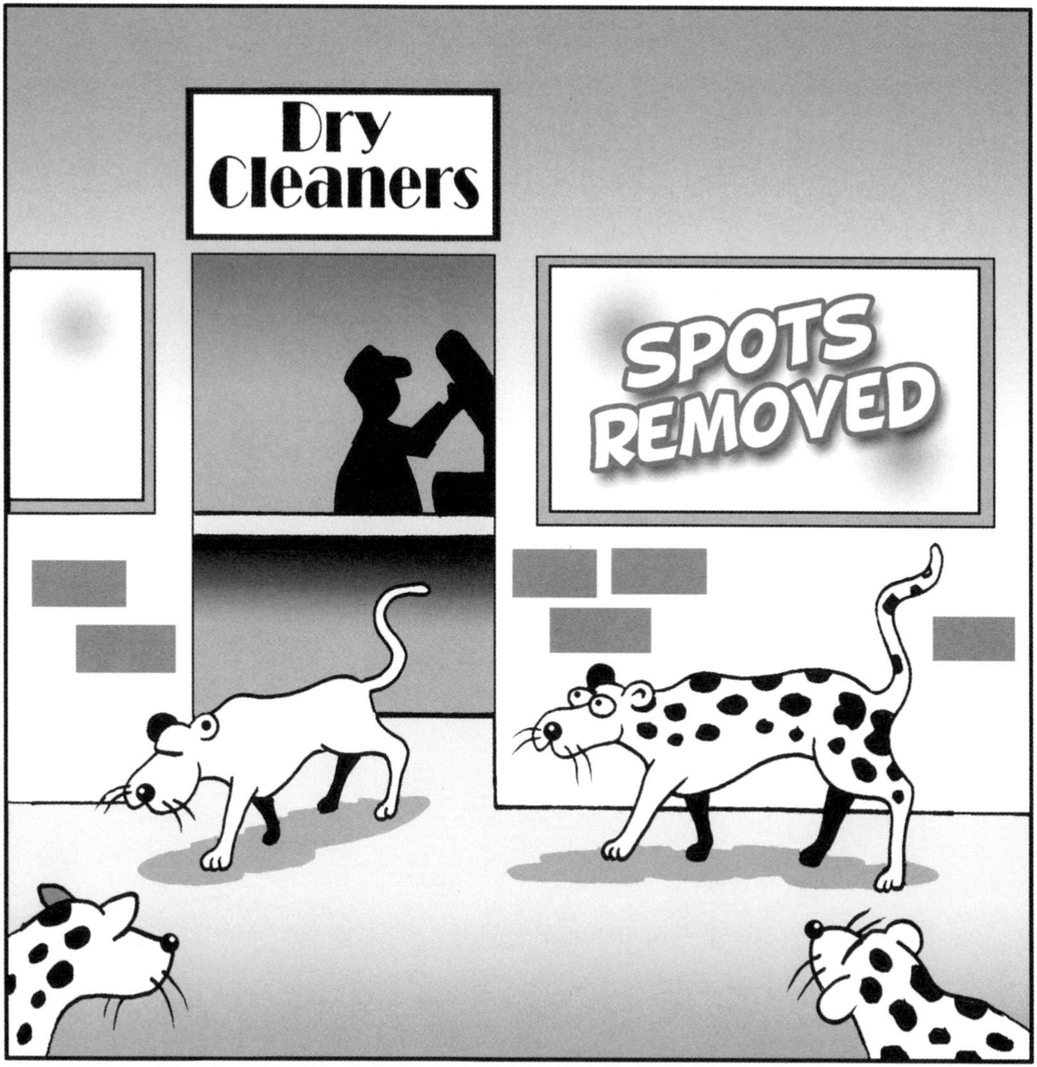
Dry Cleaners
SPOTS REMOVED

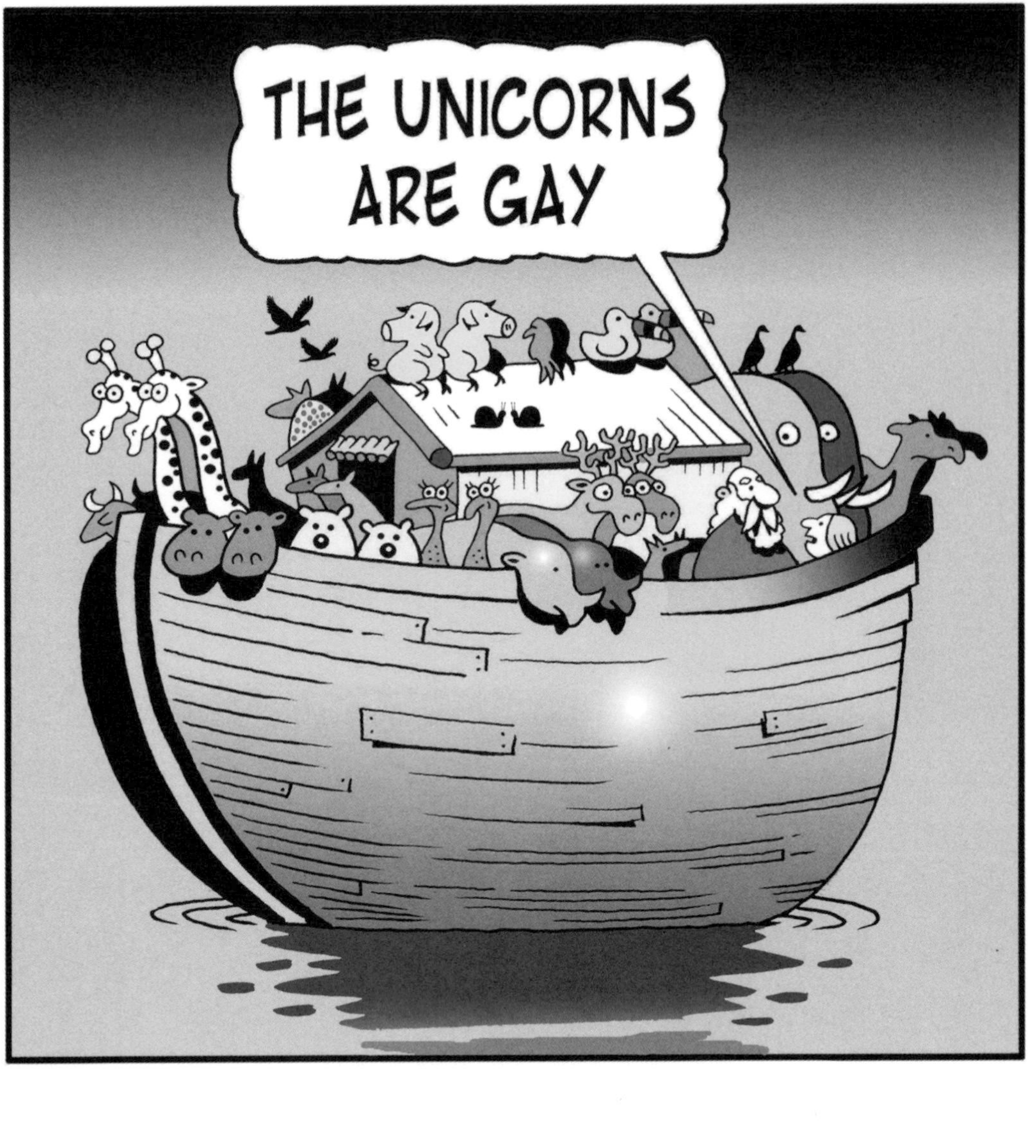
THE UNICORNS ARE GAY

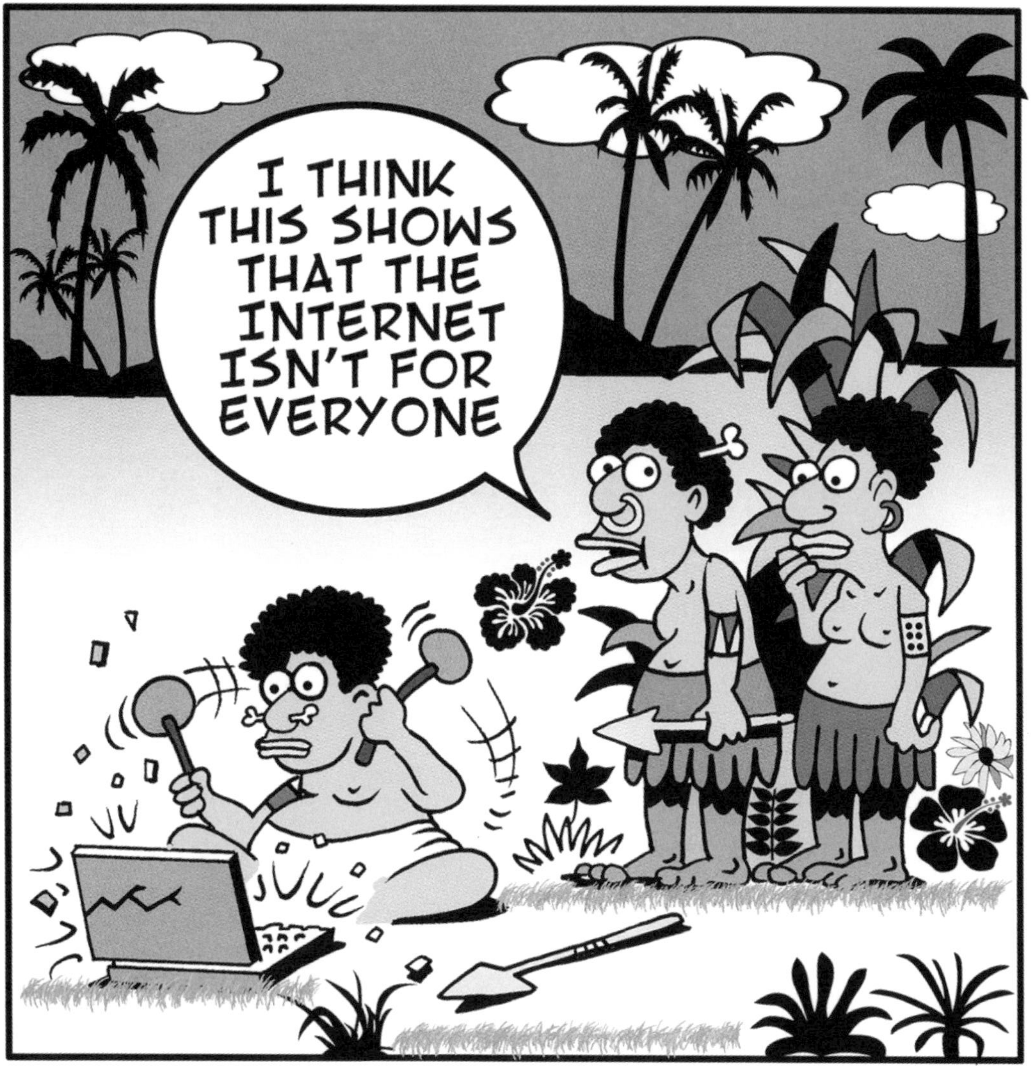
I THINK THIS SHOWS THAT THE INTERNET ISN'T FOR EVERYONE

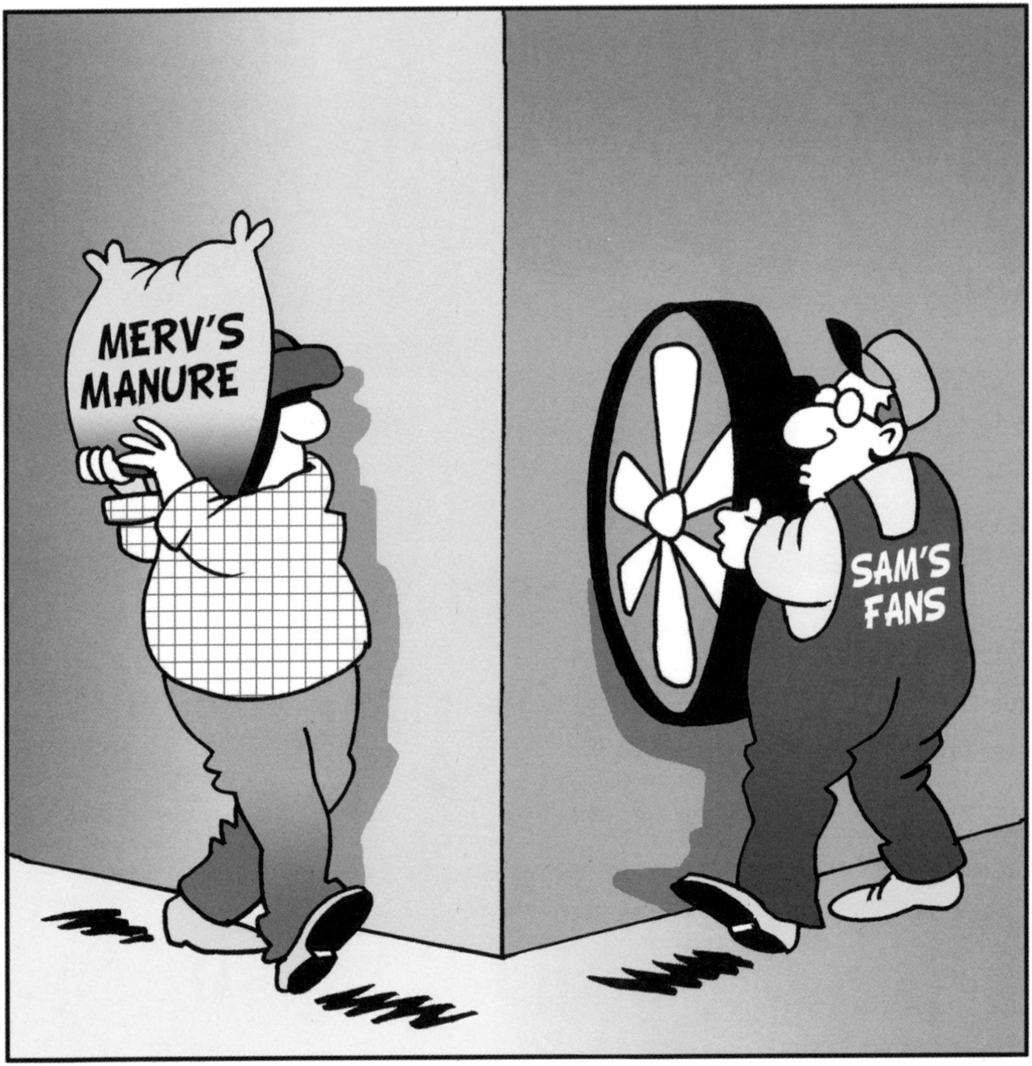
MERV'S MANURE
SAM'S FANS

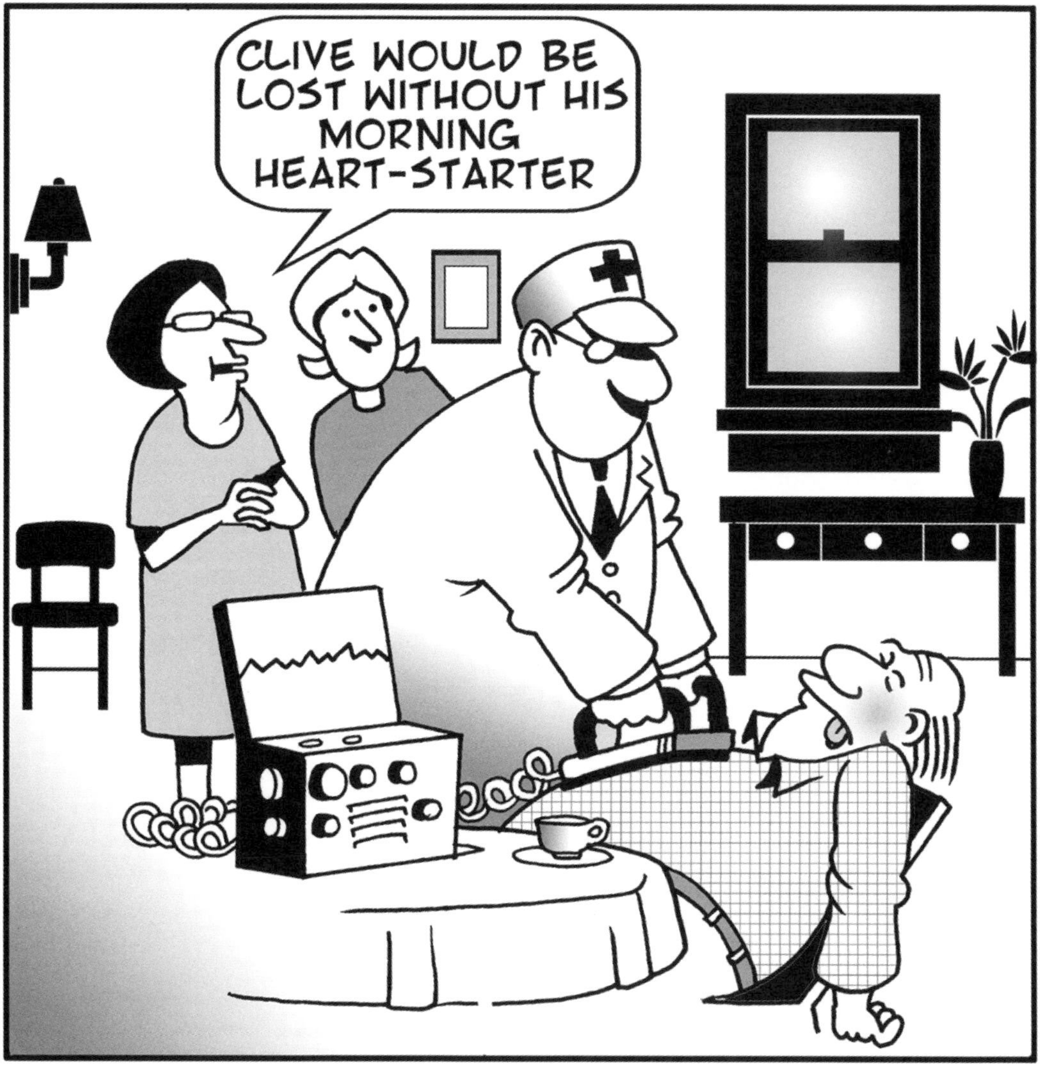
CLIVE WOULD BE LOST WITHOUT HIS MORNING HEART-STARTER

ACUTE ANIMAL MAGNETISM

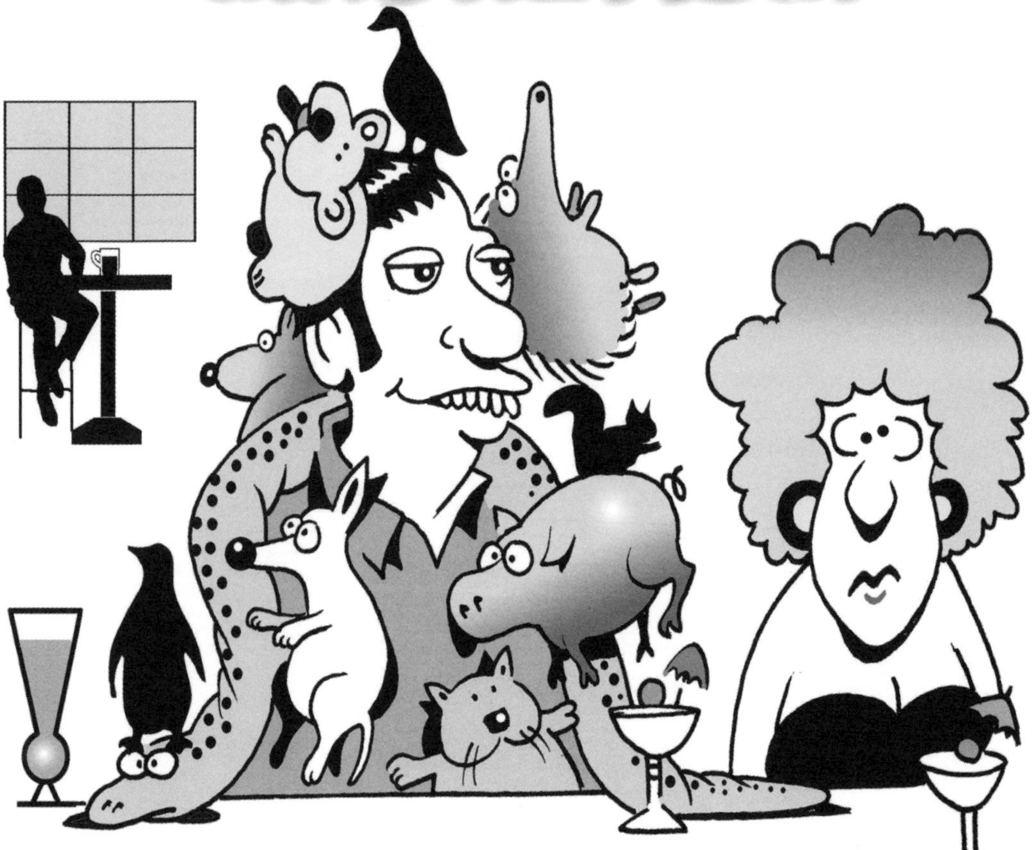

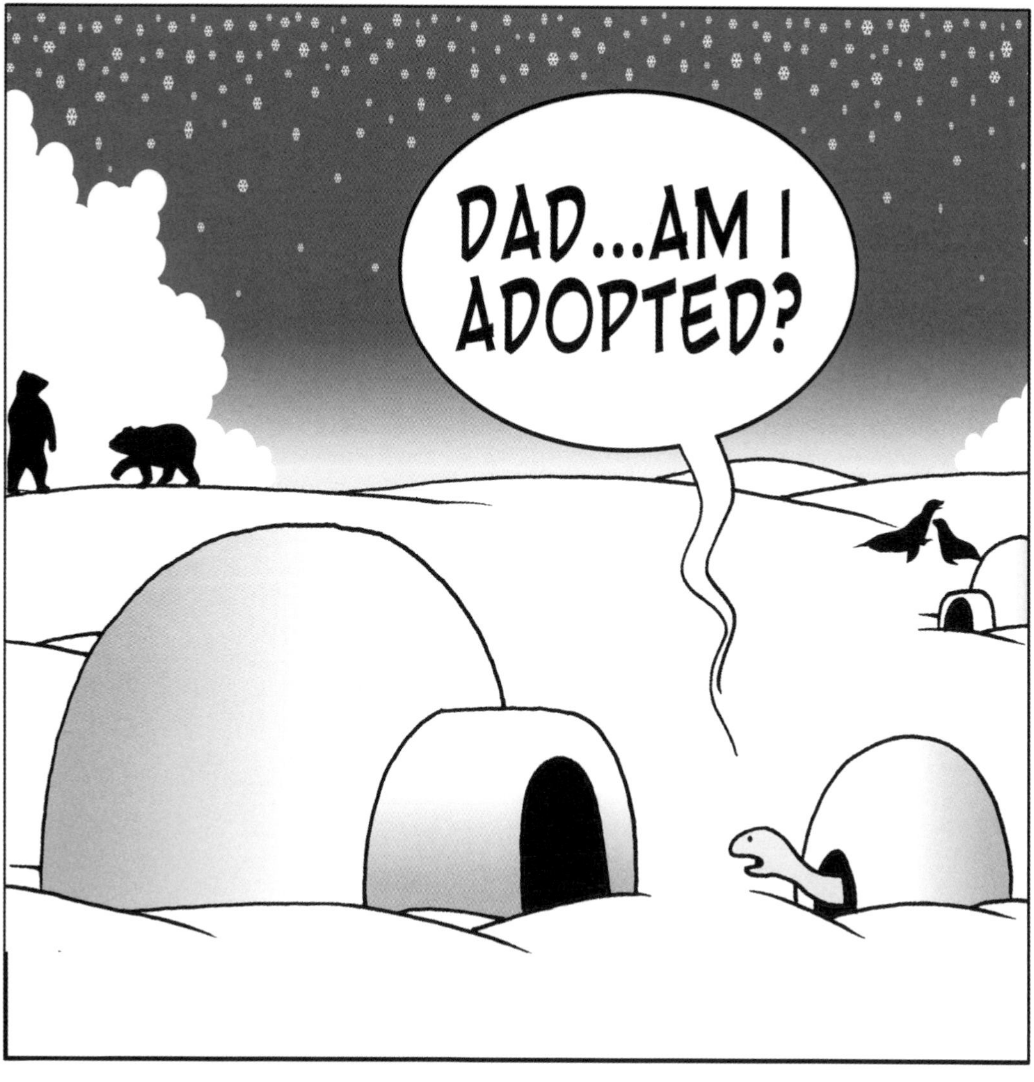
DAD...AM I ADOPTED?

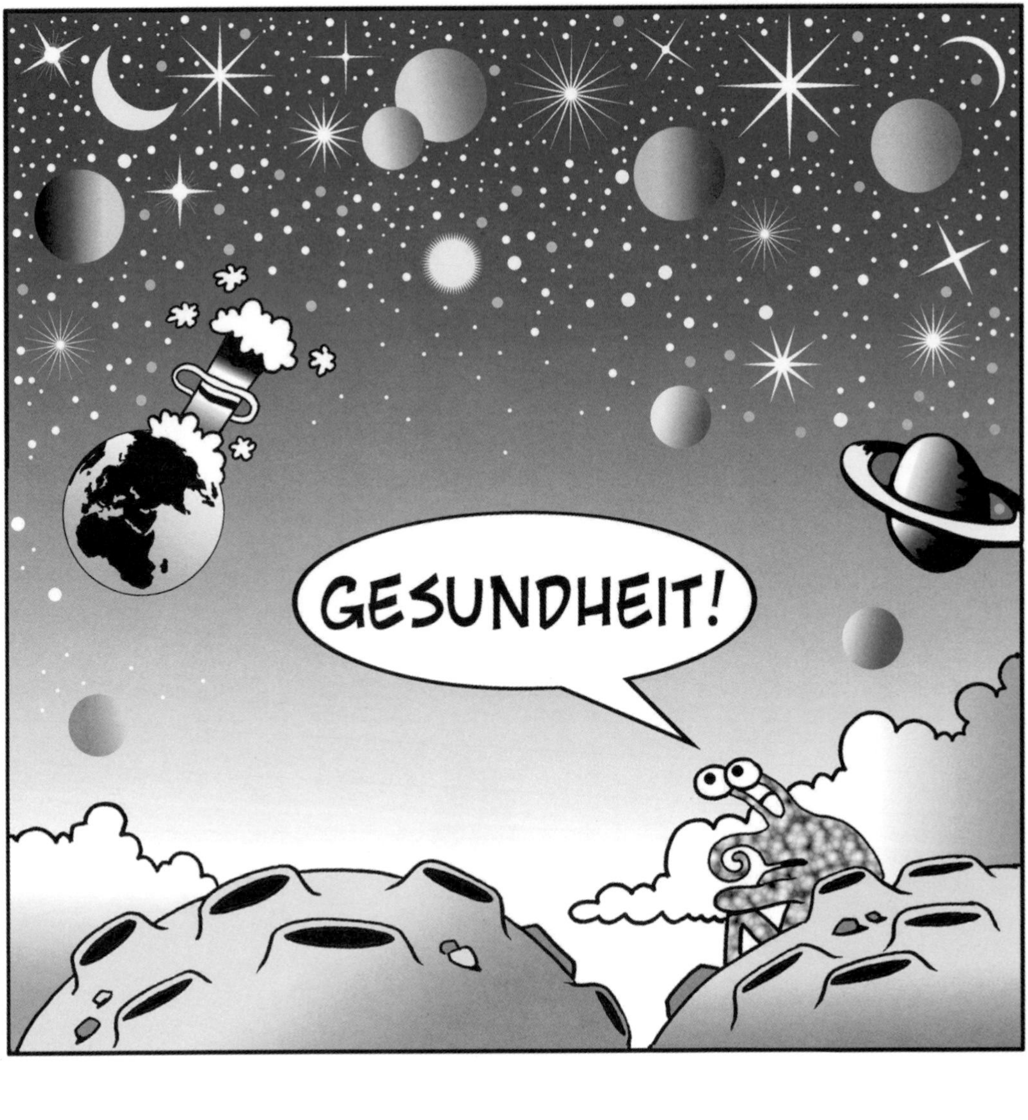
GESUNDHEIT!

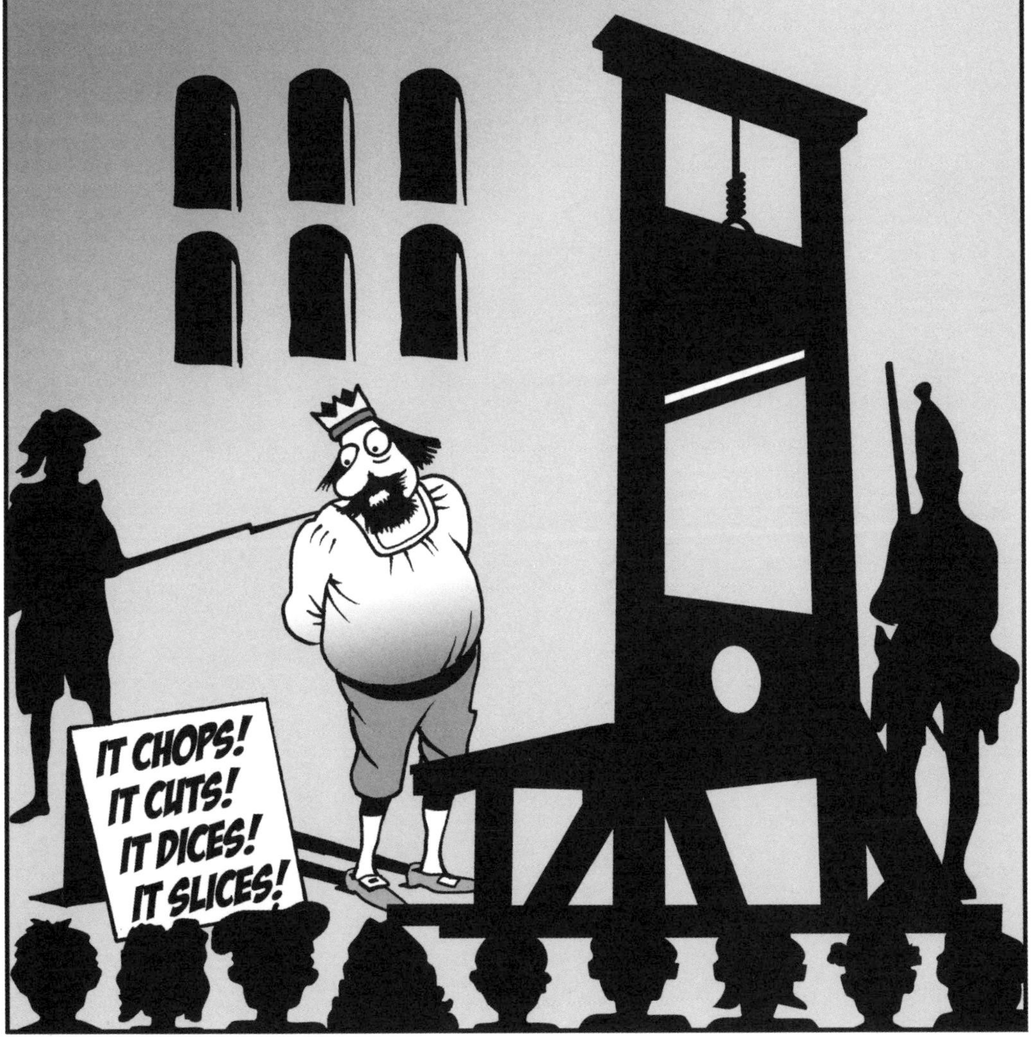
IT CHOPS!
IT CUTS!
IT DICES!
IT SLICES!

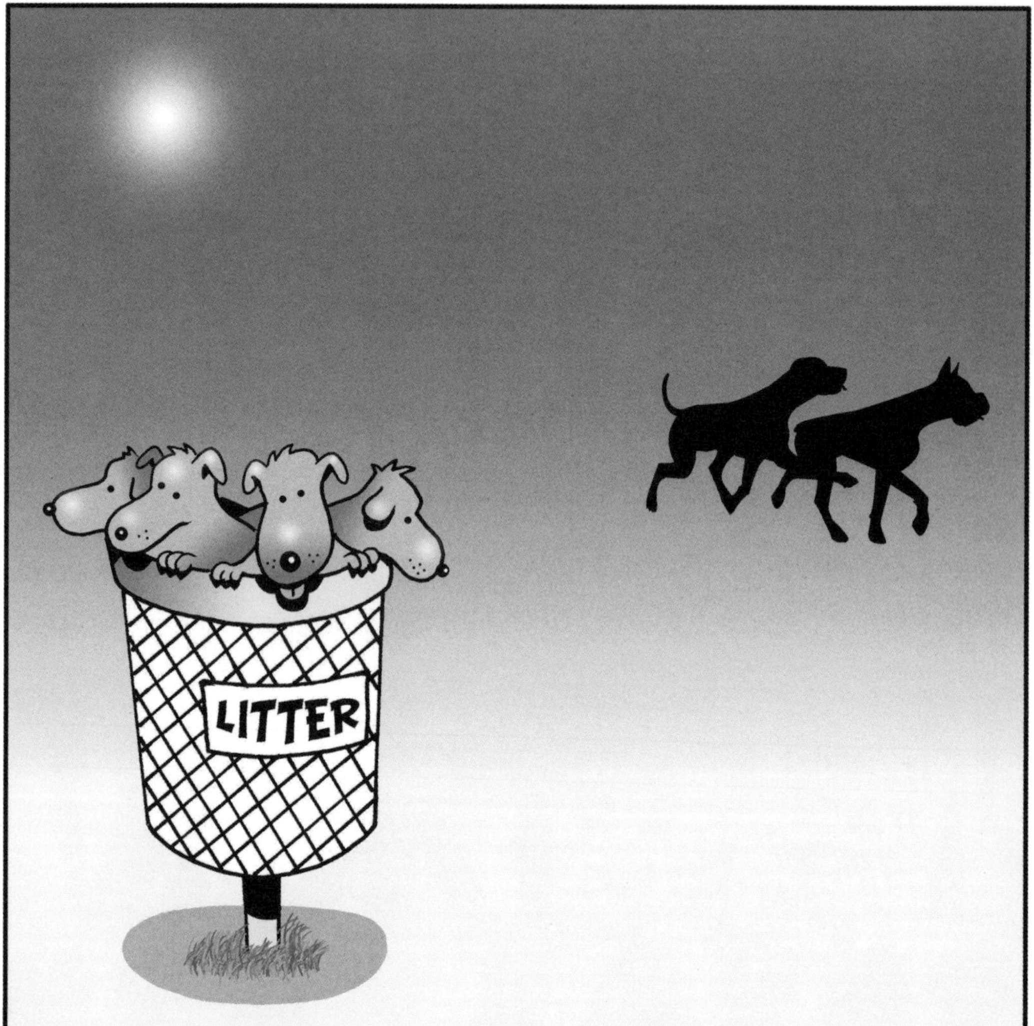
LITTER

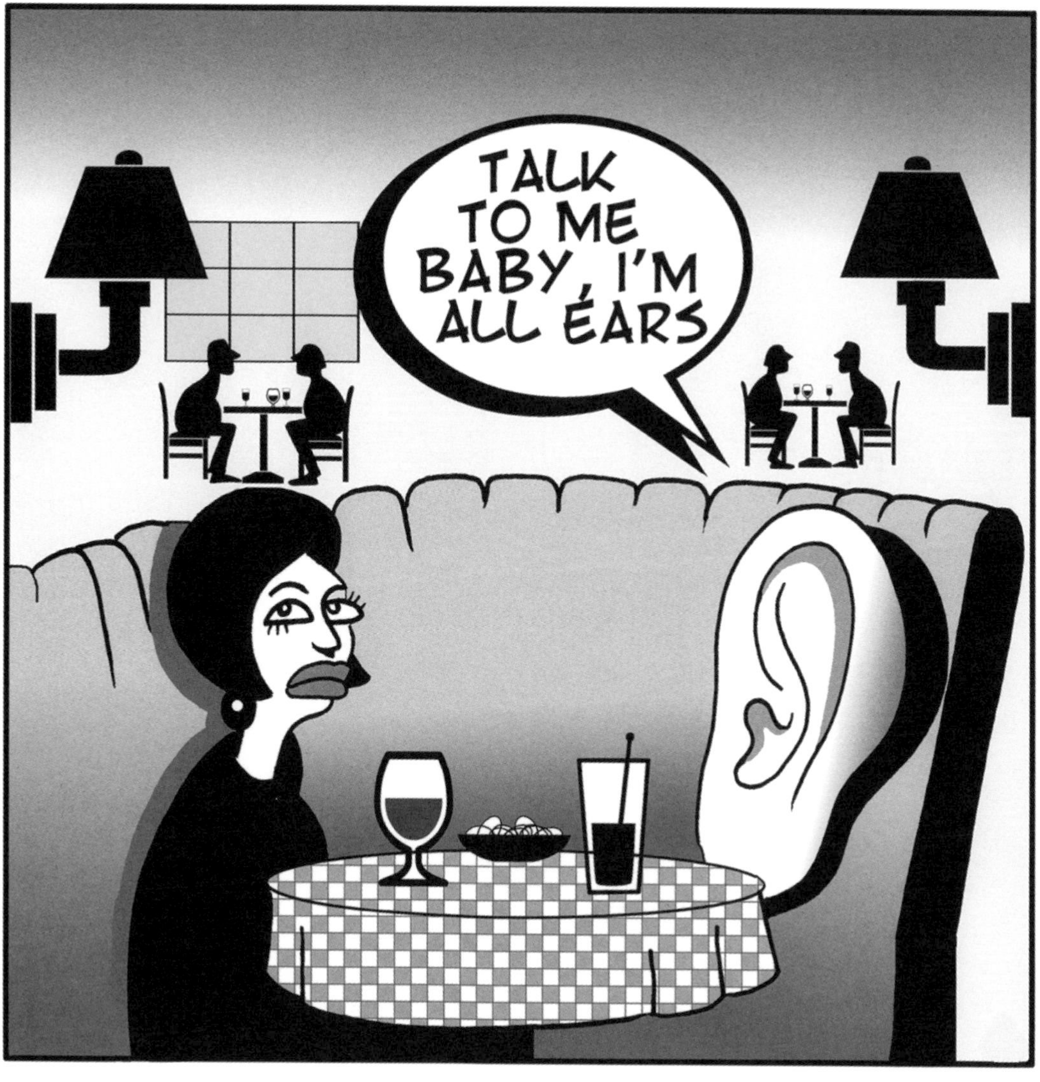
TALK TO ME BABY, I'M ALL EARS

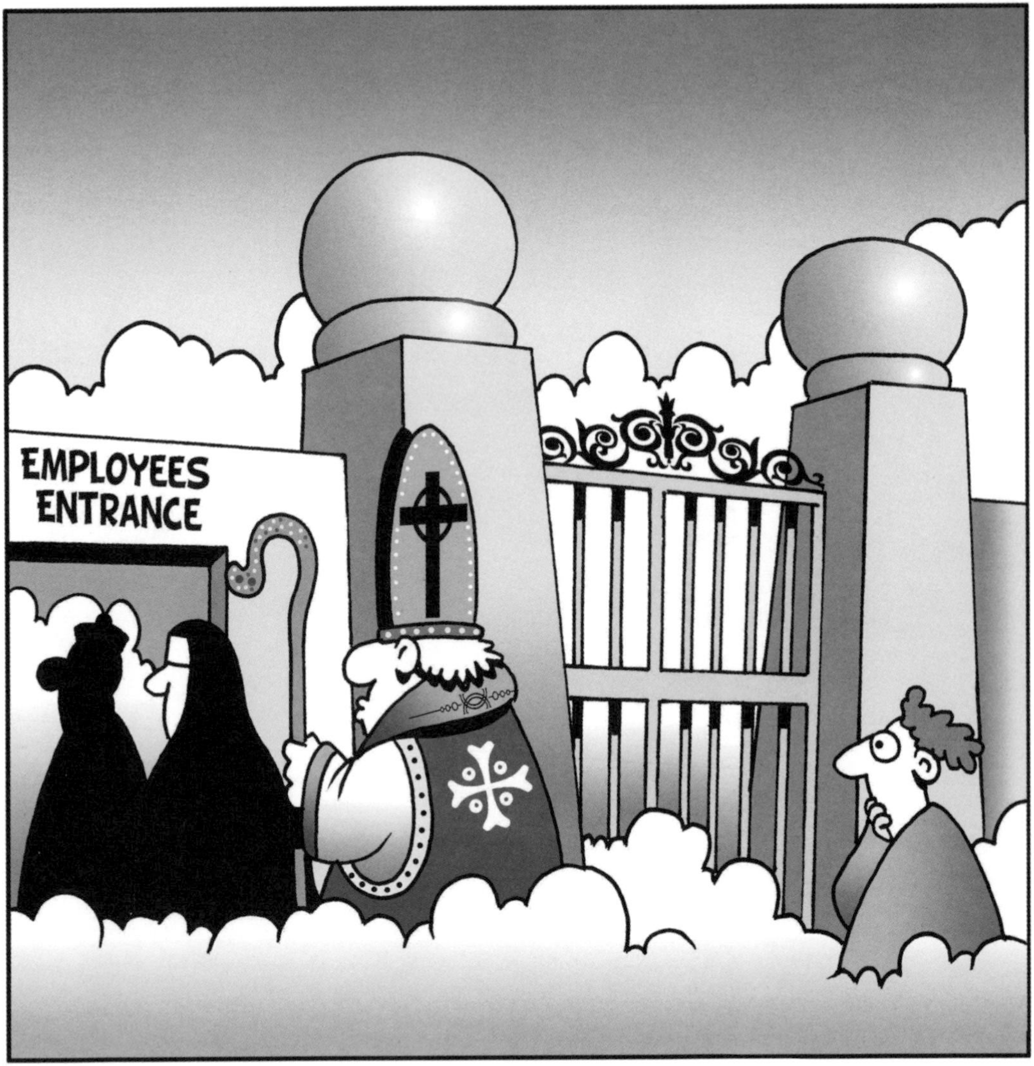
EMPLOYEES
ENTRANCE

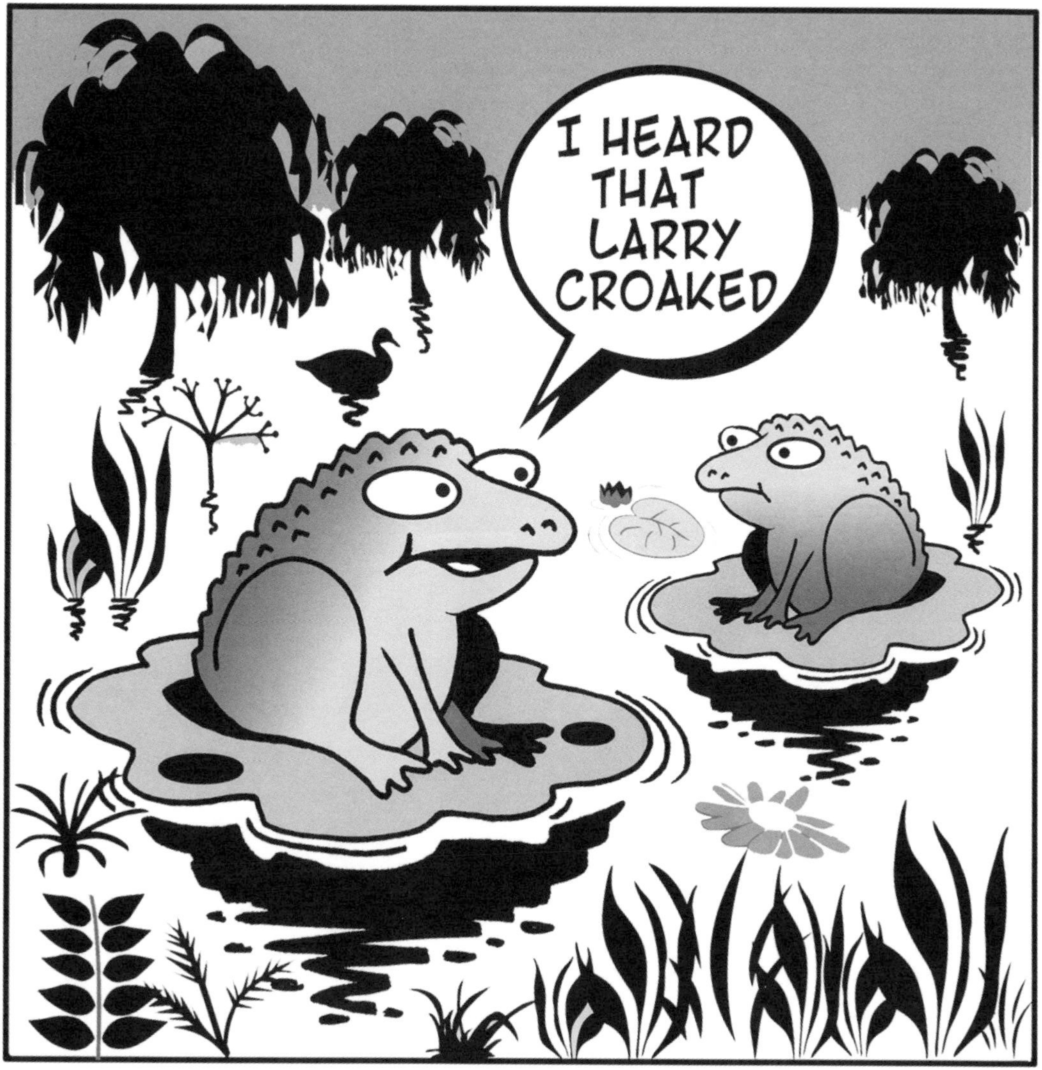
I HEARD THAT LARRY CROAKED

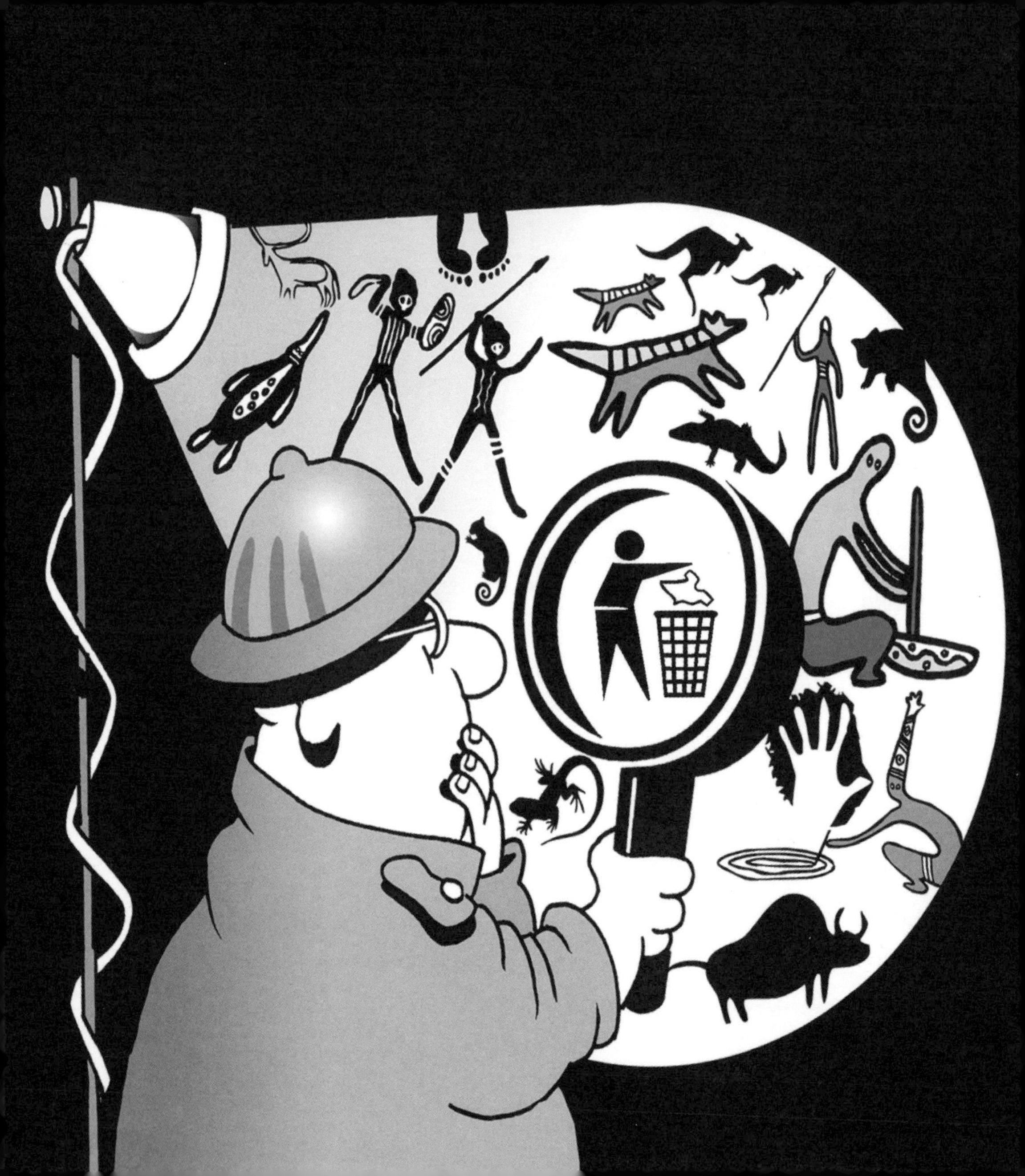

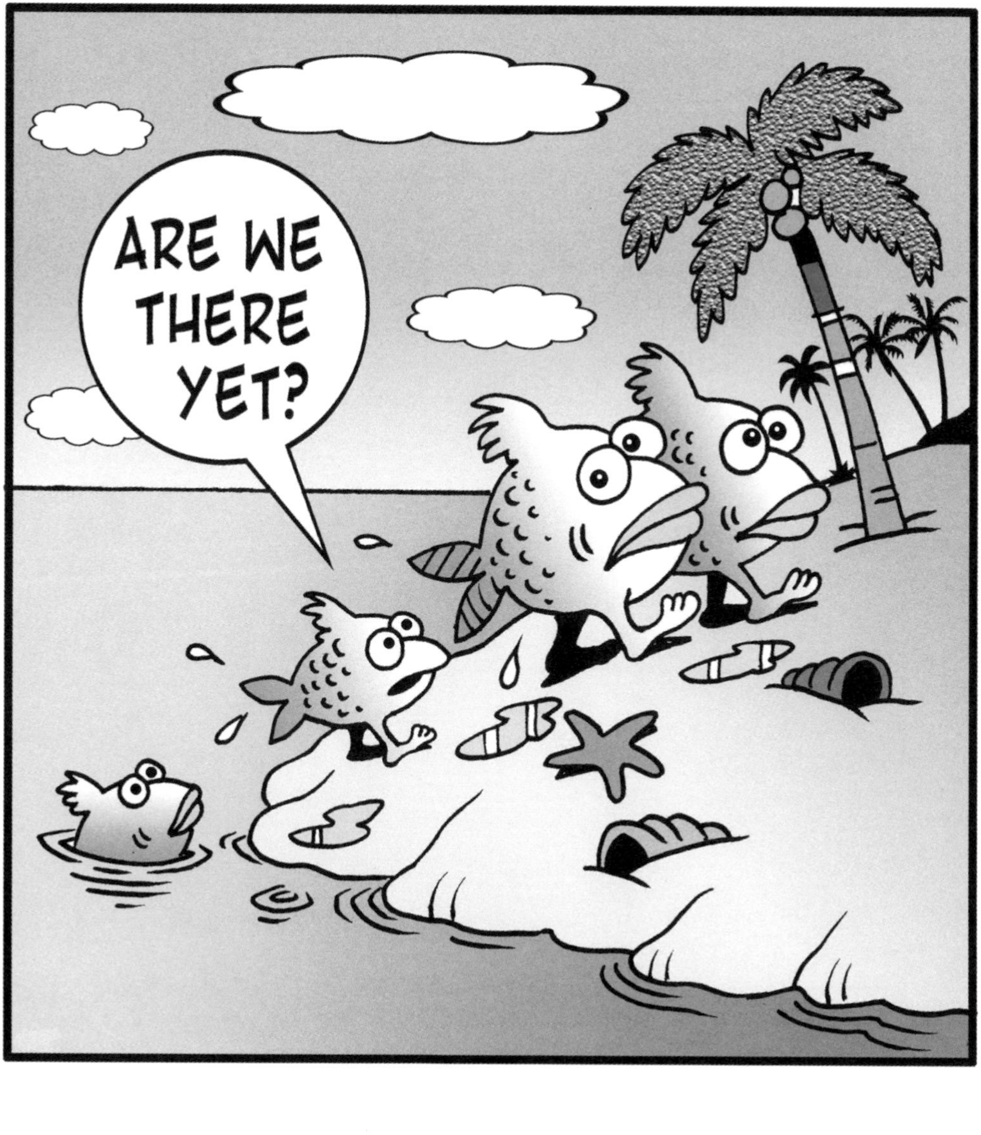
ARE WE THERE YET?

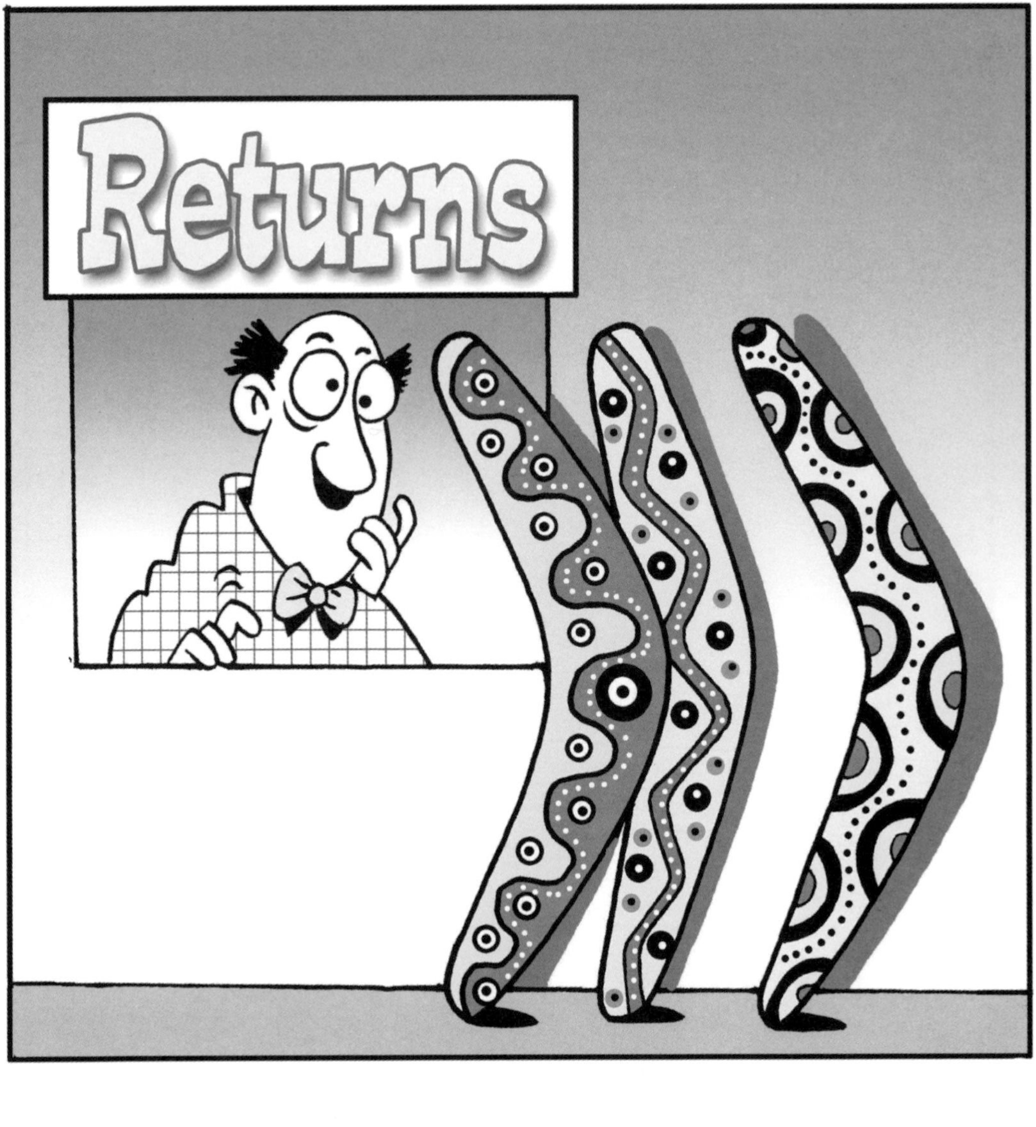
Returns

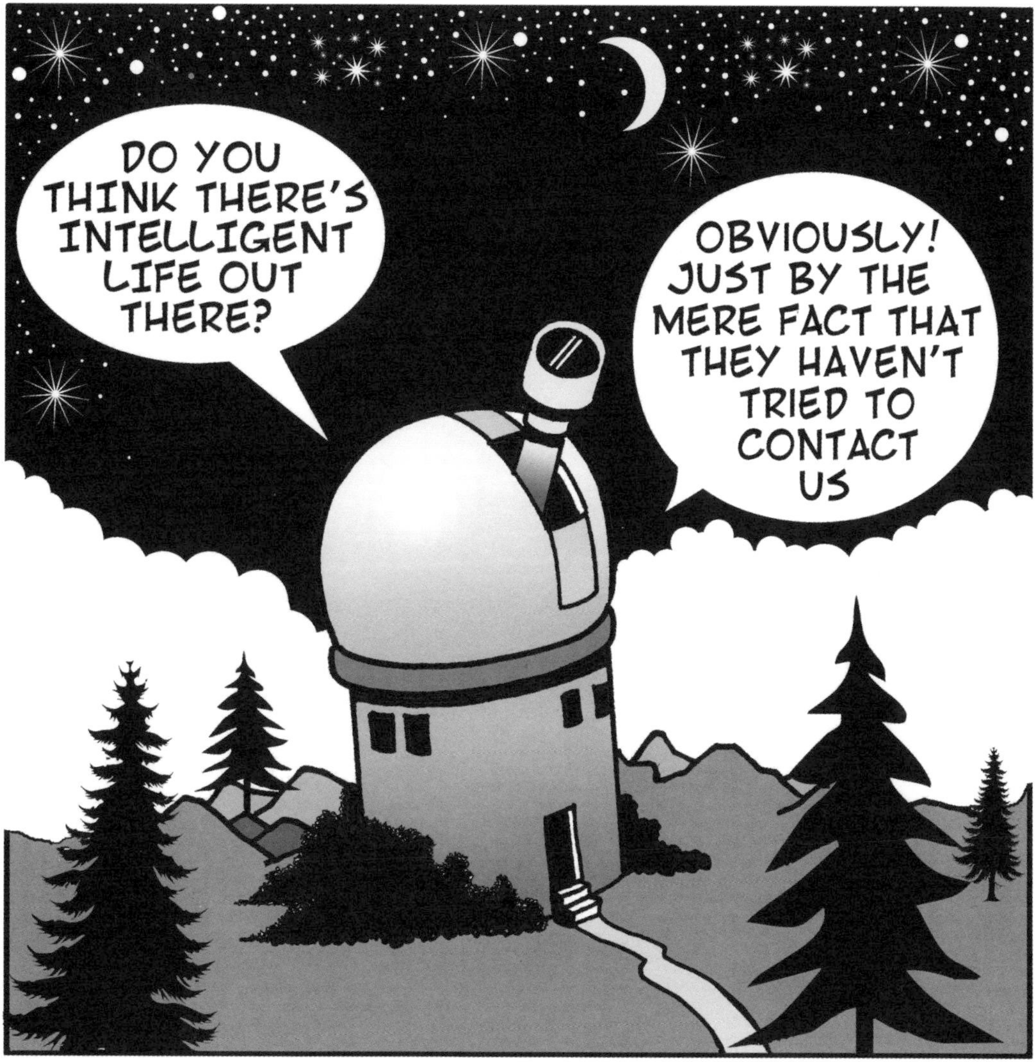
DO YOU THINK THERE'S INTELLIGENT LIFE OUT THERE?
OBVIOUSLY! JUST BY THE MERE FACT THAT THEY HAVEN'T TRIED TO CONTACT US

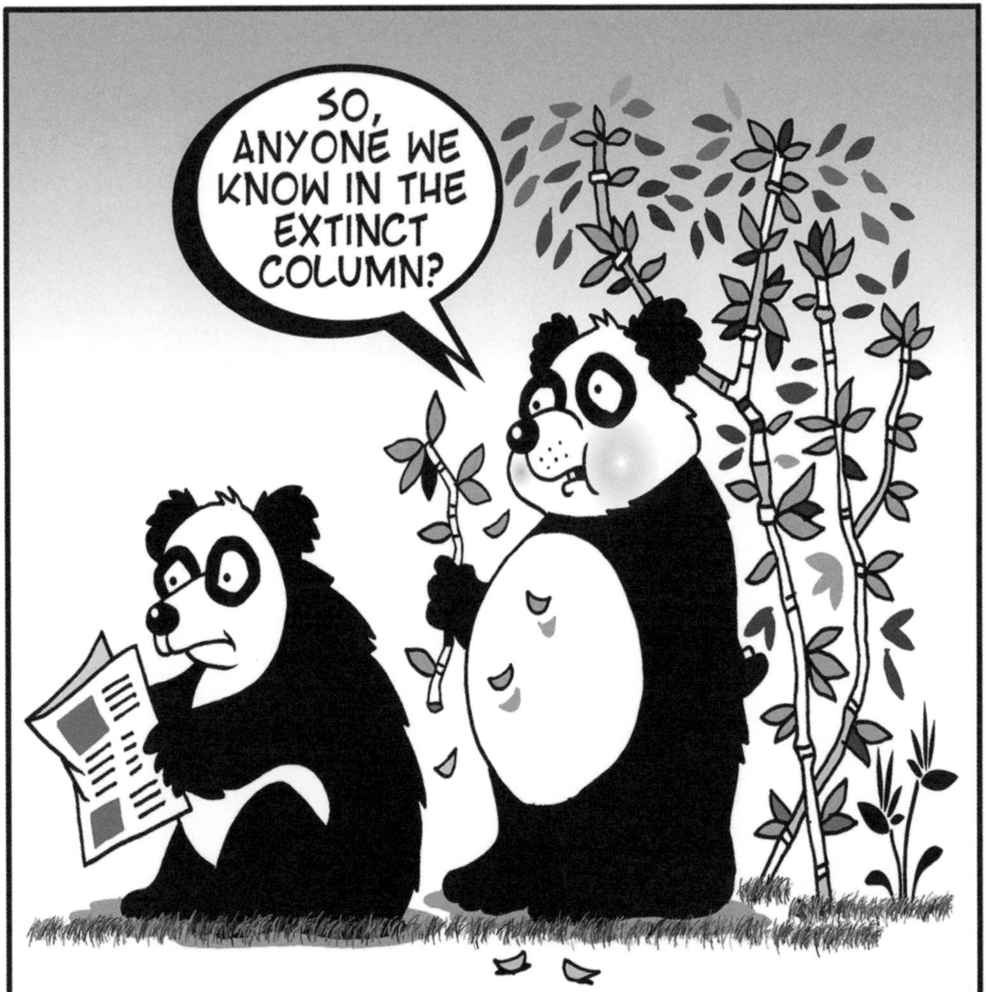
SO, ANYONE WE KNOW IN THE EXTINCT COLUMN?

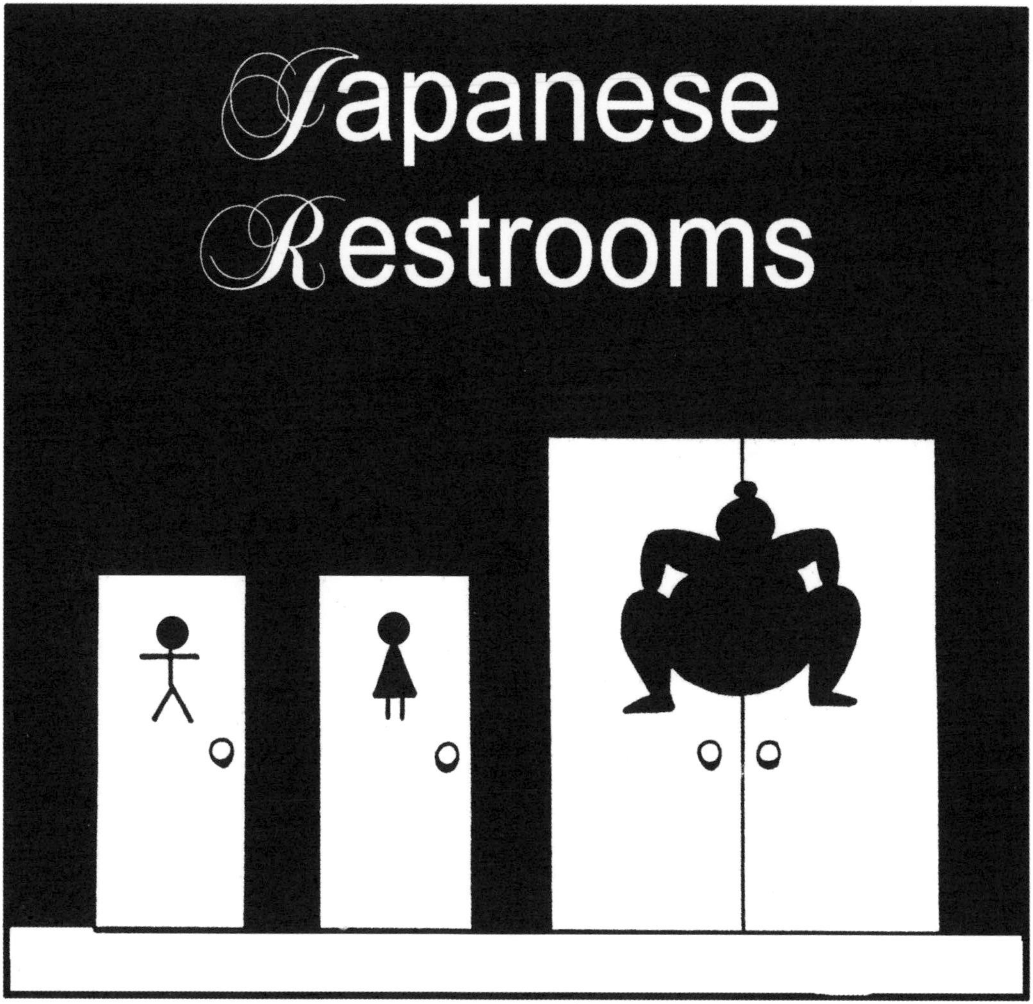
Japanese
Restrooms

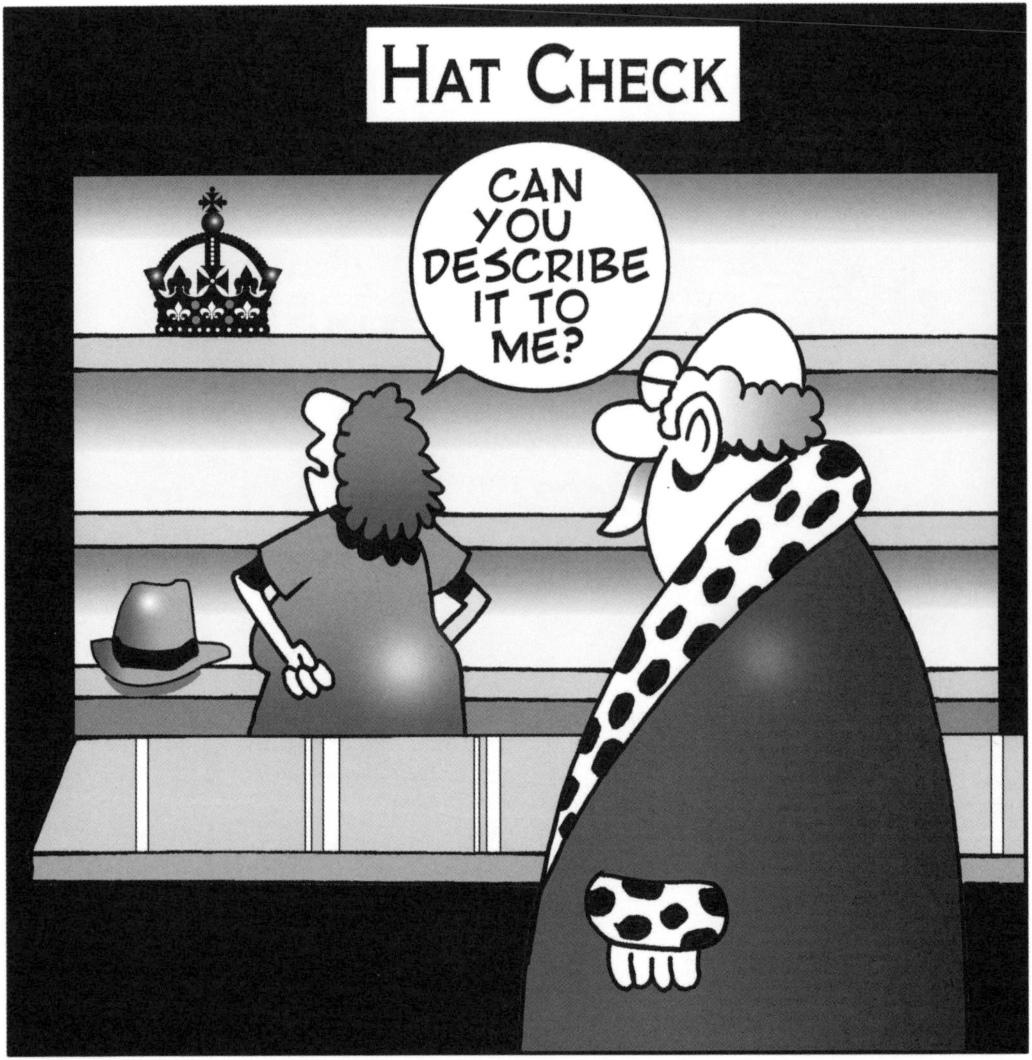
HAT CHECK
CAN YOU DESCRIBE IT TO ME?

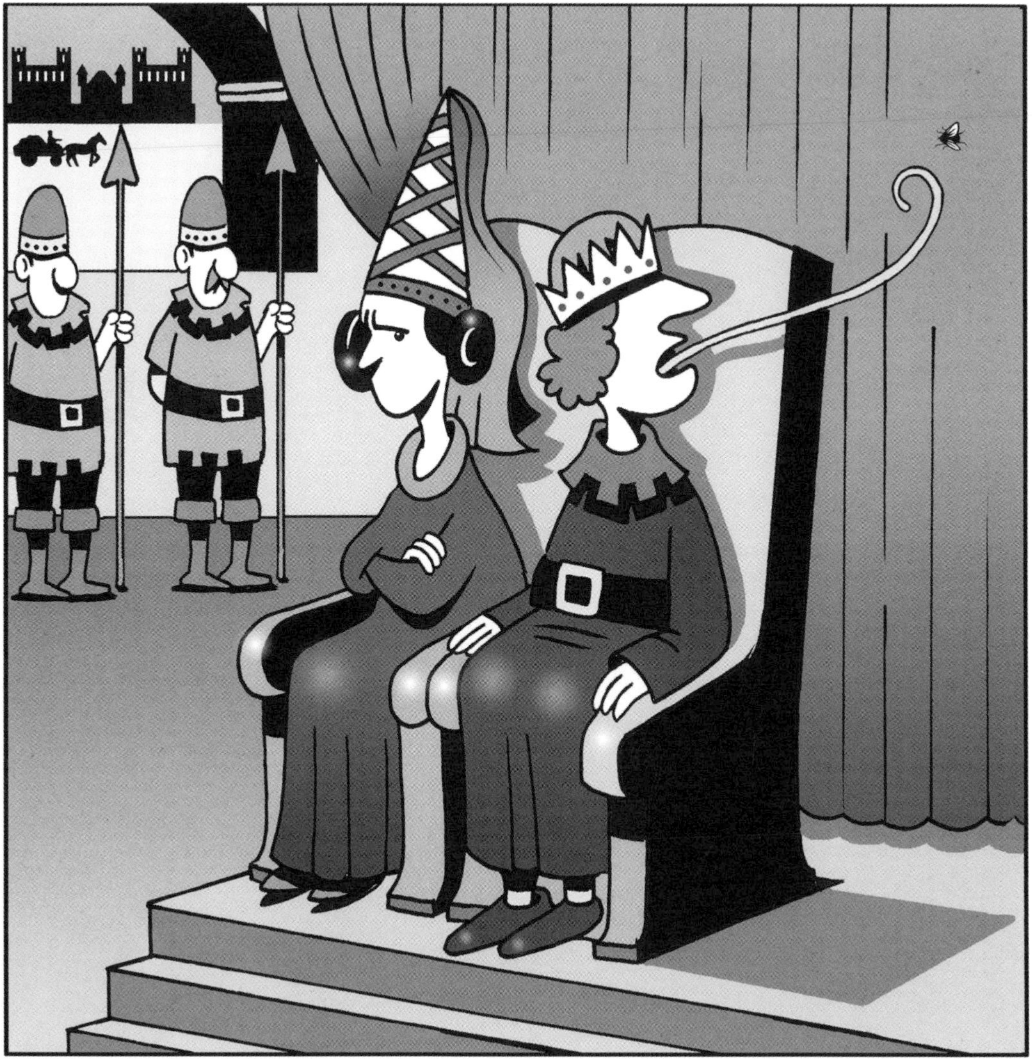

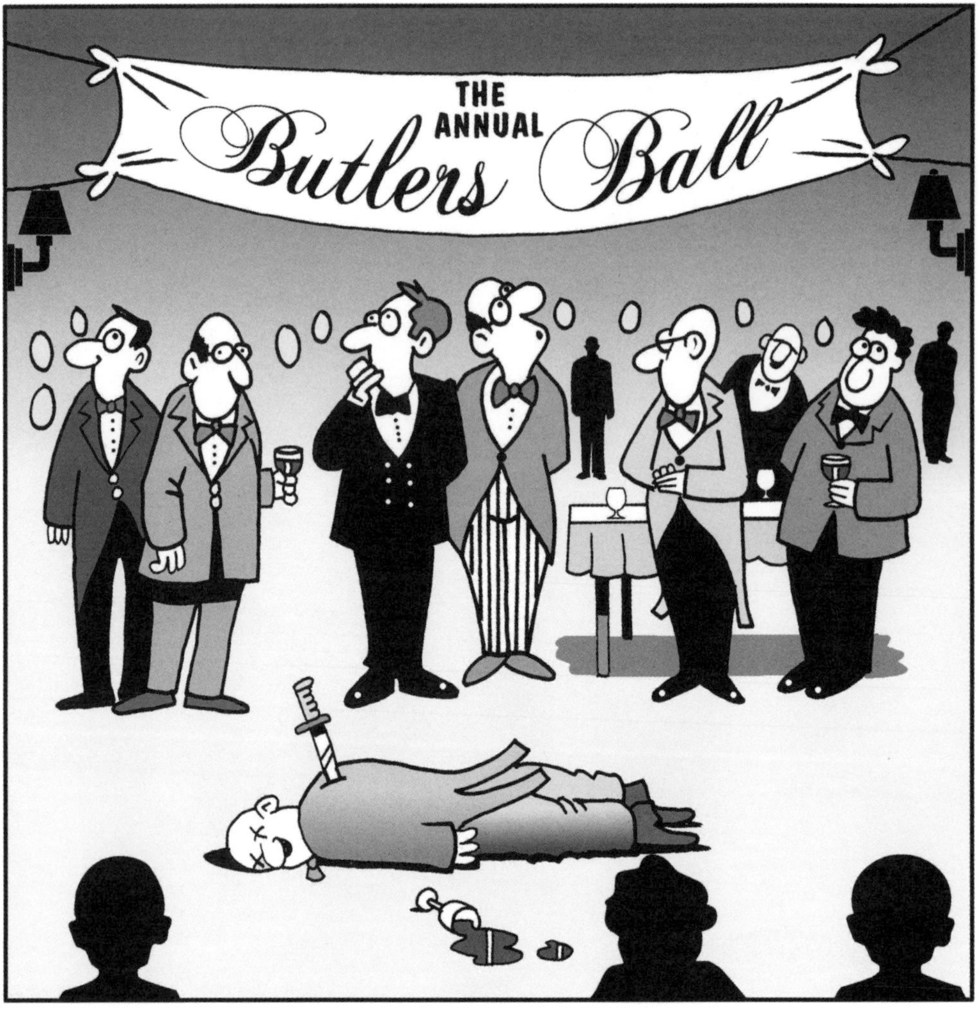
THE ANNUAL
Butlers Ball

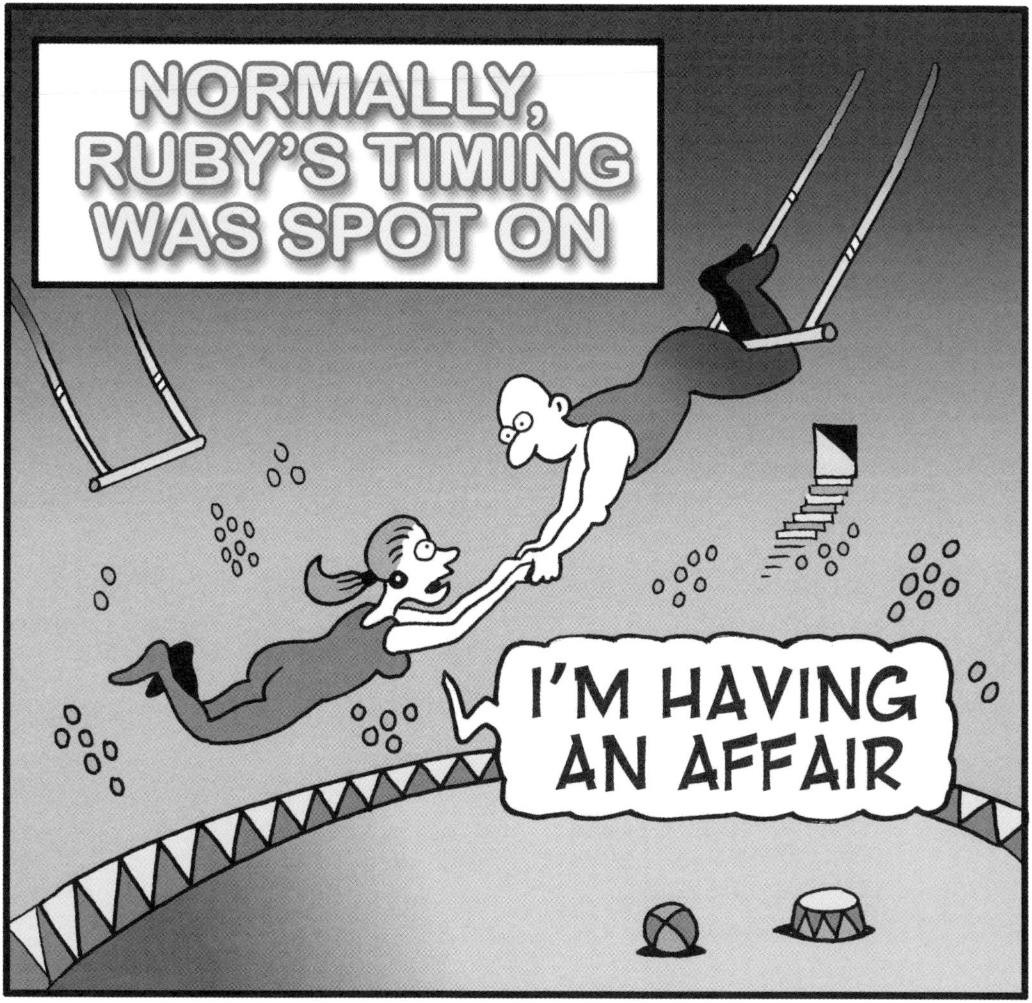
NORMALLY, RUBY'S TIMING WAS SPOT ON
I'M HAVING AN AFFAIR

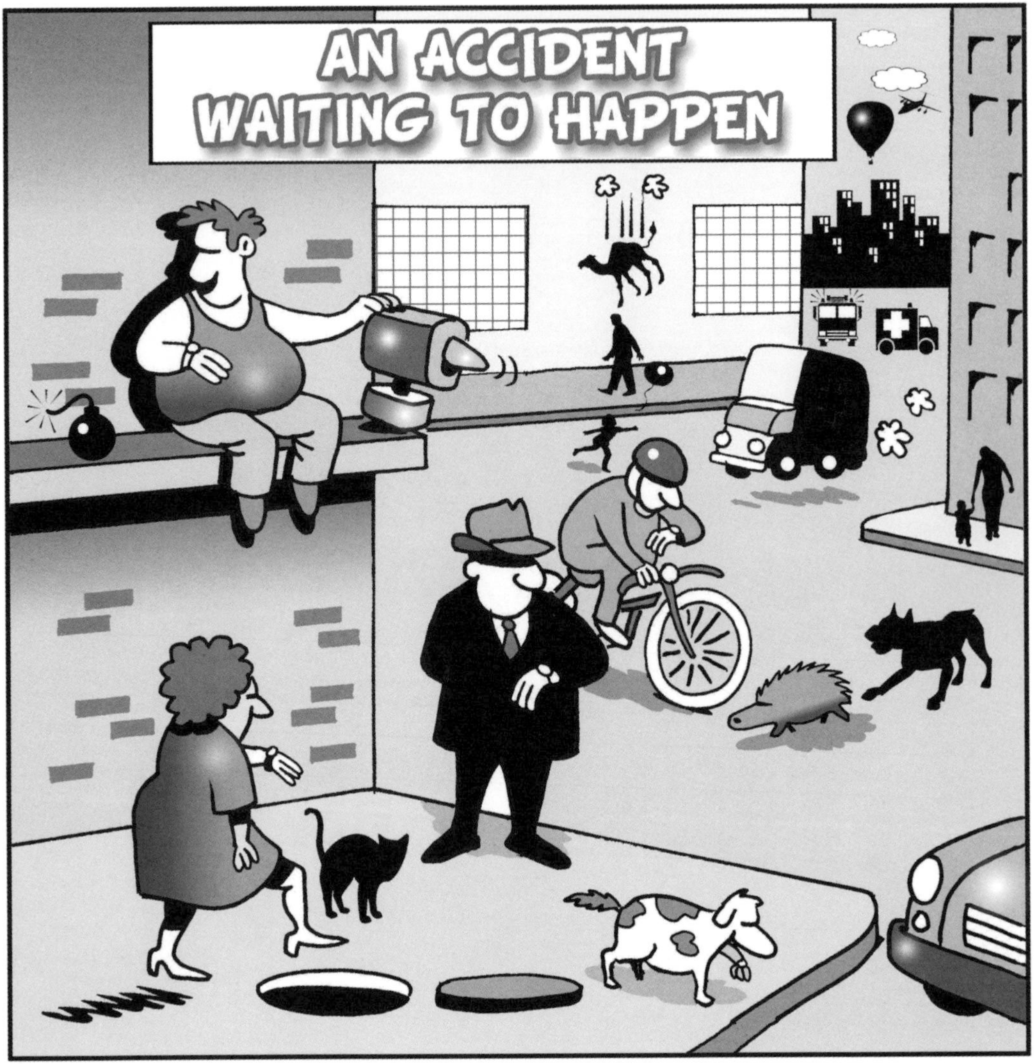
AN ACCIDENT
WAITING TO HAPPEN

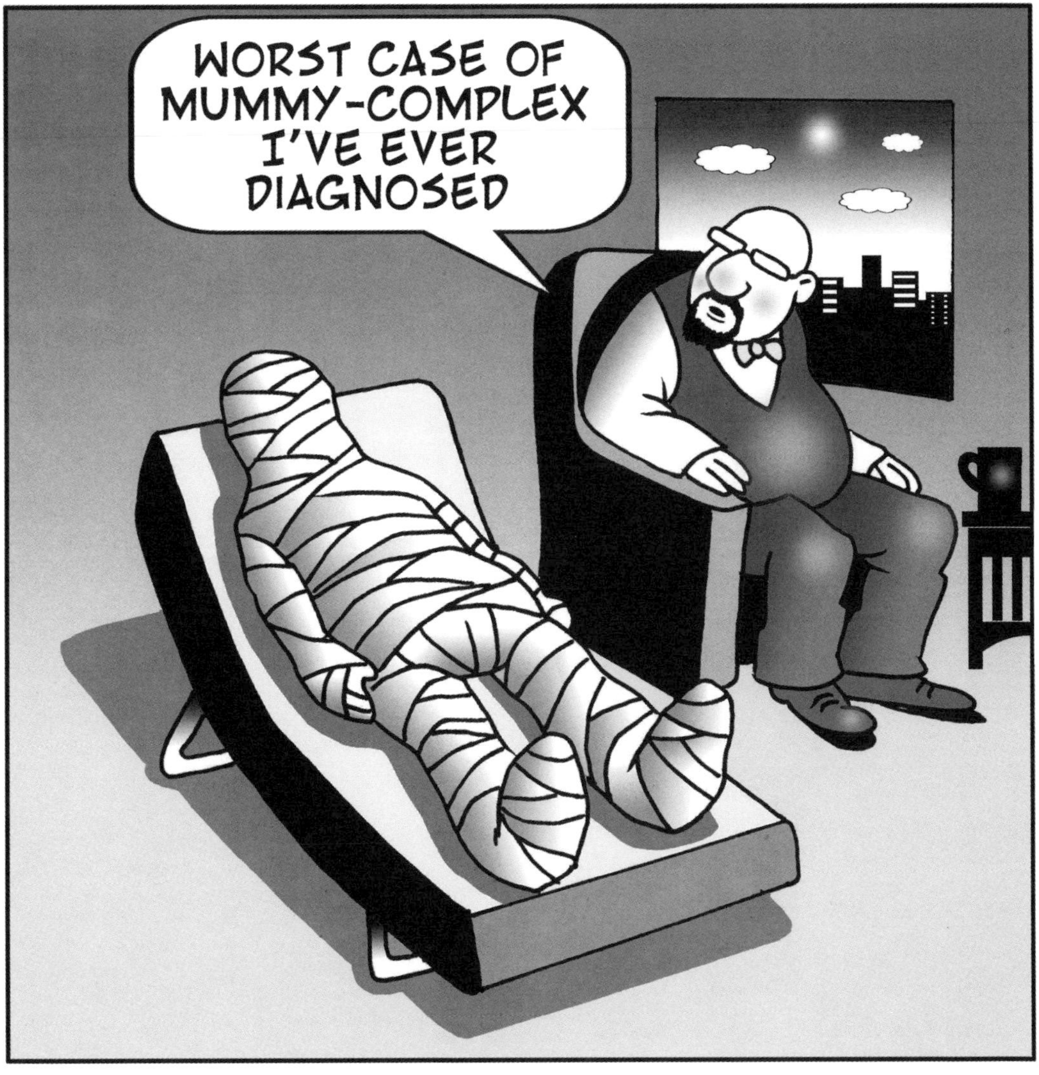
WORST CASE OF MUMMY-COMPLEX I'VE EVER DIAGNOSED

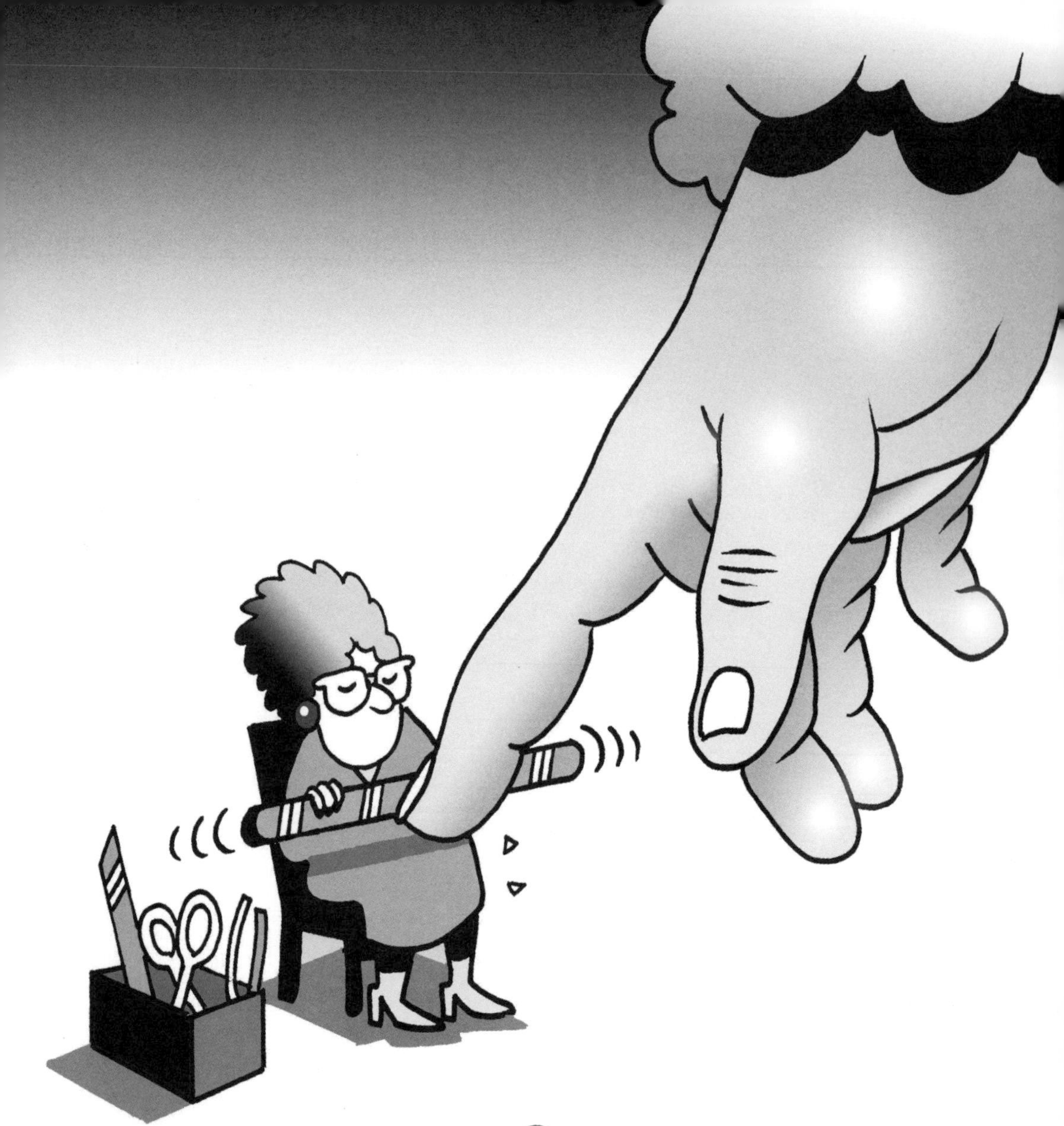

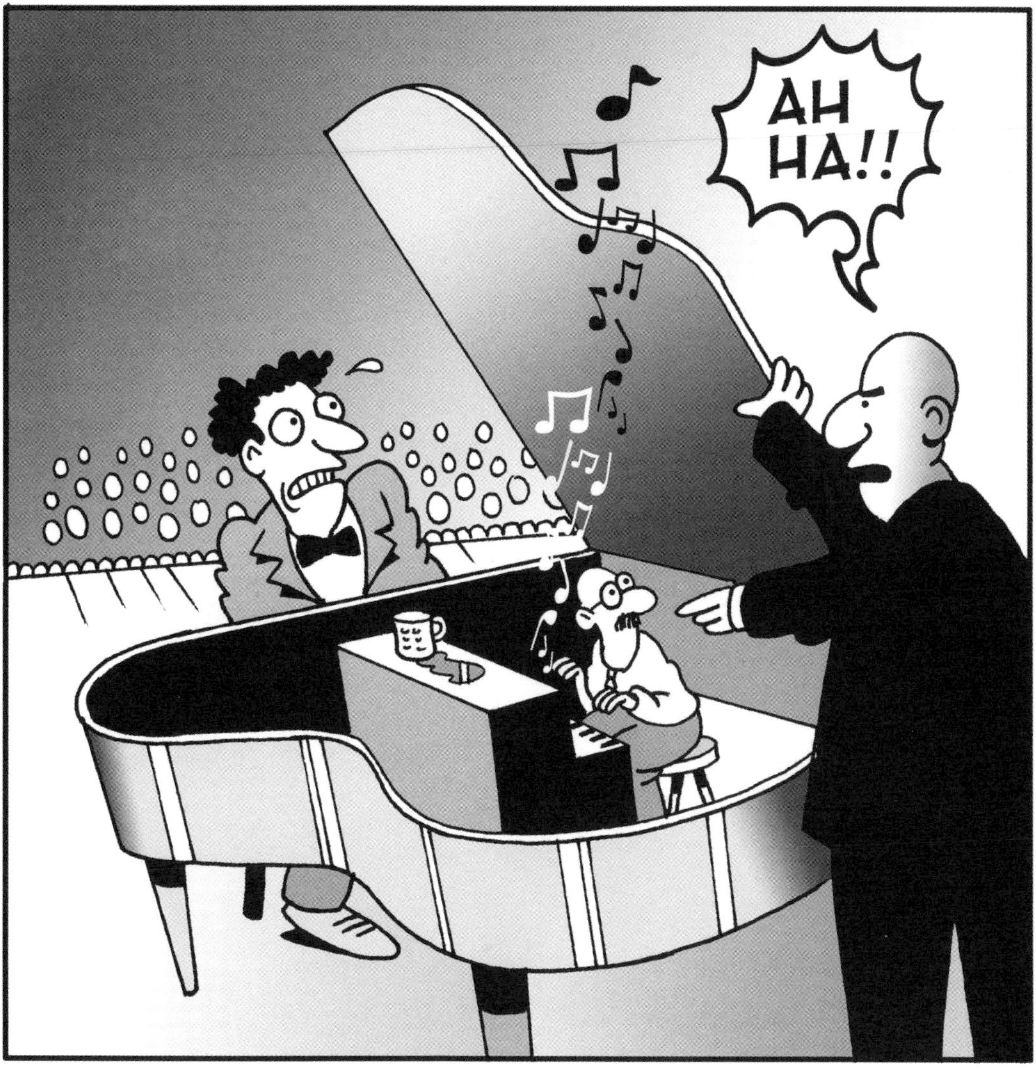
AH HA!!

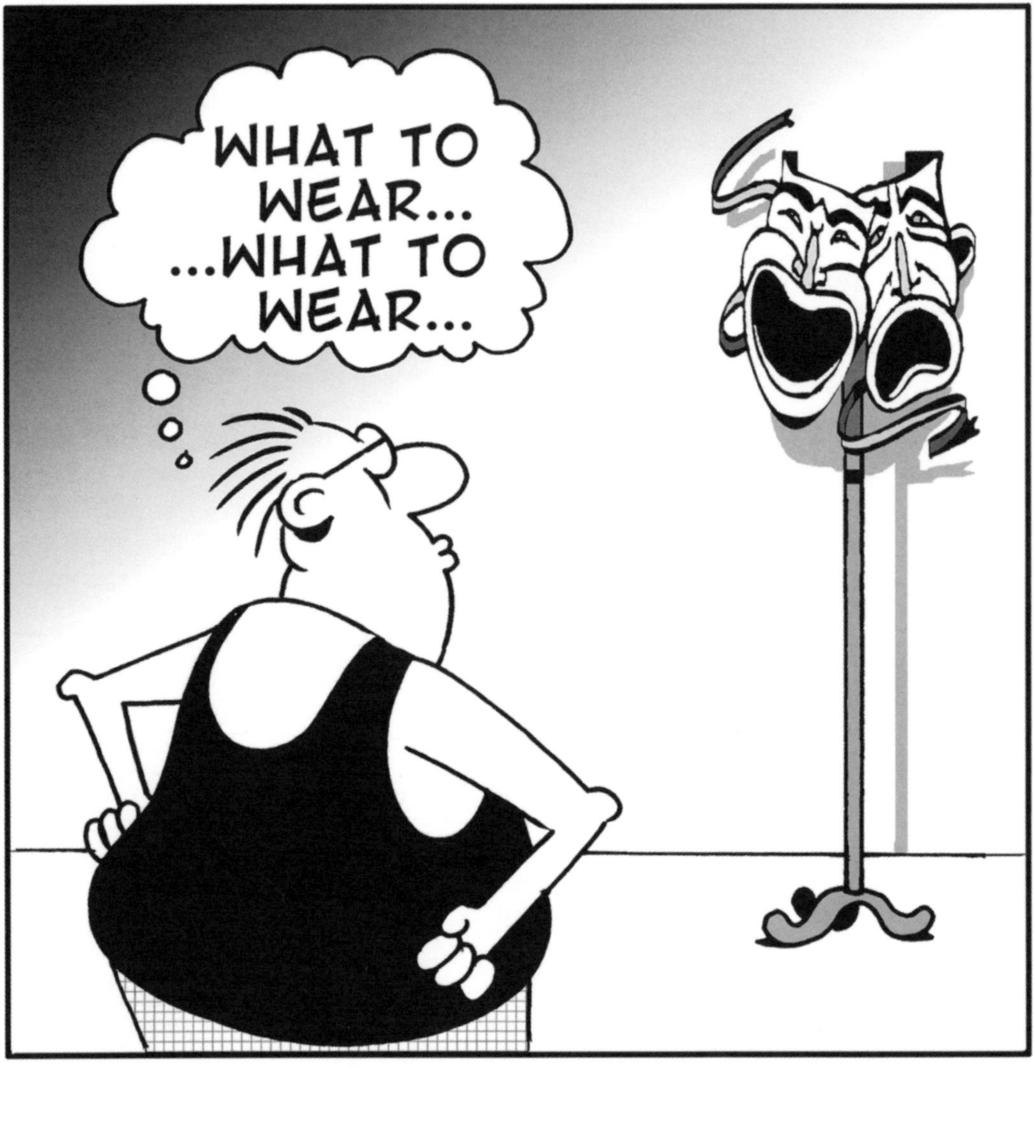
WHAT TO WEAR... ...WHAT TO WEAR...

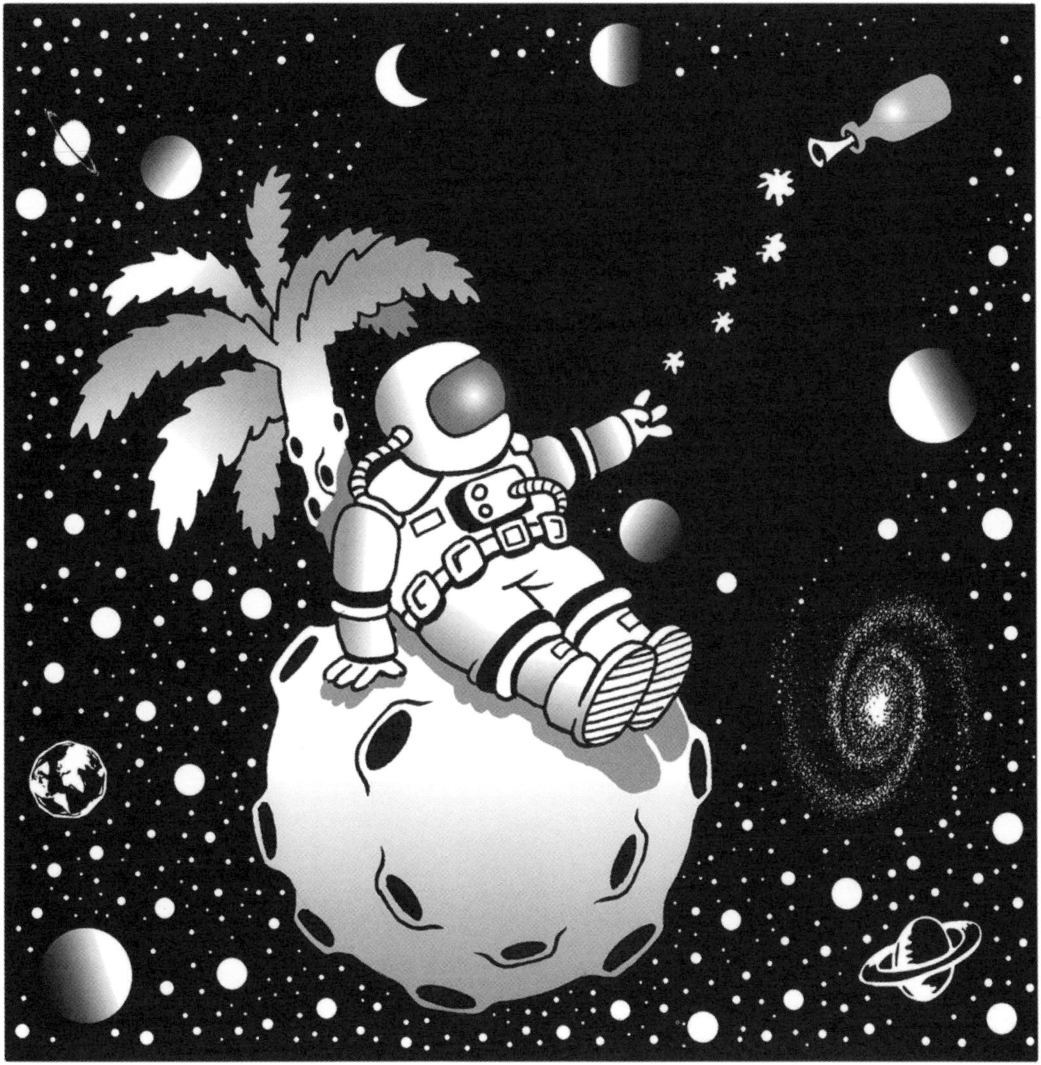

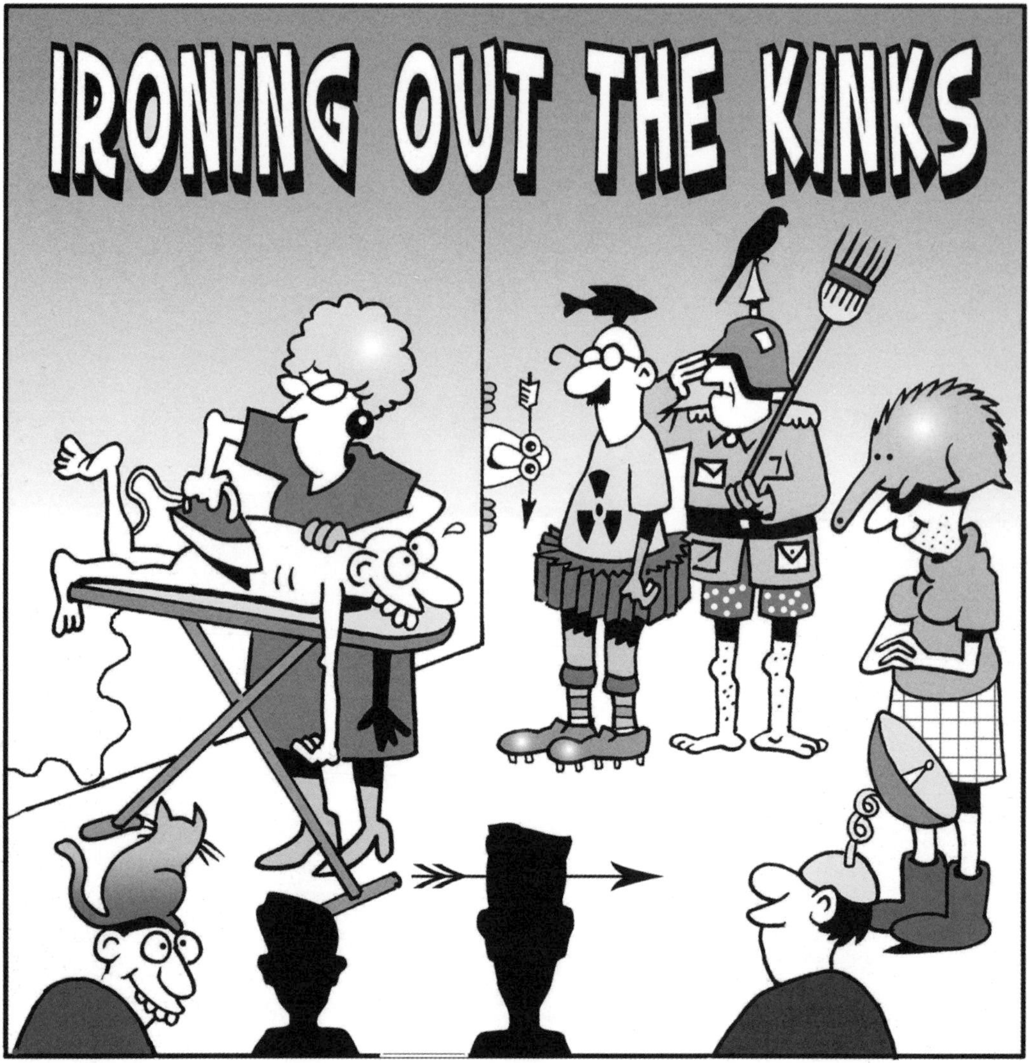
IRONING OUT THE KINKS

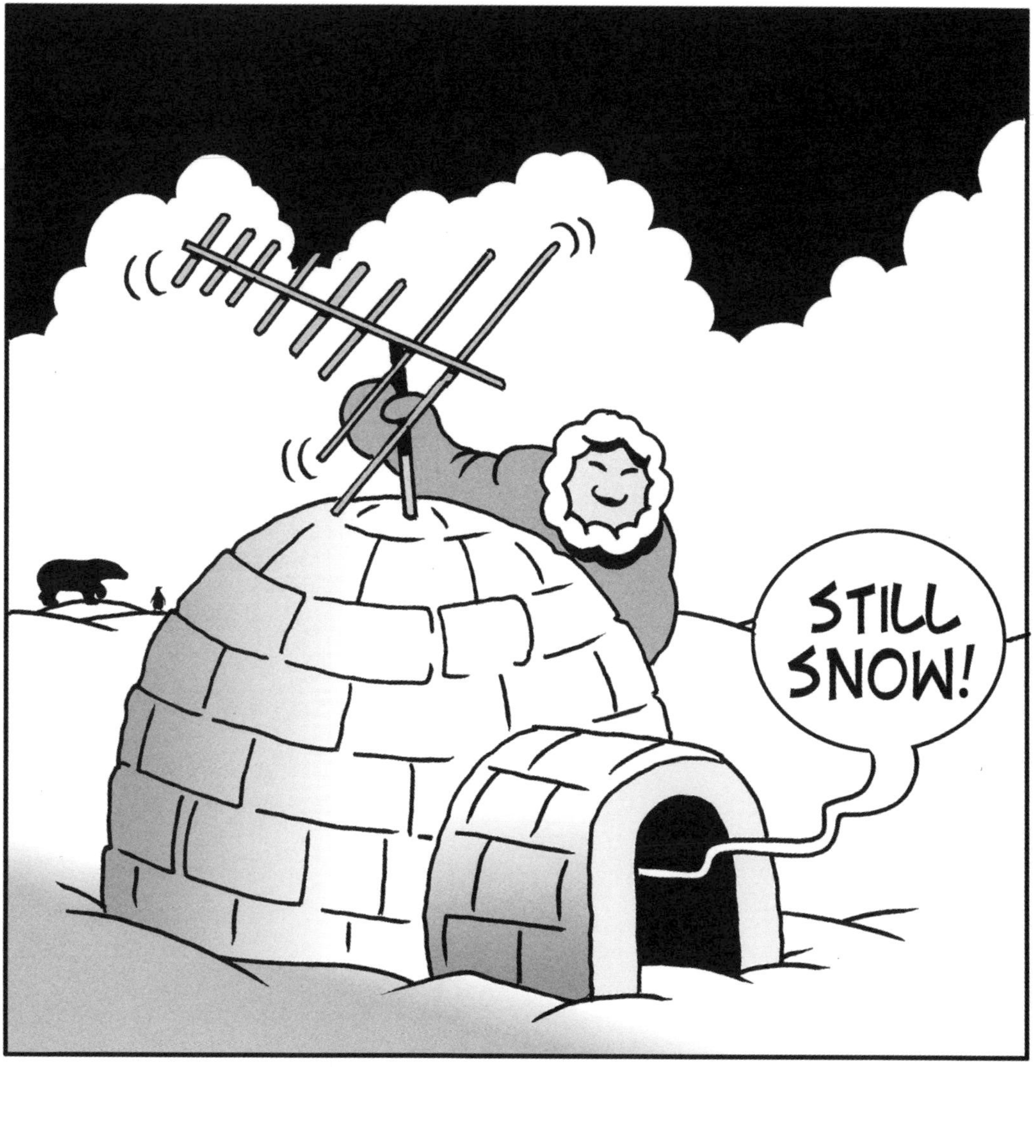
STILL SNOW!

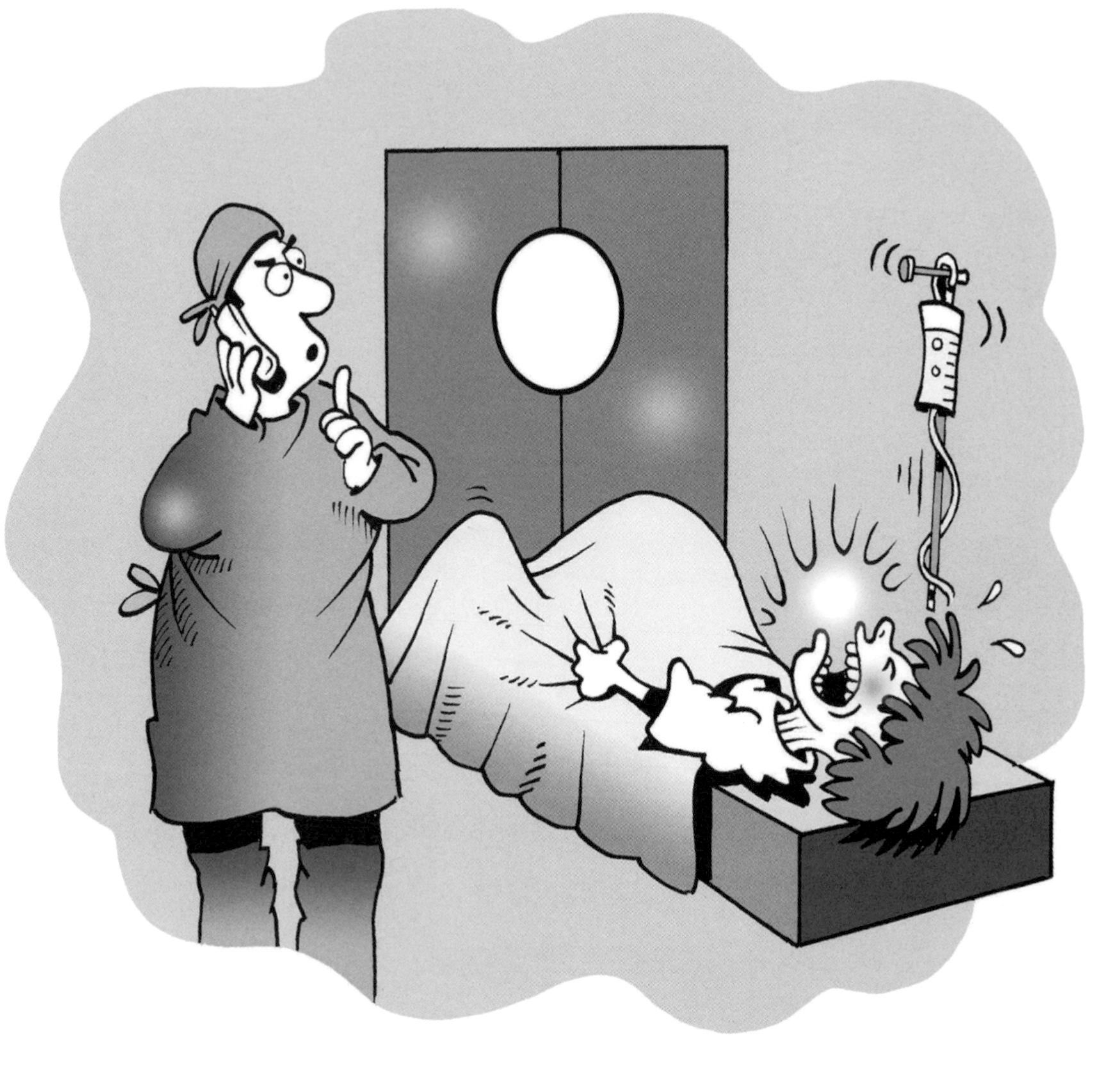

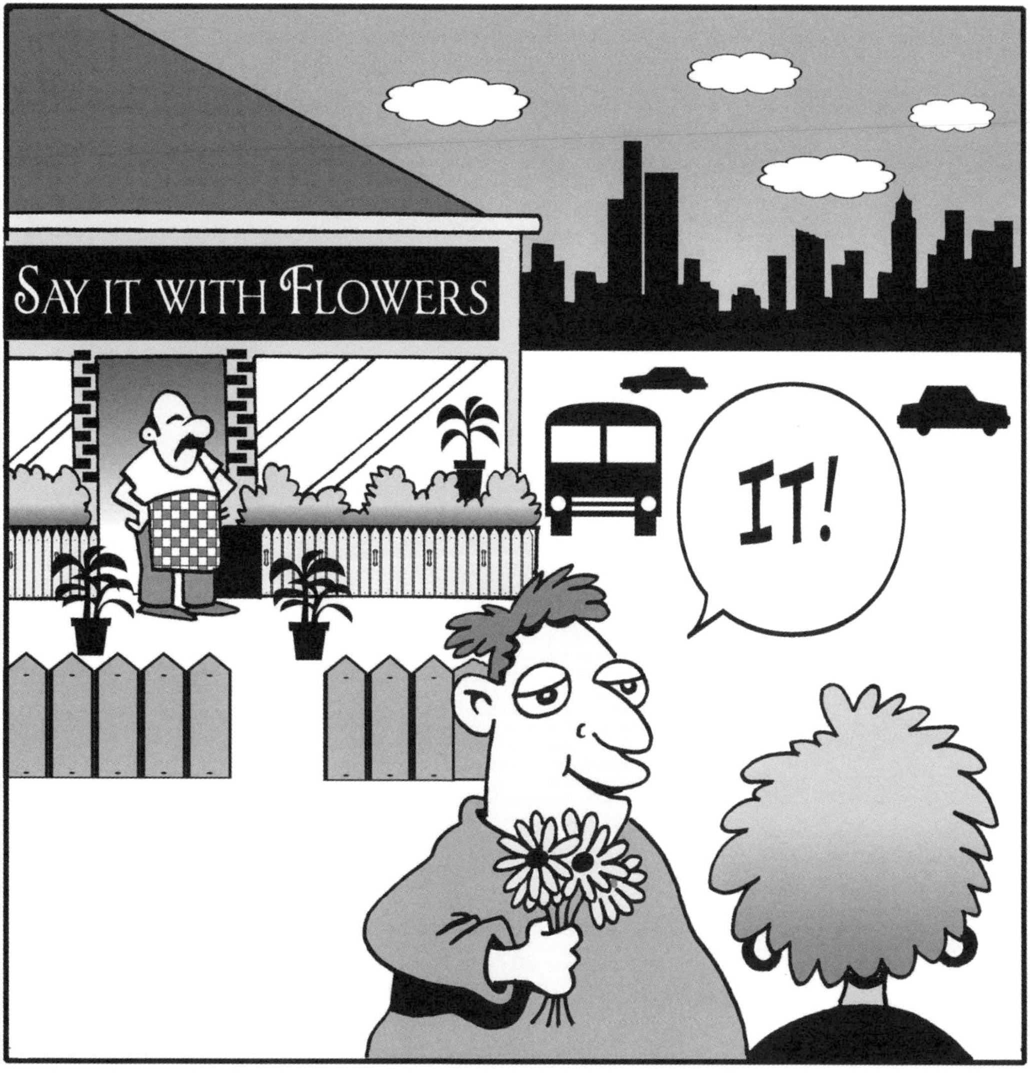
SAY IT WITH FLOWERS
IT!

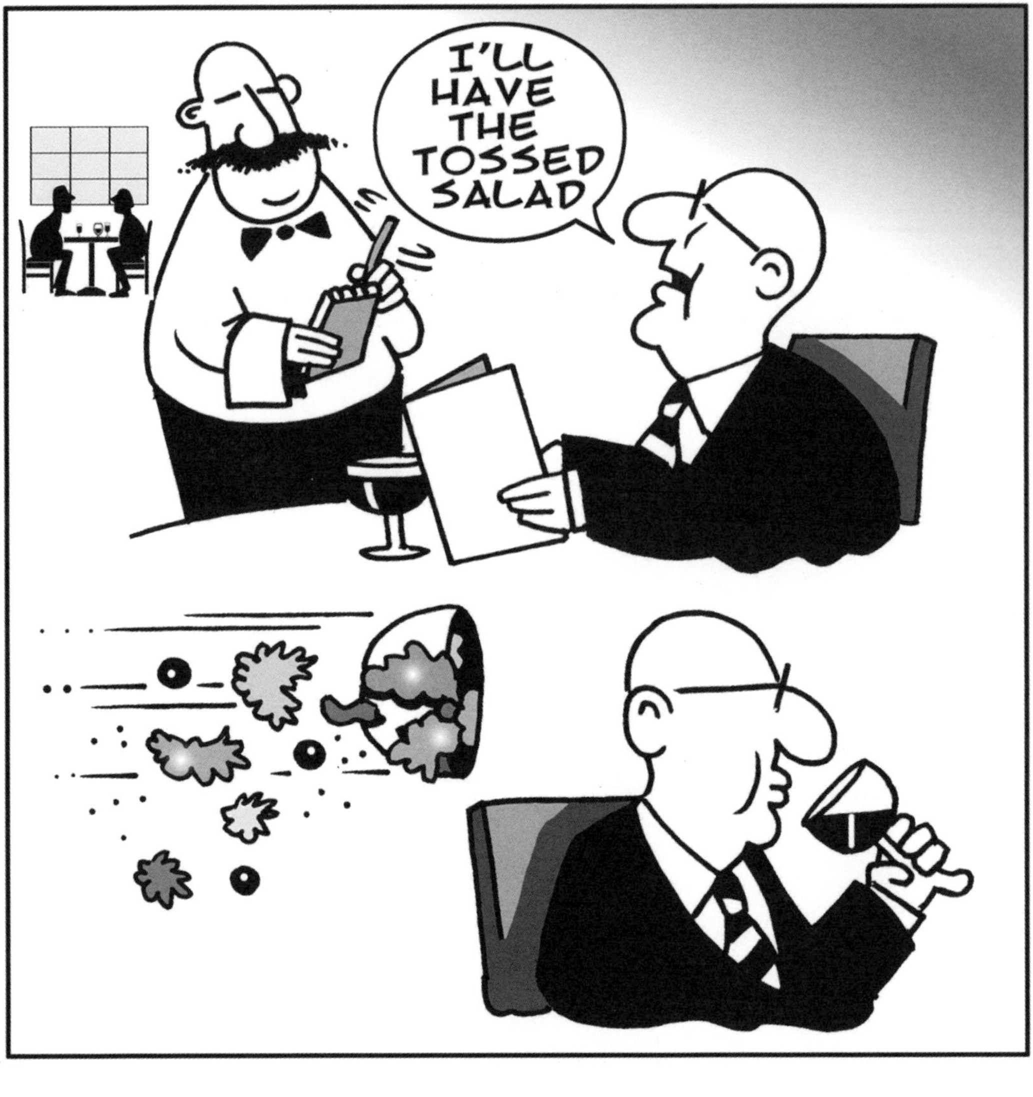
I'LL HAVE THE TOSSED SALAD

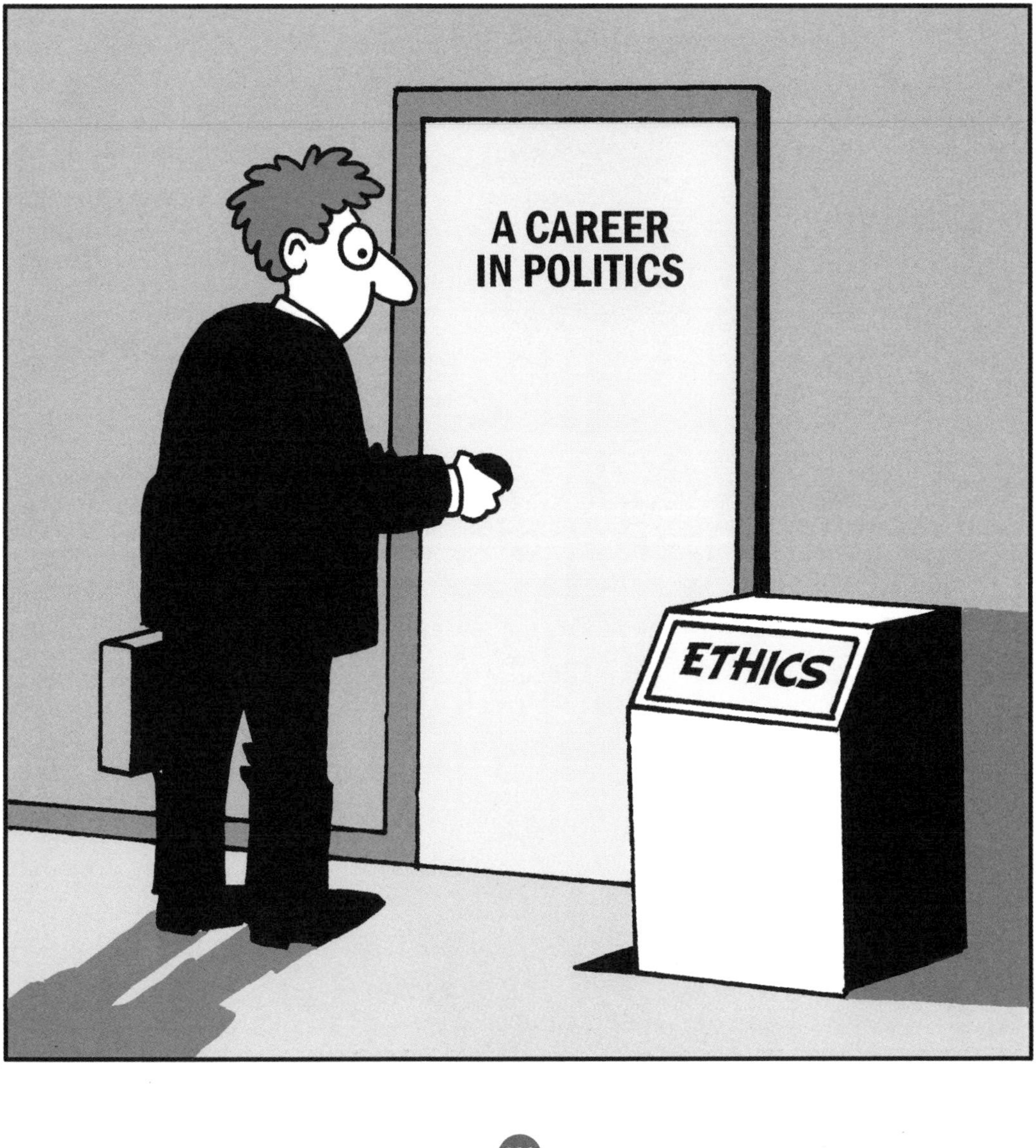
A CAREER
IN POLITICS
ETHICS

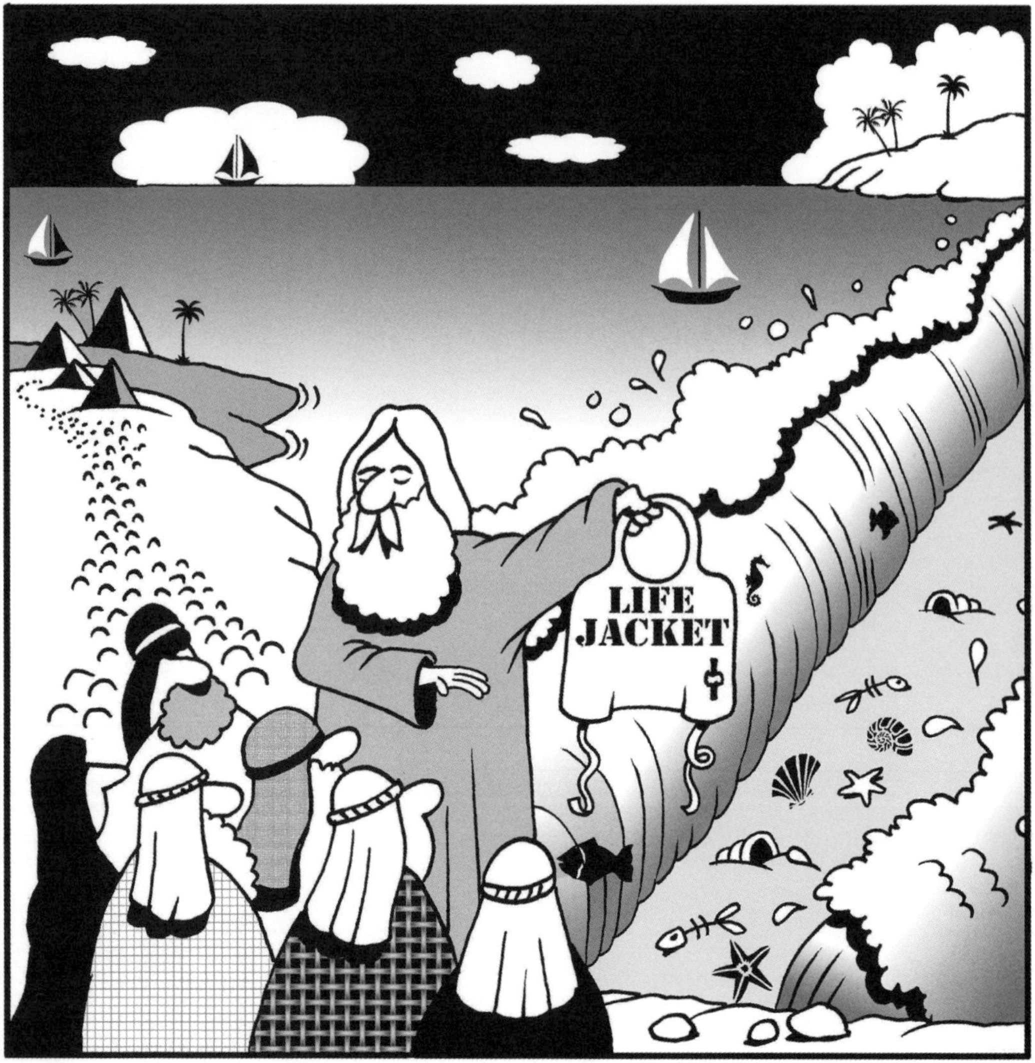
LIFE
JACKET

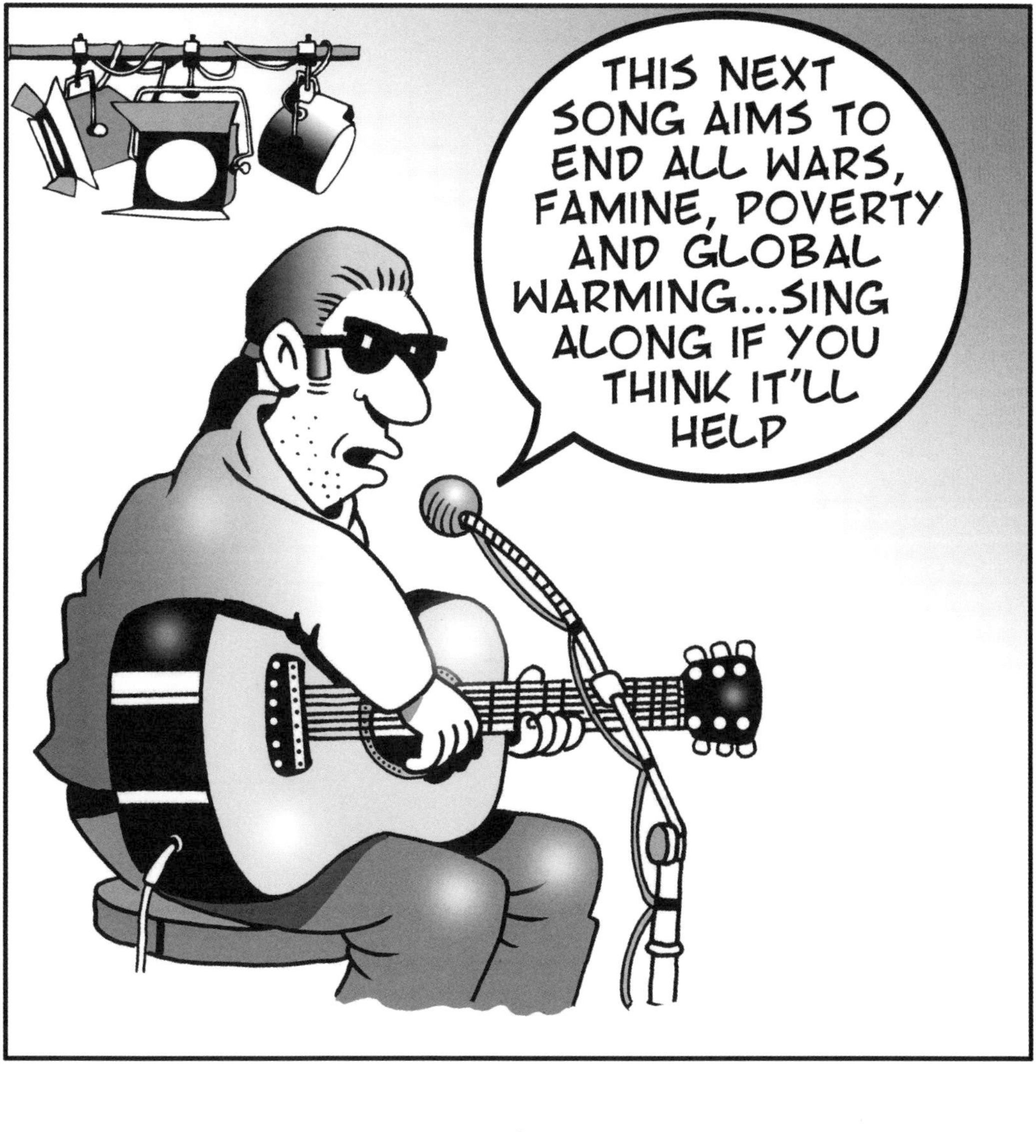
THIS NEXT SONG AIMS TO END ALL WARS, FAMINE, POVERTY AND GLOBAL WARMING...SING ALONG IF YOU THINK IT'LL HELP

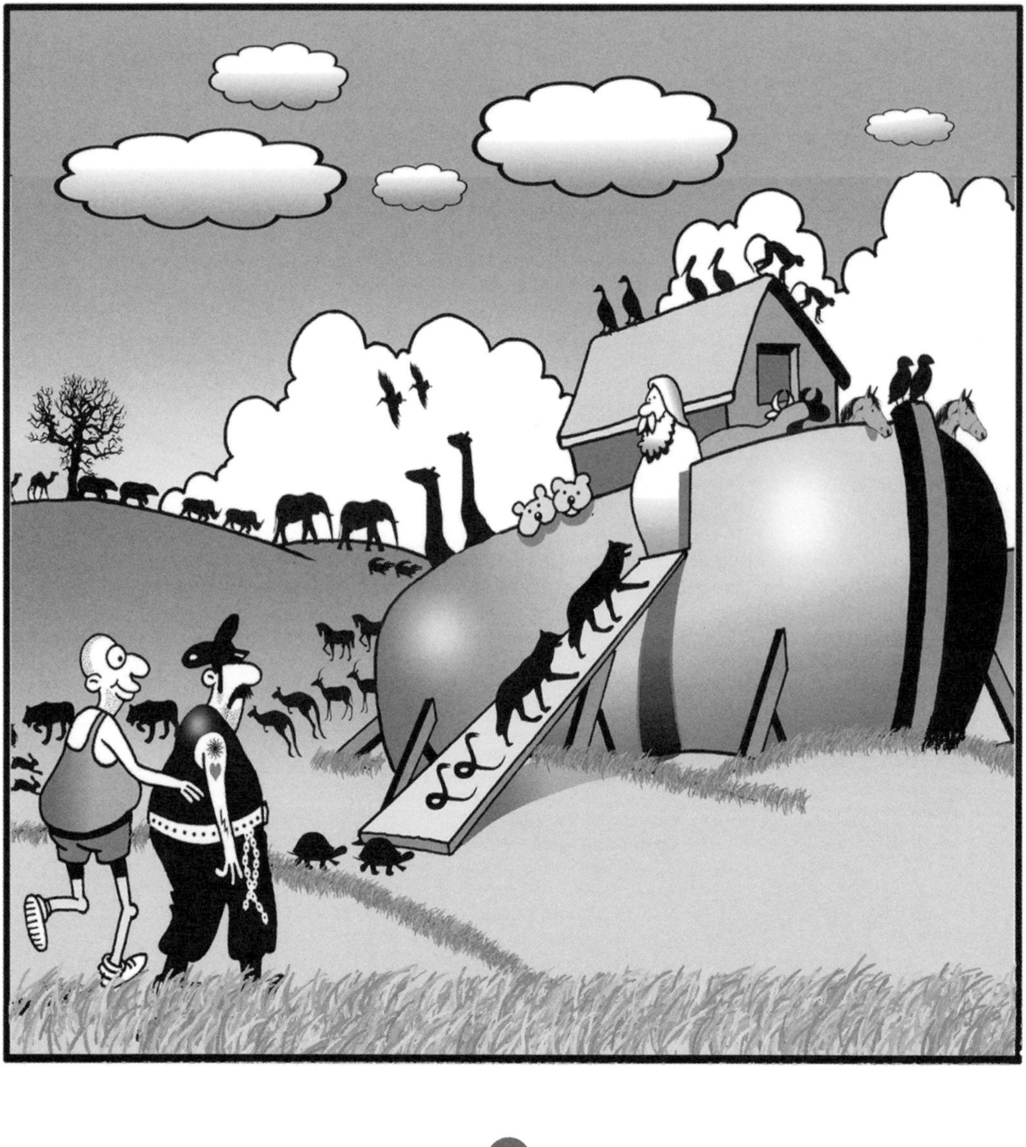

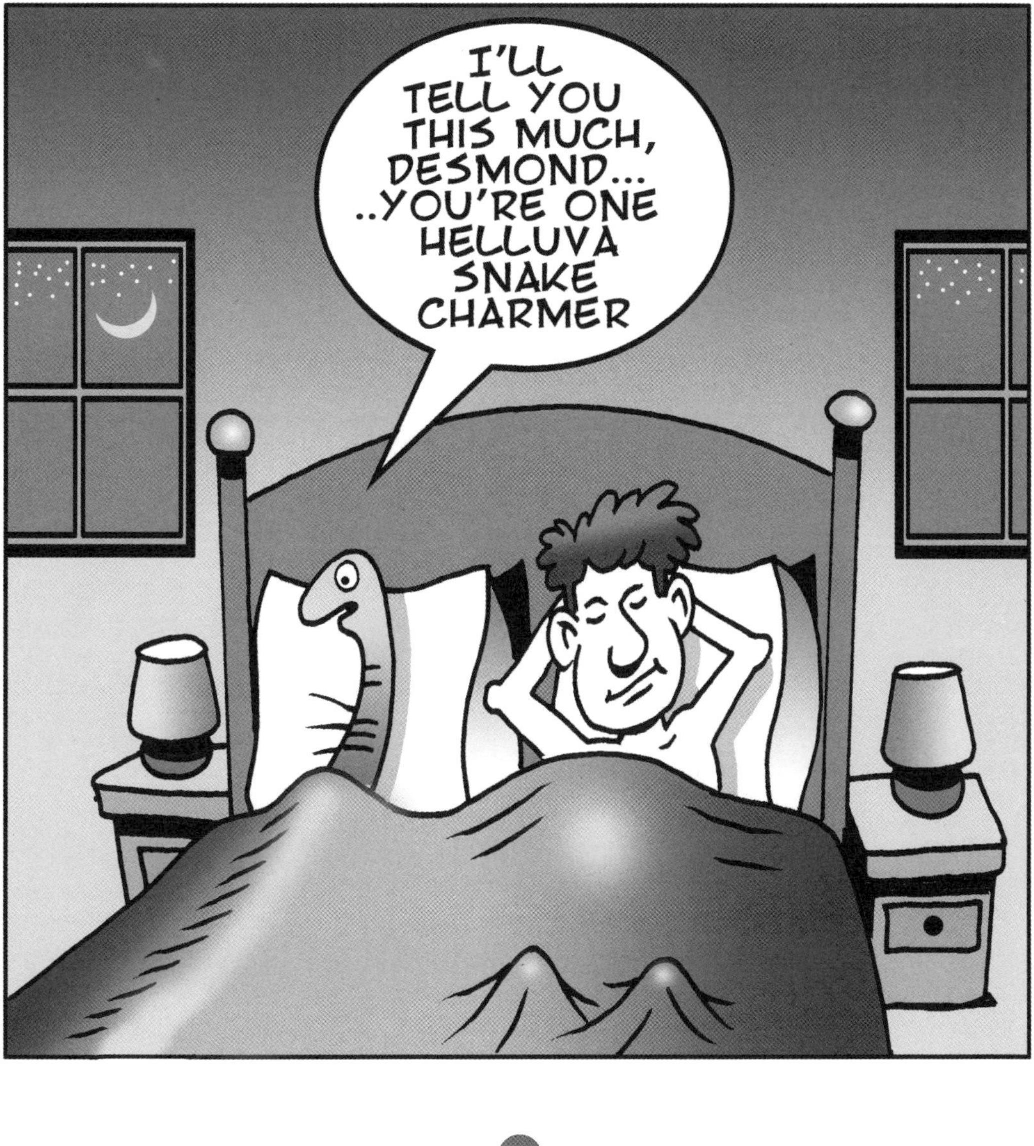
I'LL TELL YOU THIS MUCH, DESMOND... ..YOU'RE ONE HELLUVA SNAKE CHARMER

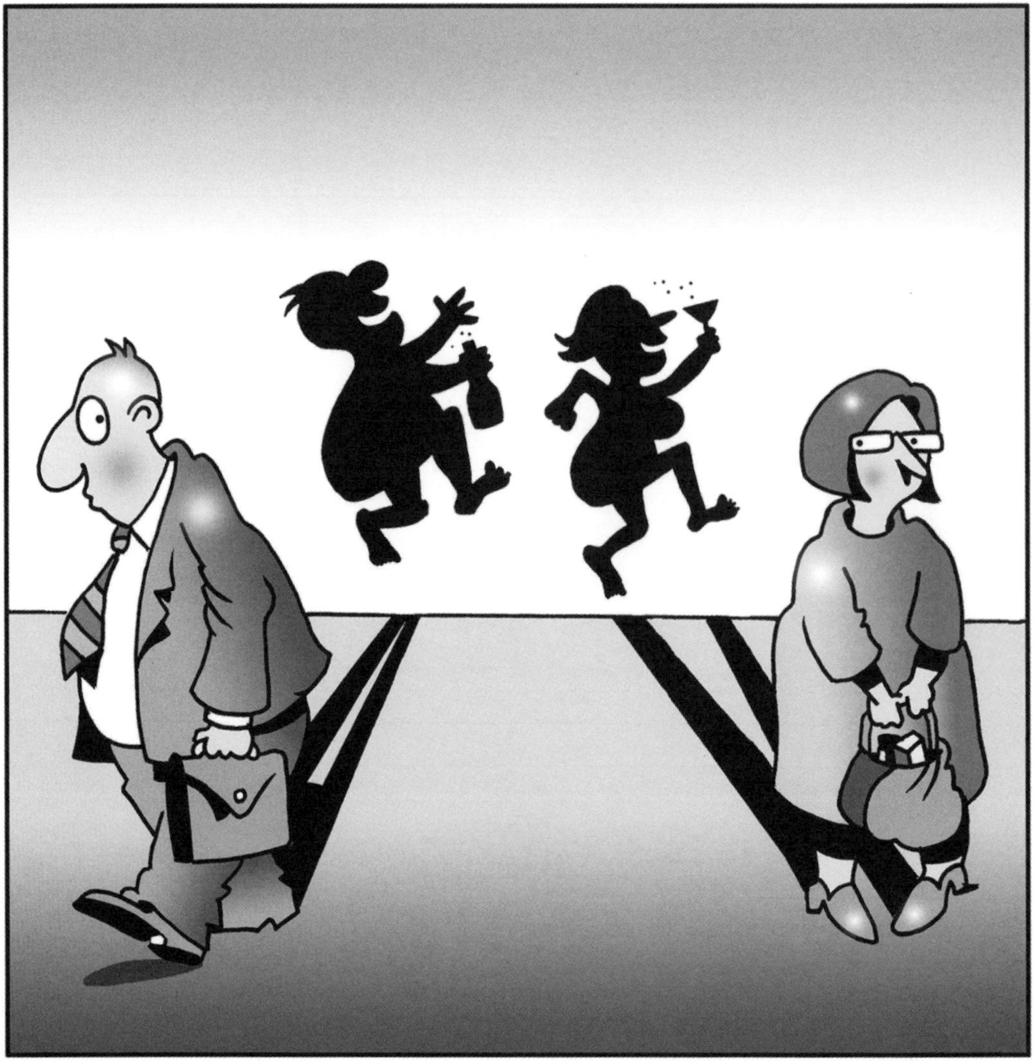

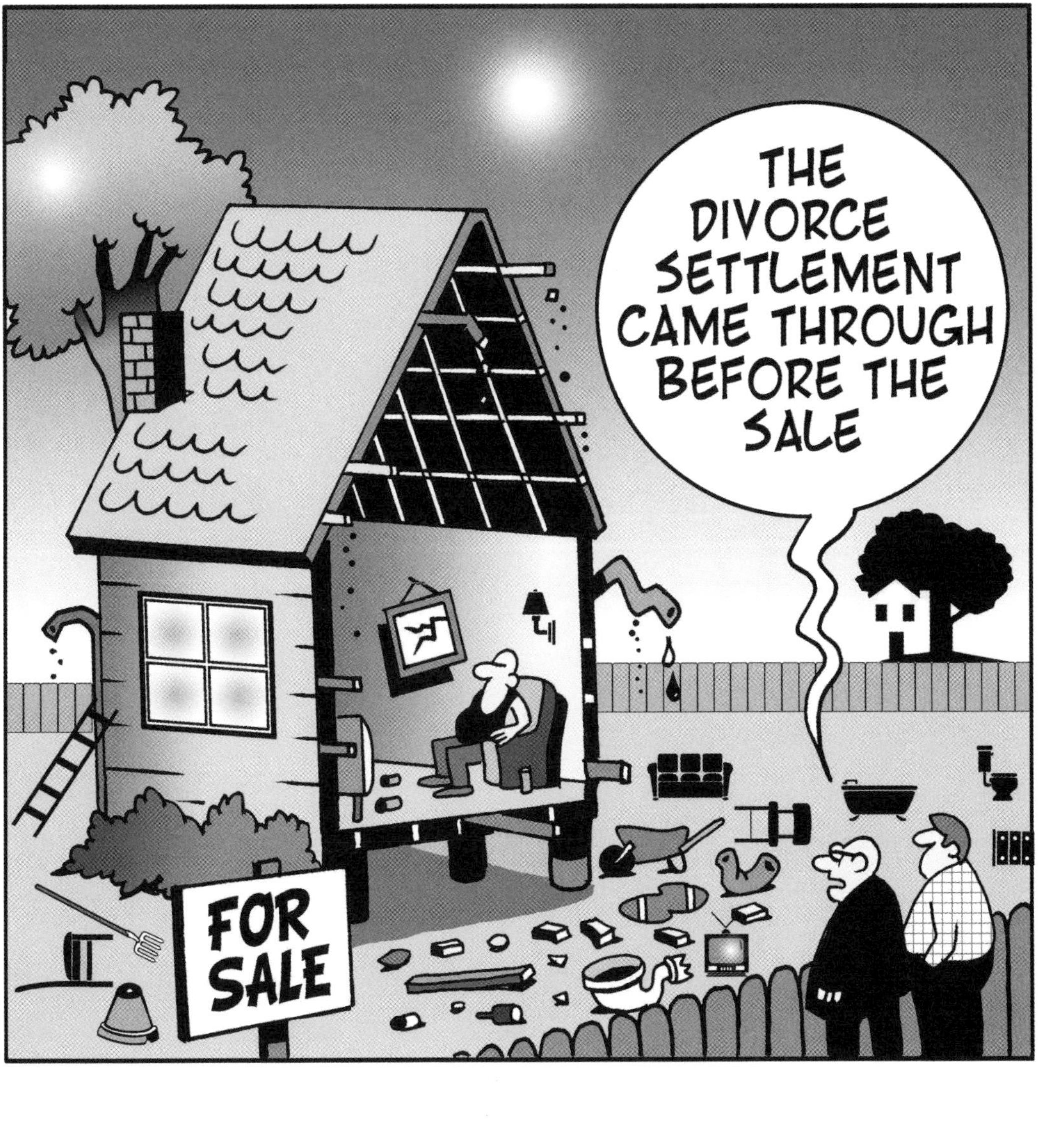
THE DIVORCE SETTLEMENT CAME THROUGH BEFORE THE SALE
FOR SALE

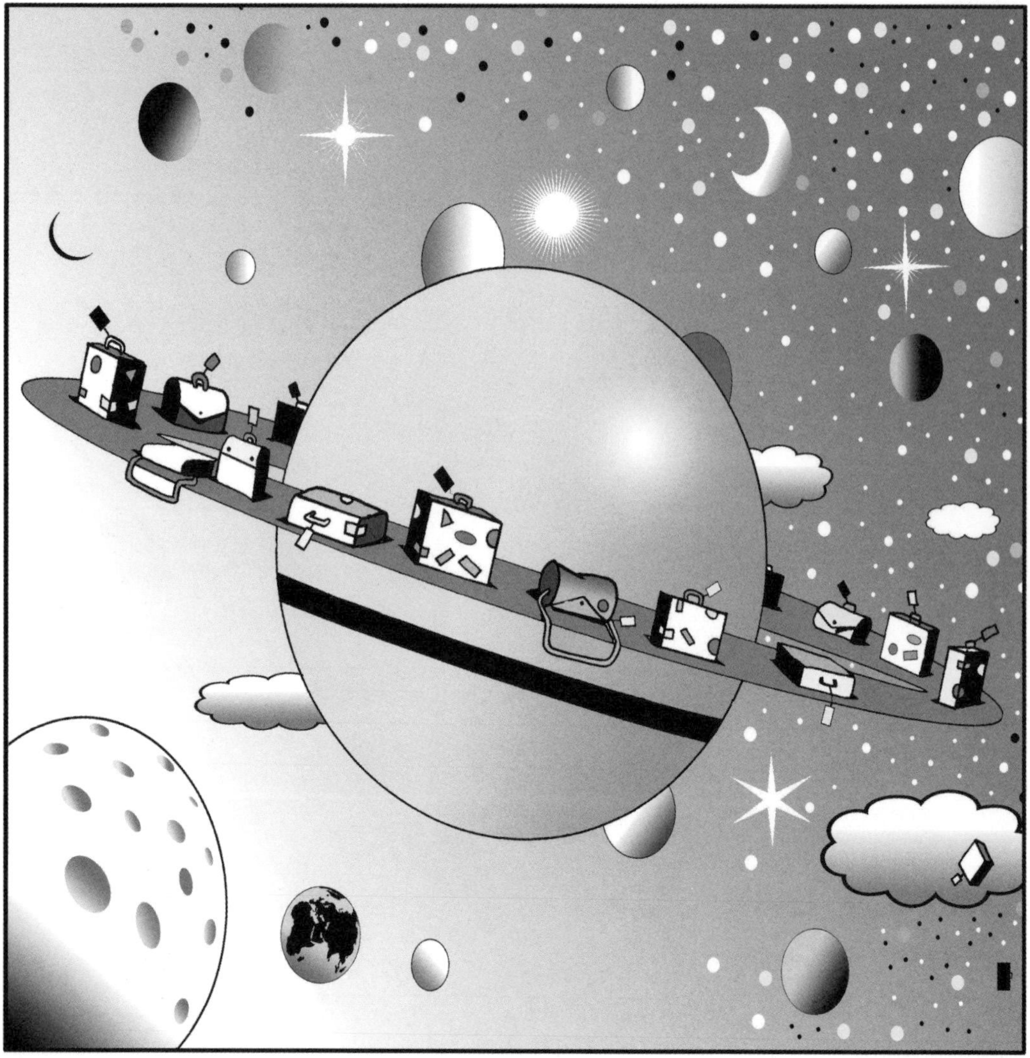

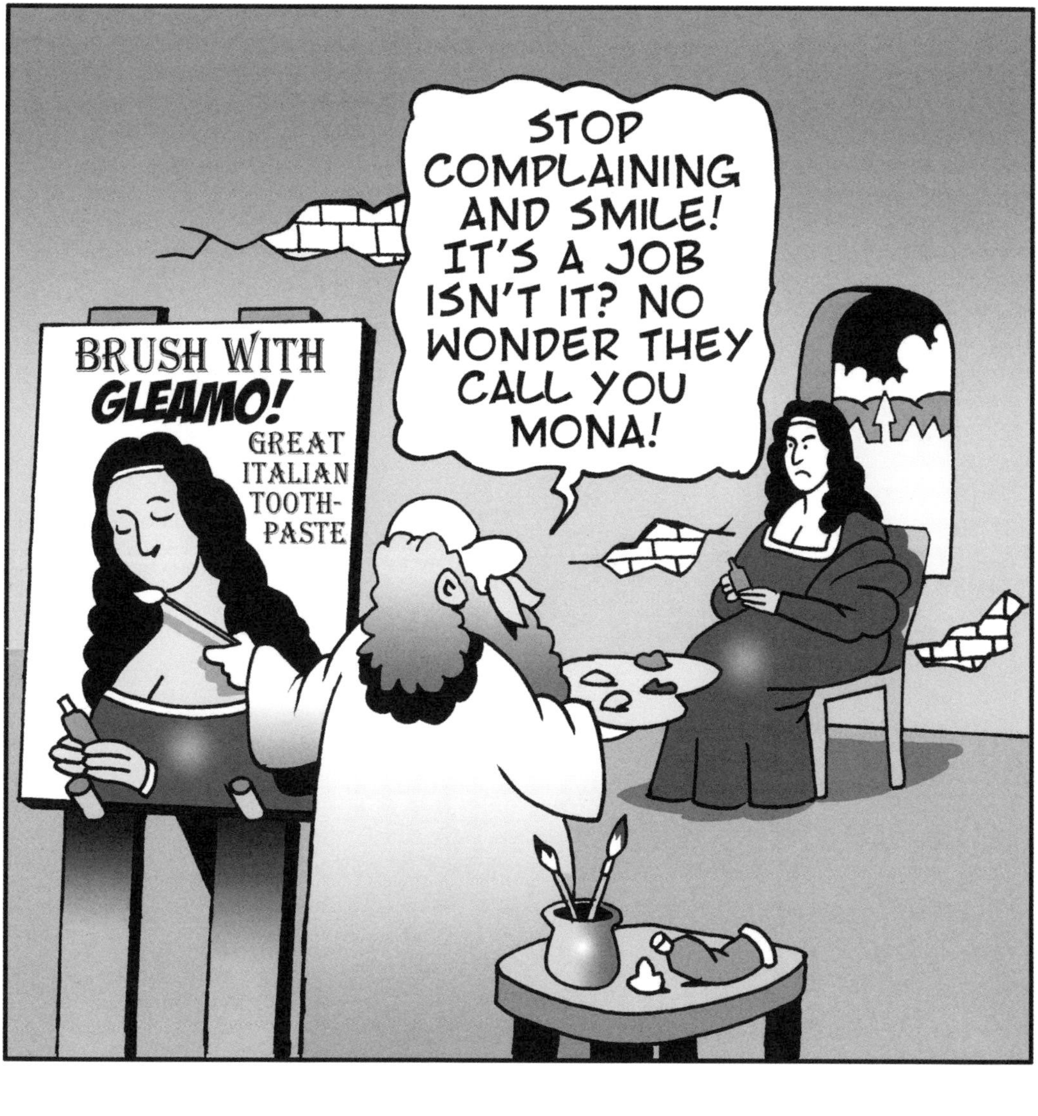
BRUSH WITH GLEAMO!
GREAT ITALIAN TOOTH-PASTE
STOP COMPLAINING AND SMILE! IT'S A JOB ISN'T IT? NO WONDER THEY CALL YOU MONA!

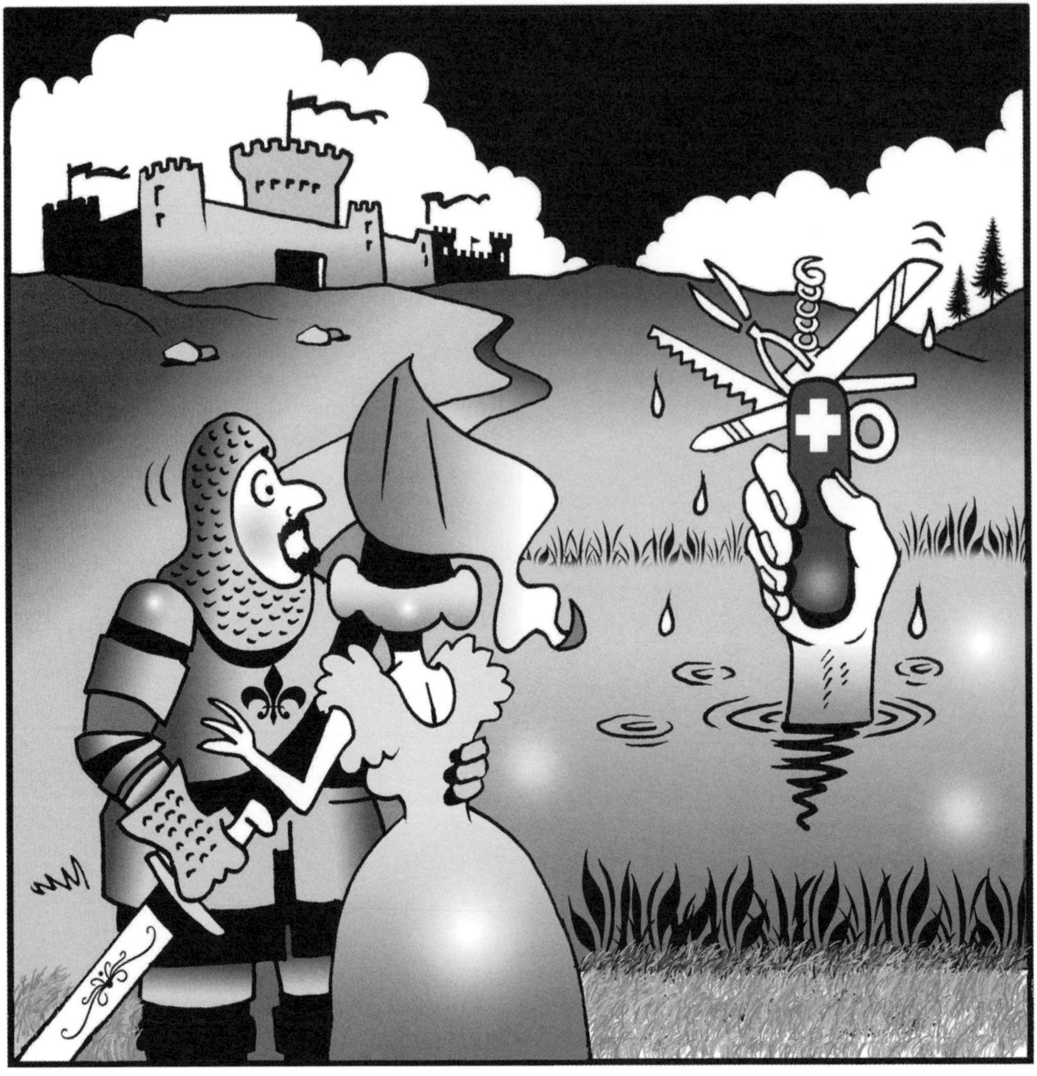

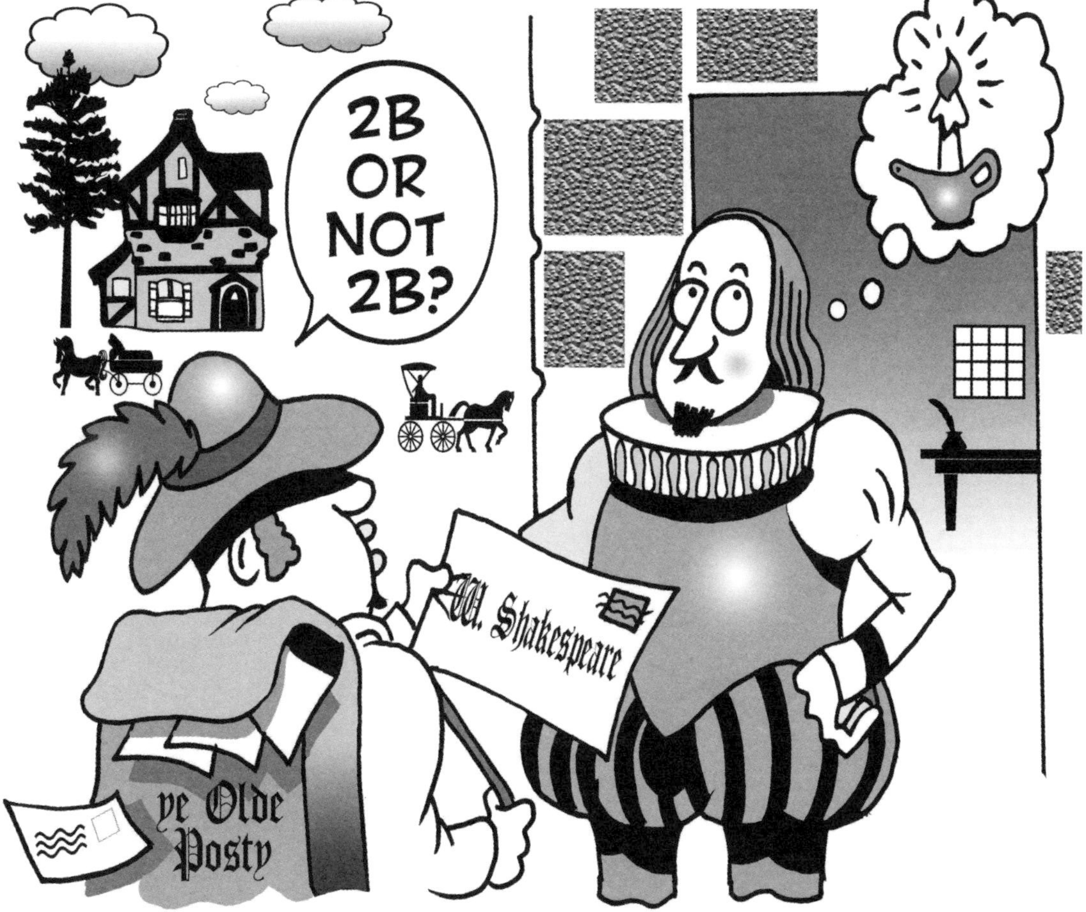
2B OR NOT 2B?
W. Shakespeare
ye Olde Posty

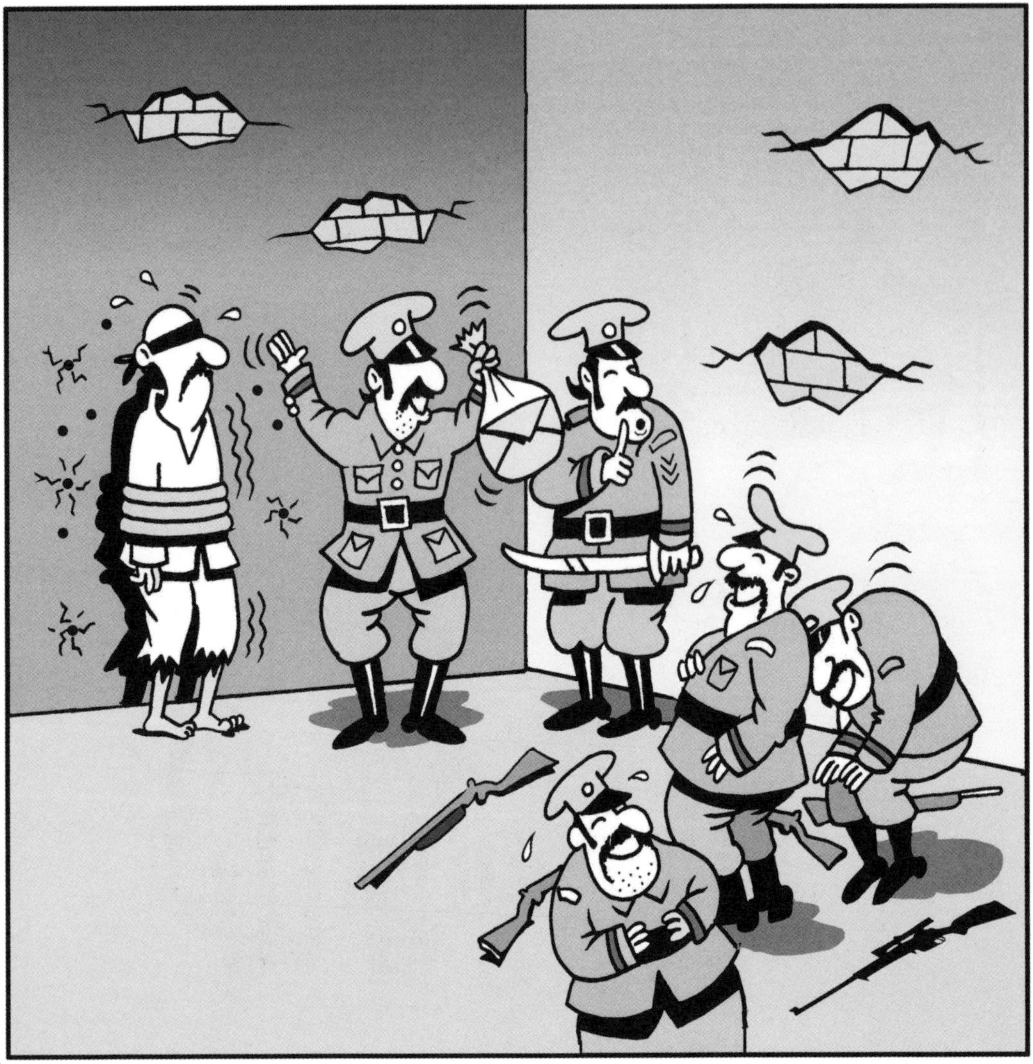

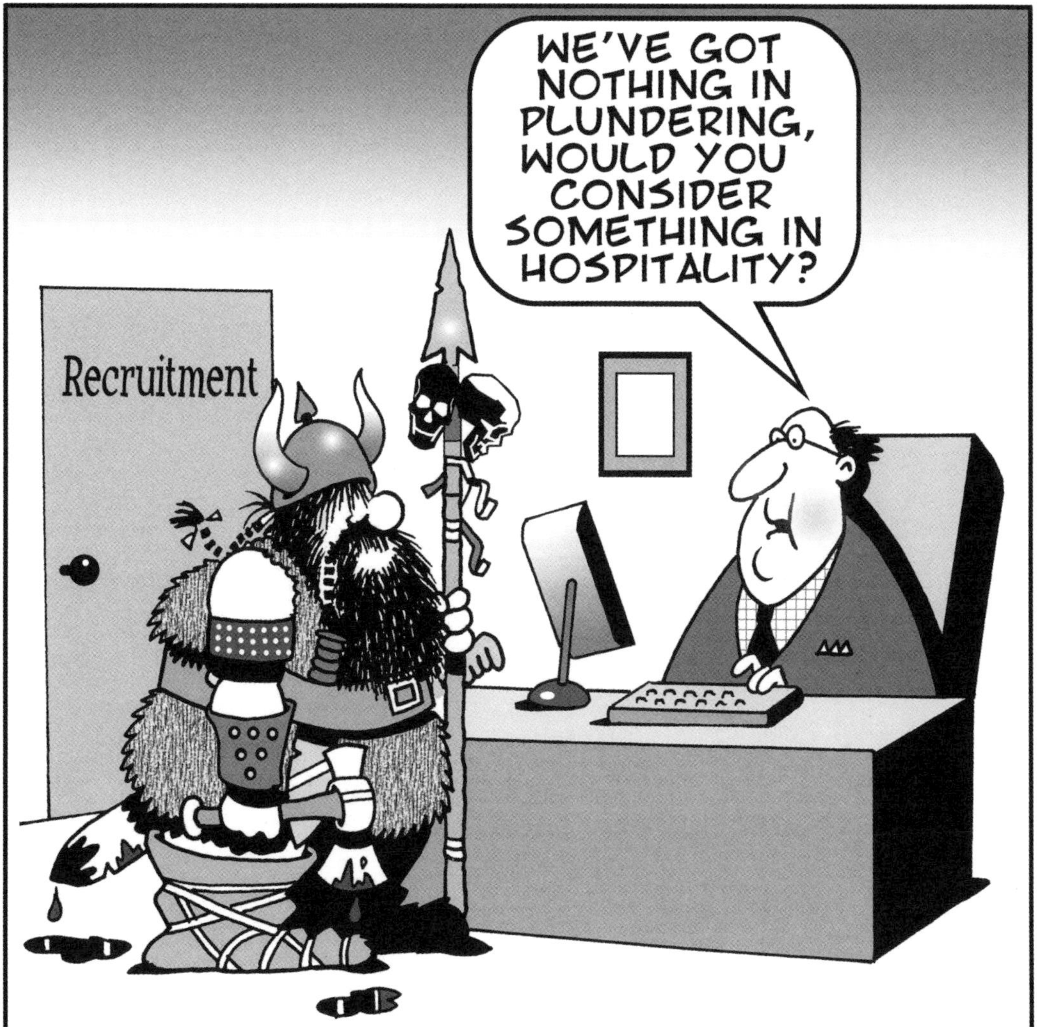
Recruitment
WE'VE GOT NOTHING IN PLUNDERING, WOULD YOU CONSIDER SOMETHING IN HOSPITALITY?

JOAN OF ARC, THE MOTHER OF ADVERTISING

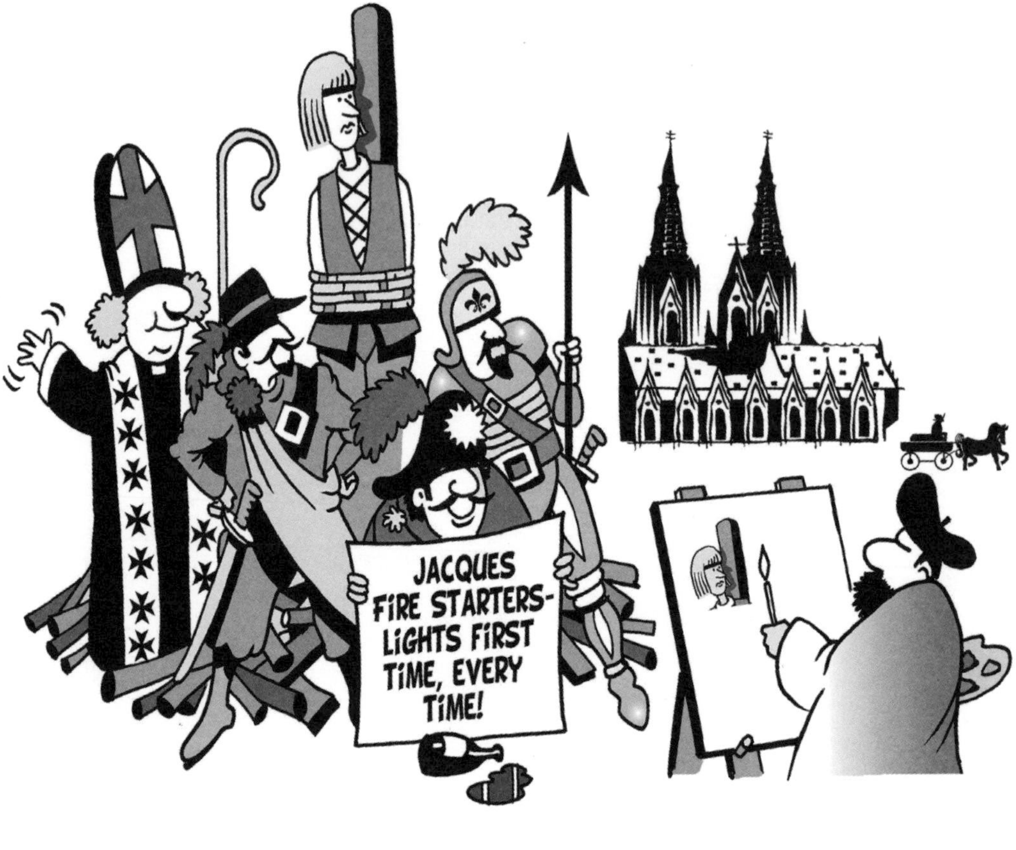
JACQUES
FIRE STARTERS-
LIGHTS FIRST
TIME, EVERY
TIME!

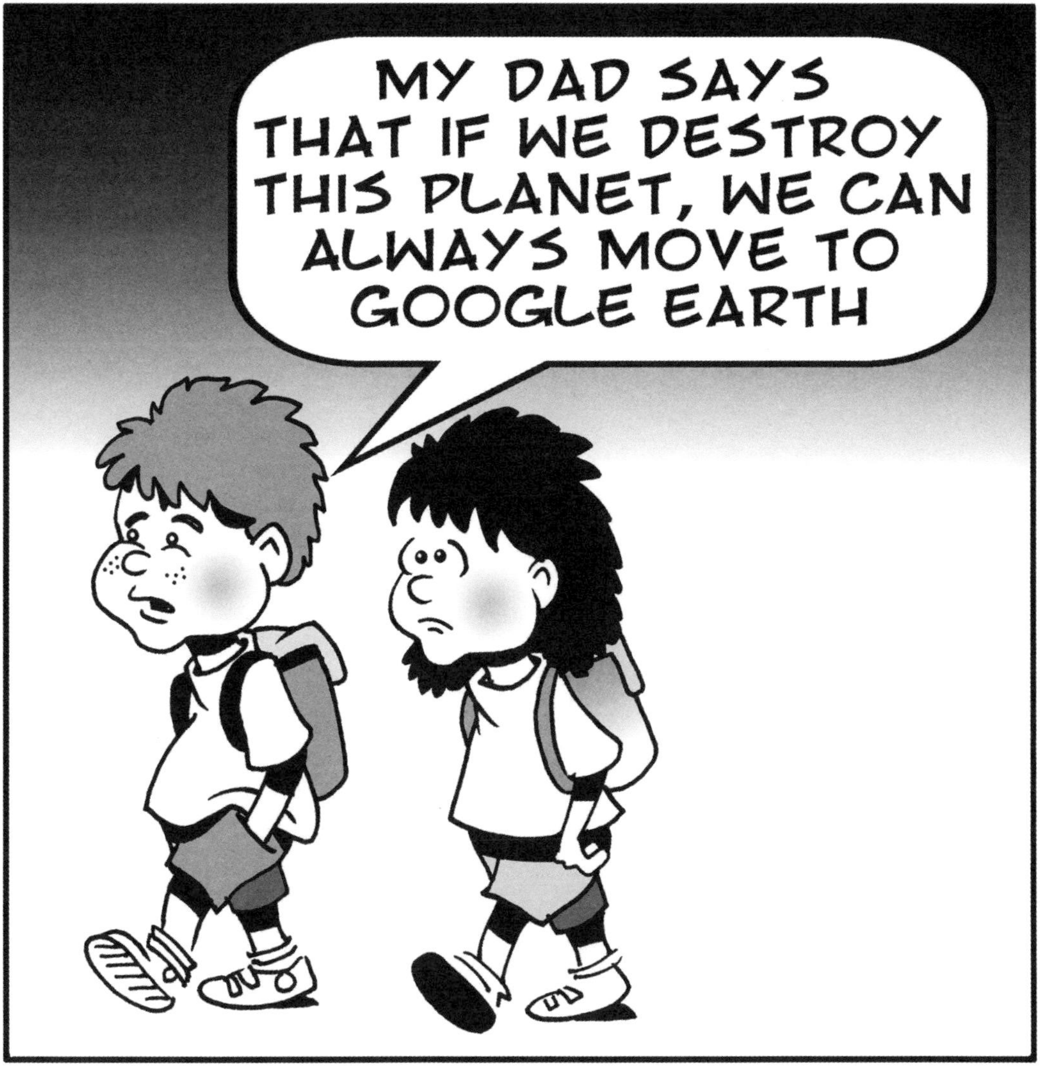
MY DAD SAYS THAT IF WE DESTROY THIS PLANET, WE CAN ALWAYS MOVE TO GOOGLE EARTH

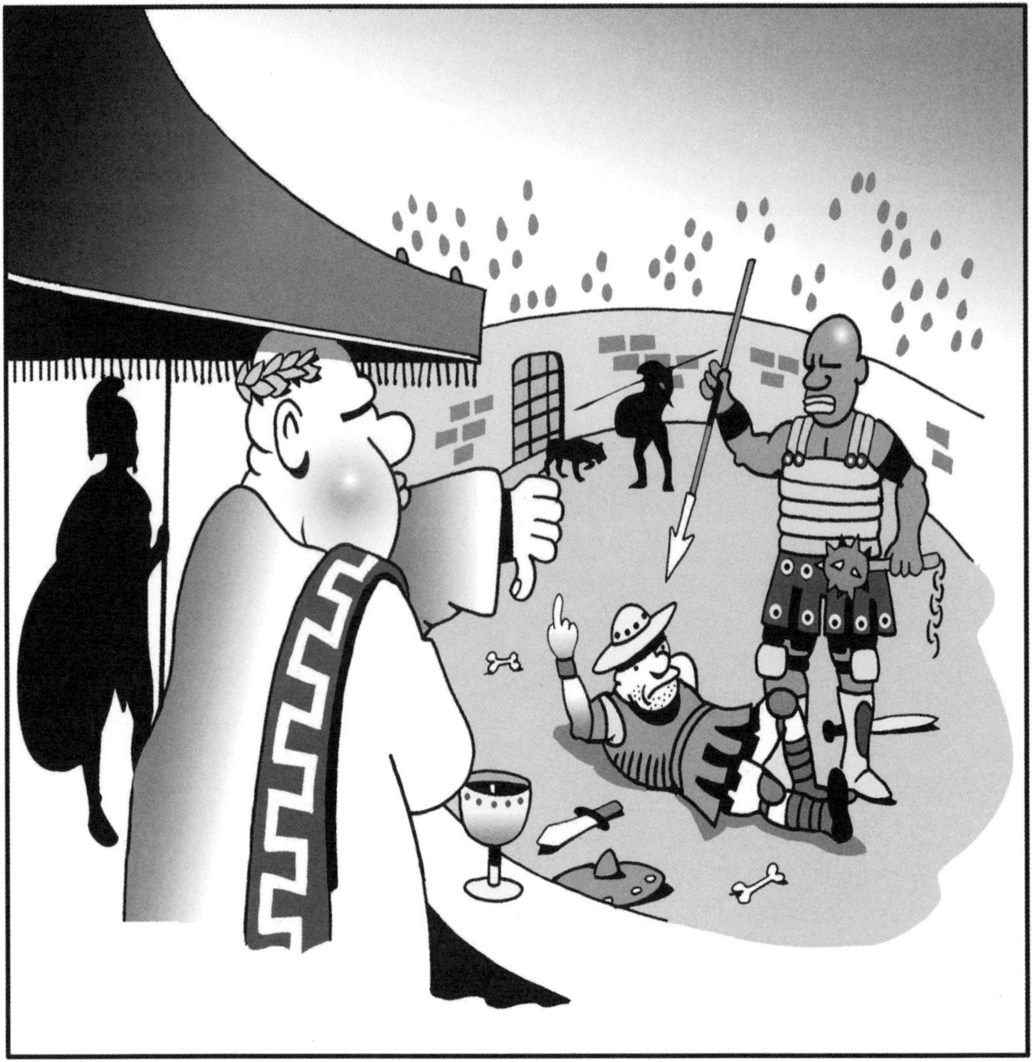

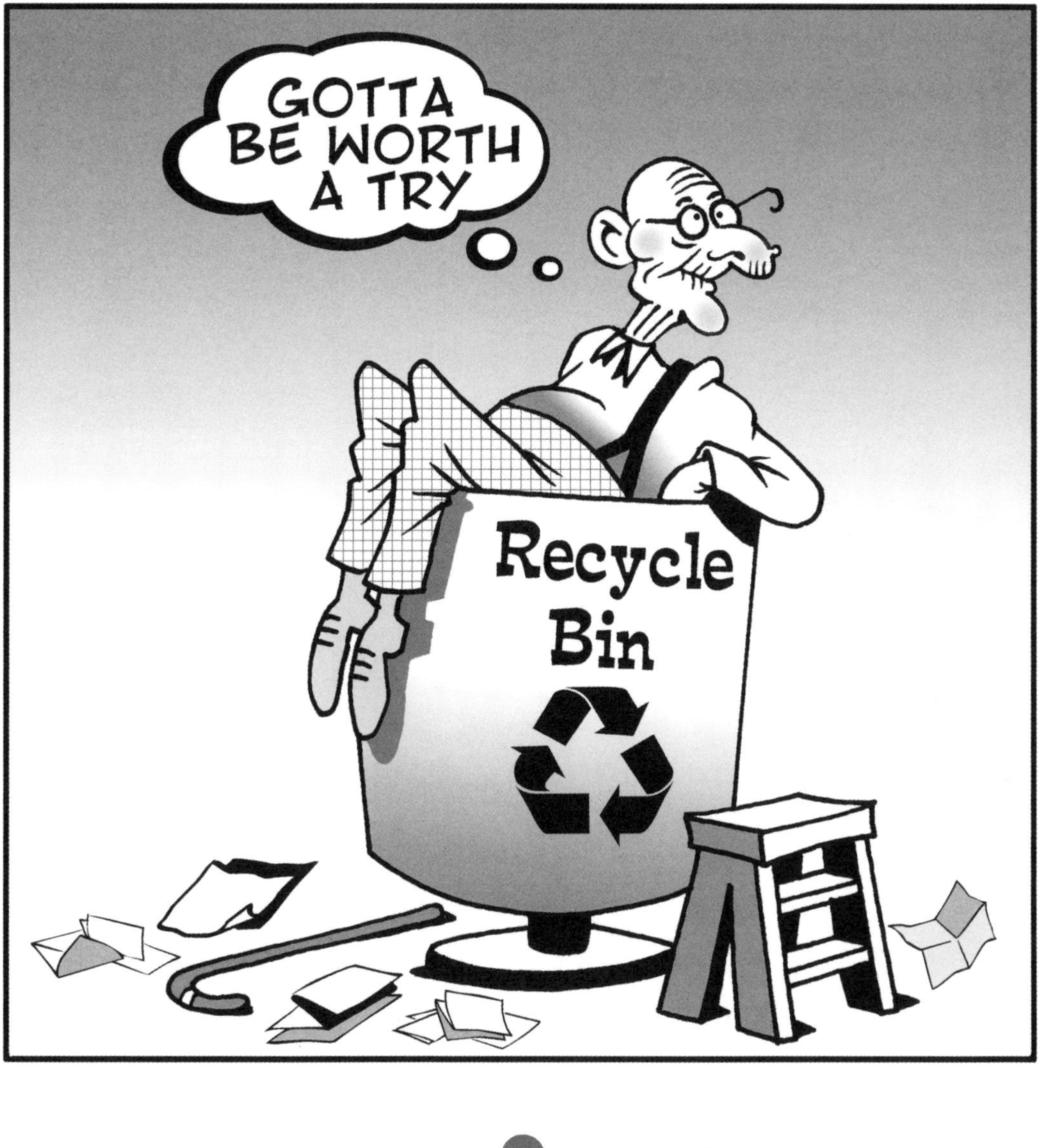
GOTTA BE WORTH A TRY
Recycle Bin

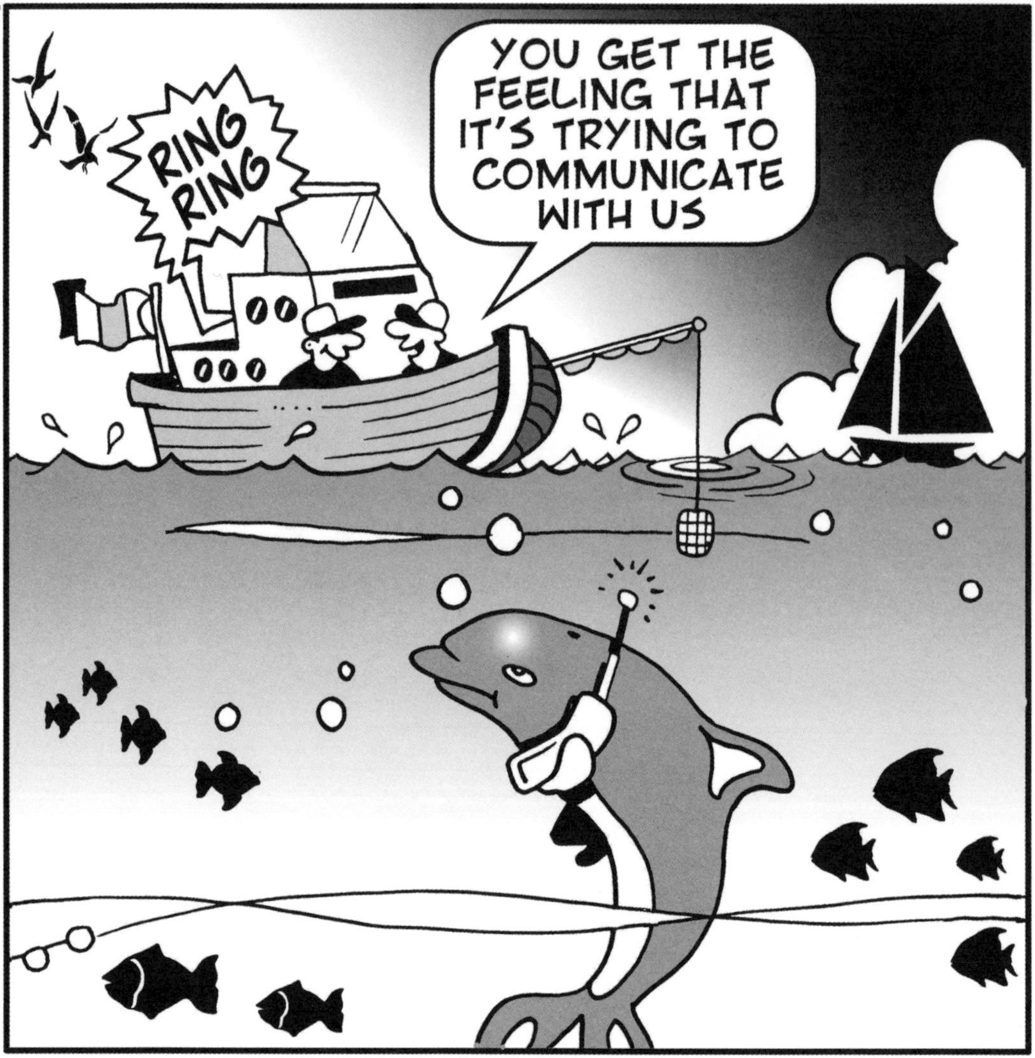
RING RING
YOU GET THE FEELING THAT IT'S TRYING TO COMMUNICATE WITH US

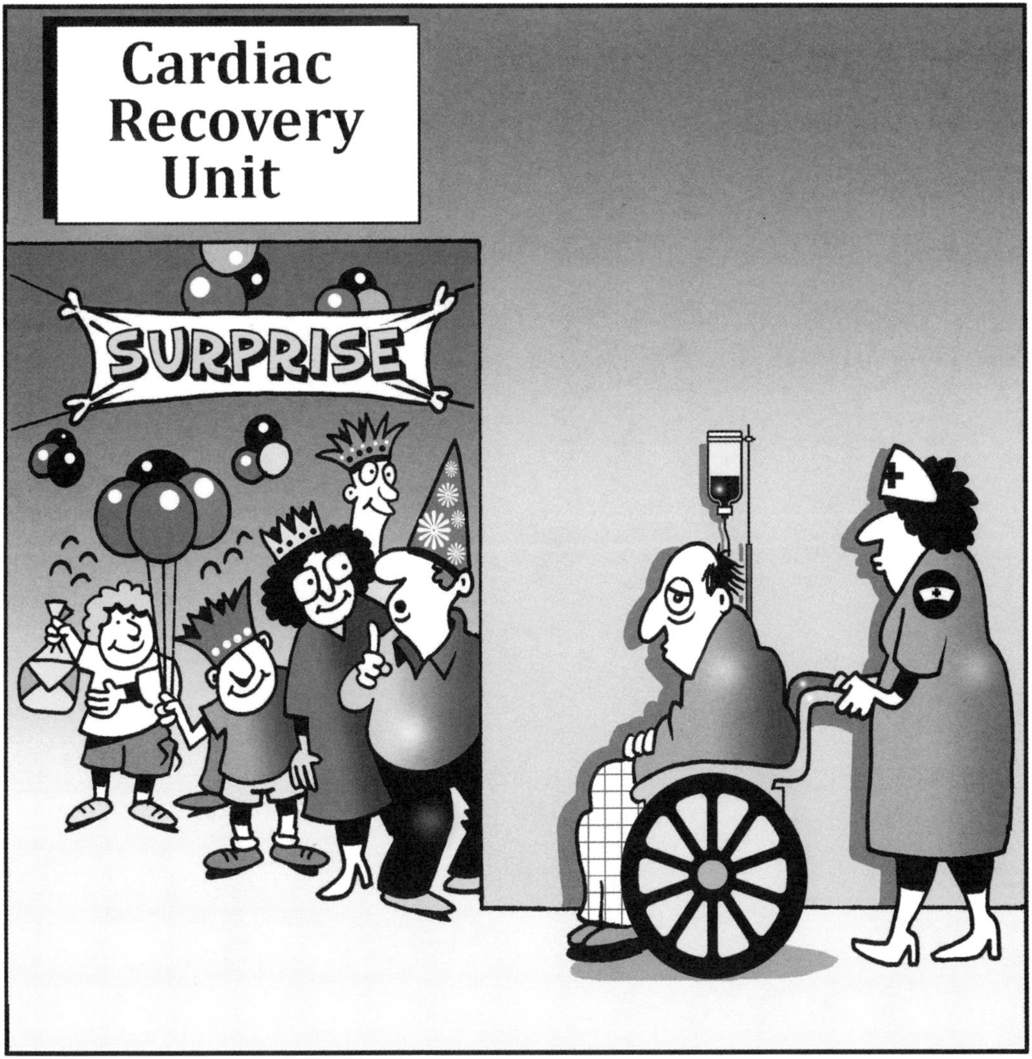
Cardiac
Recovery
Unit
SURPRISE

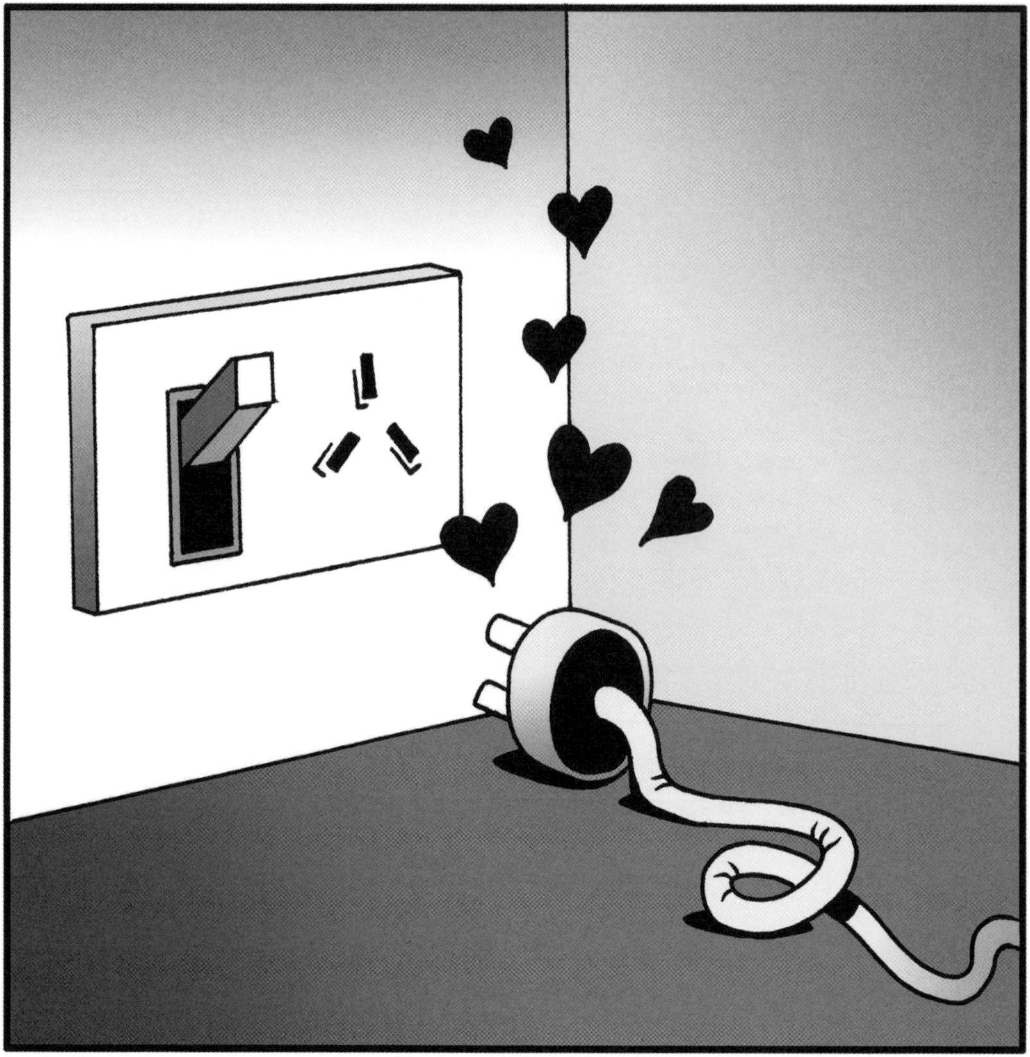

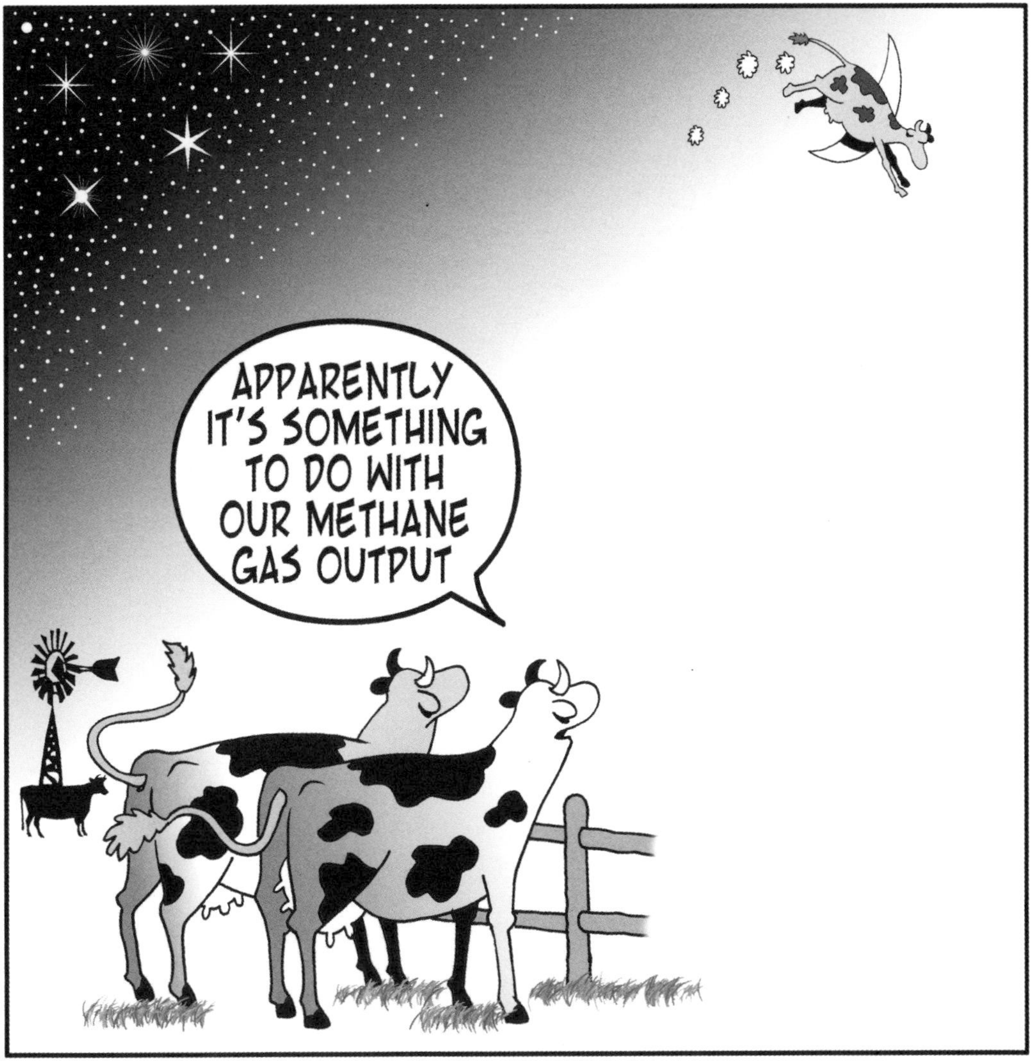
APPARENTLY IT'S SOMETHING TO DO WITH OUR METHANE GAS OUTPUT

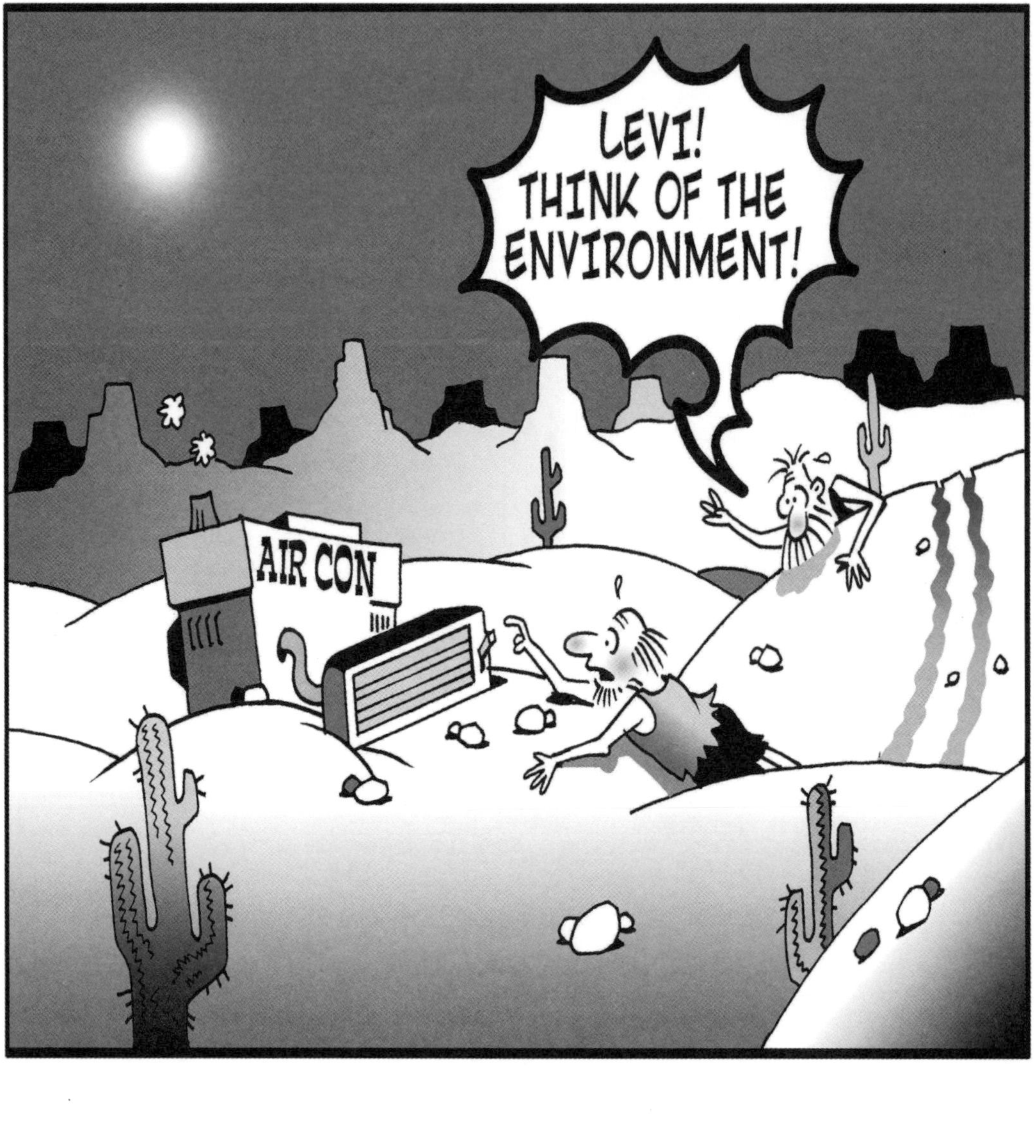
LEVI! THINK OF THE ENVIRONMENT!
AIR CON

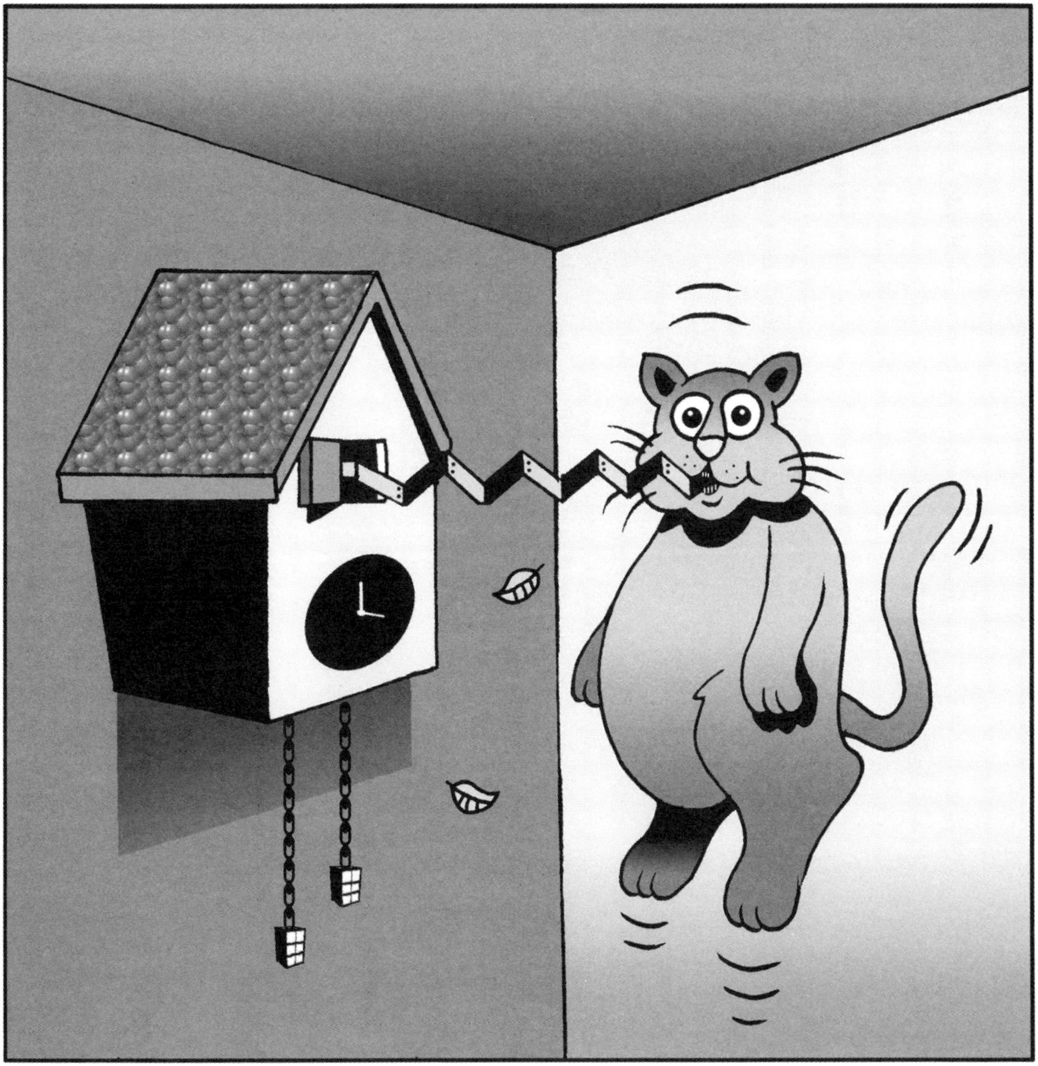

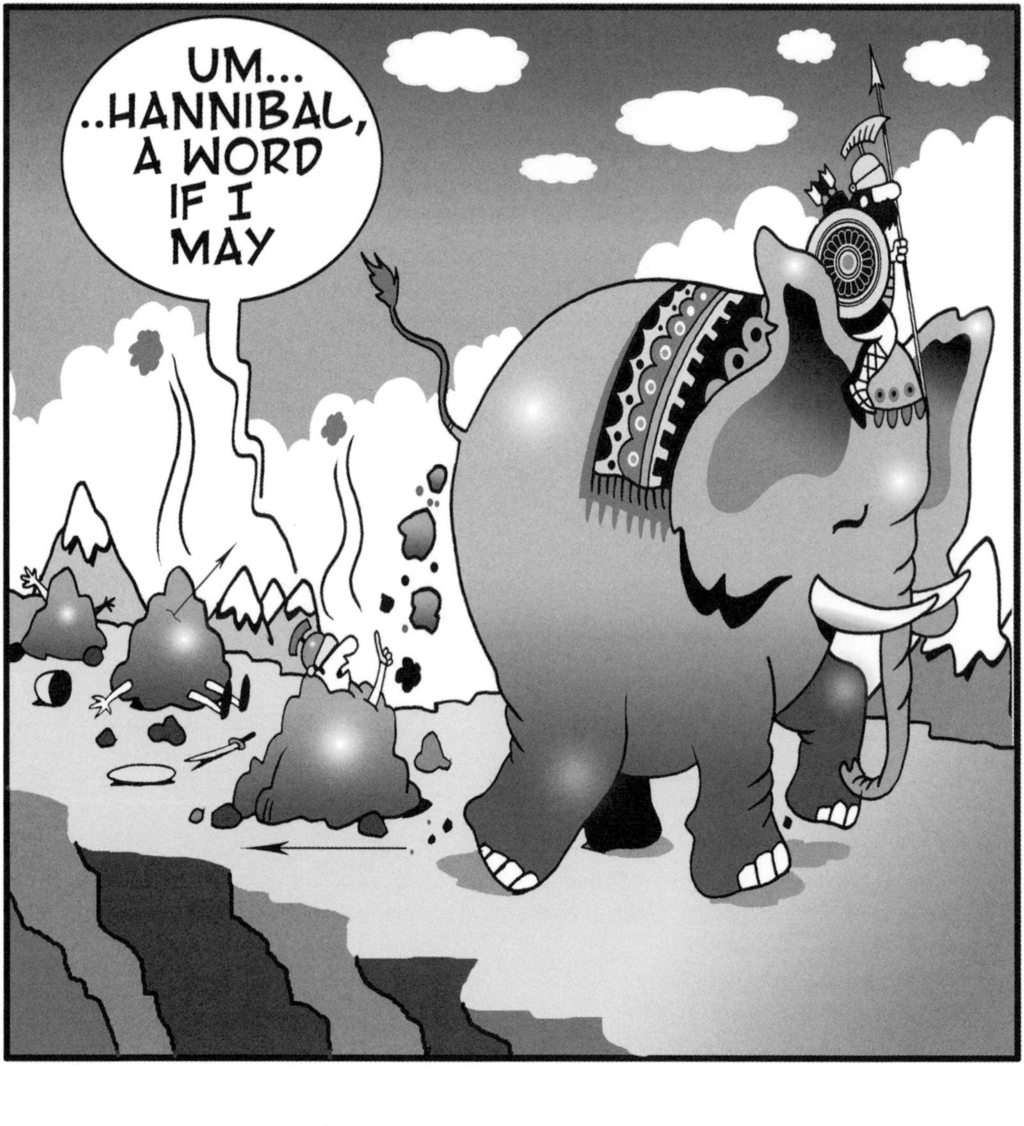
UM...
..HANNIBAL,
A WORD
IF I
MAY

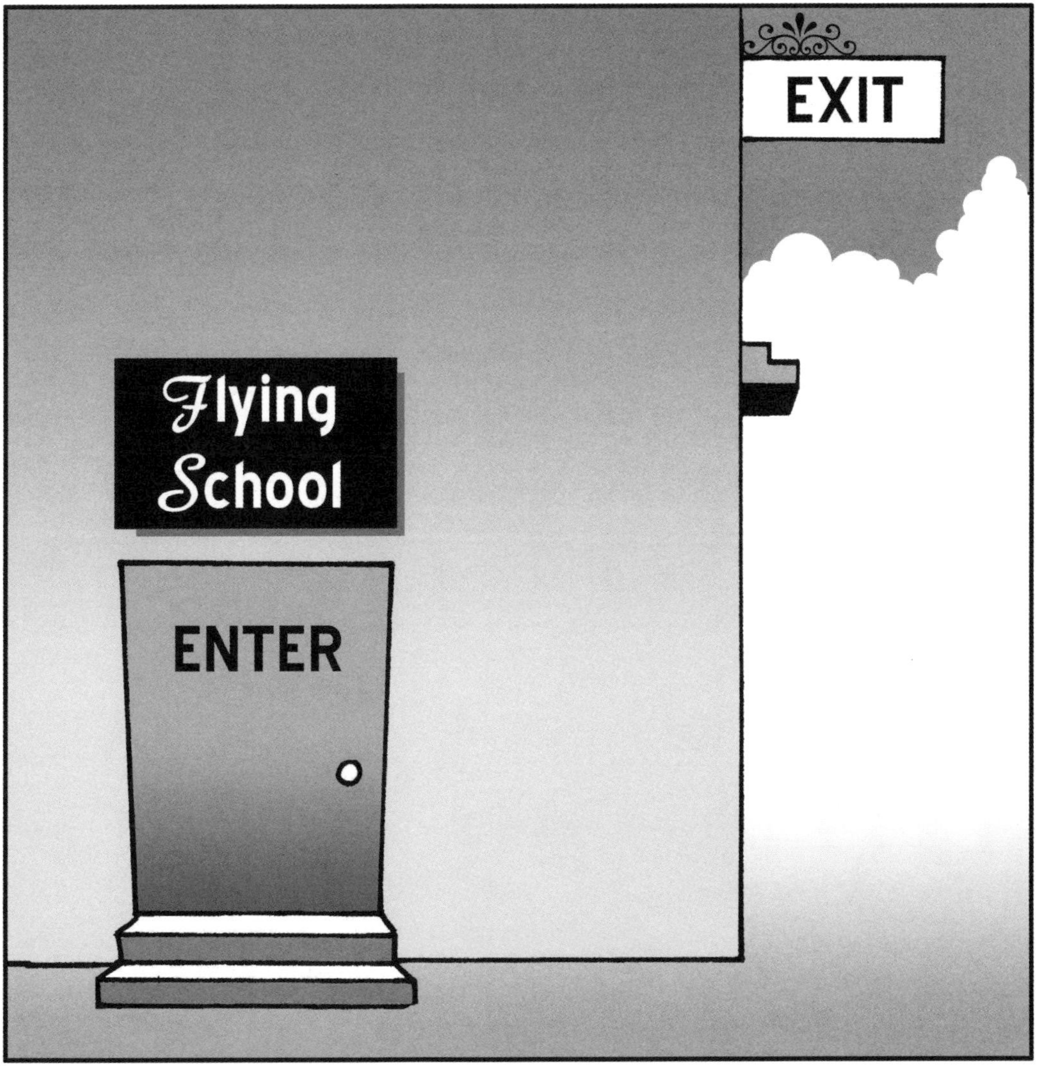

EXIT
Flying School
ENTER

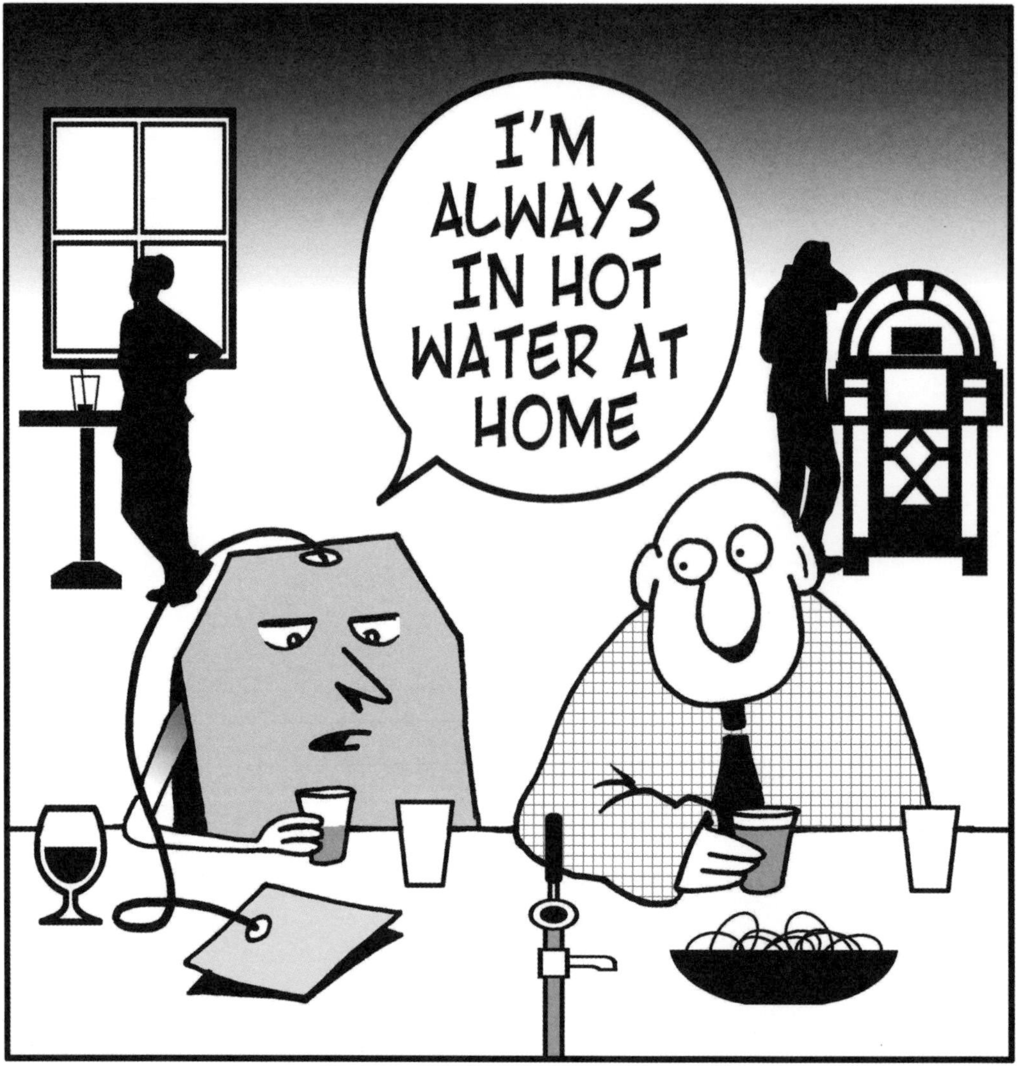
I'M ALWAYS IN HOT WATER AT HOME

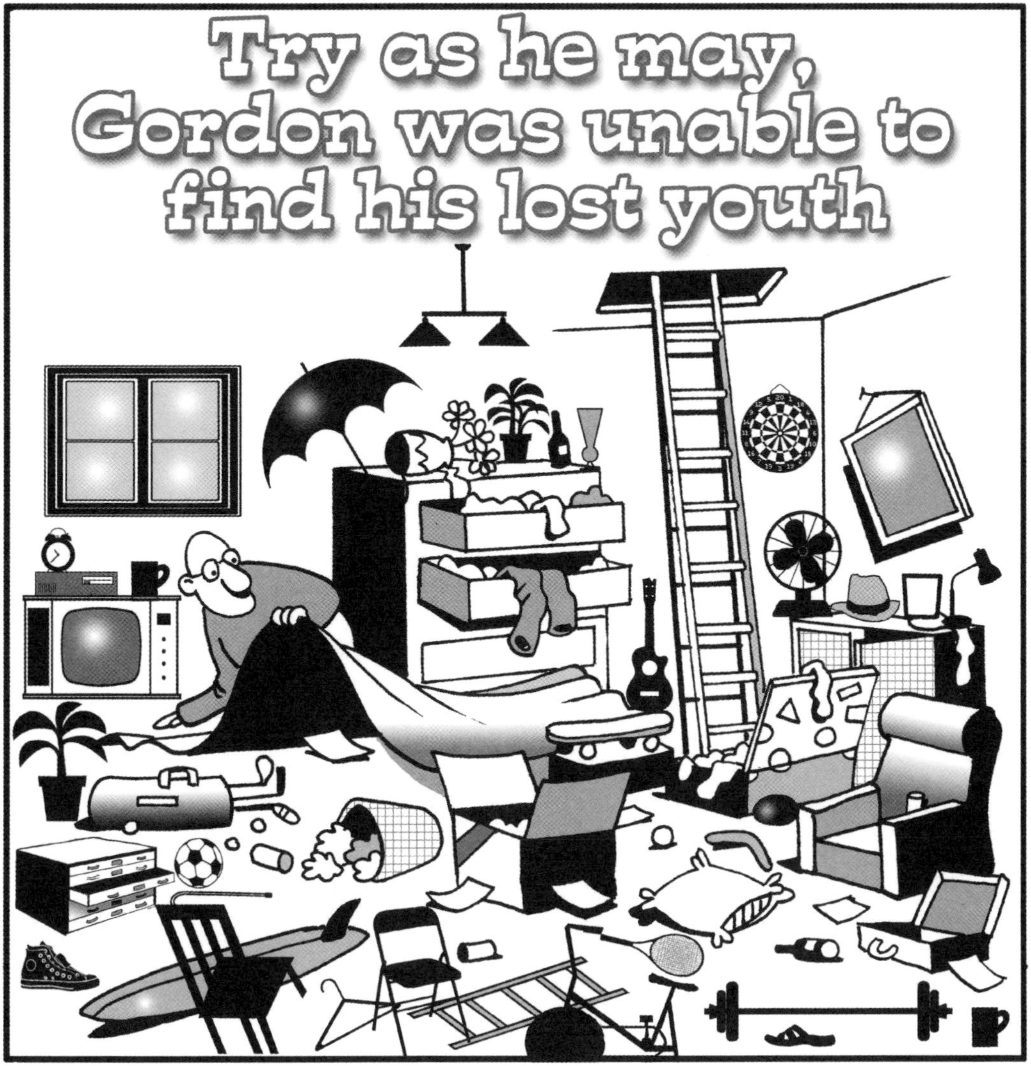
Try as he may,
Gordon was unable to
find his lost youth

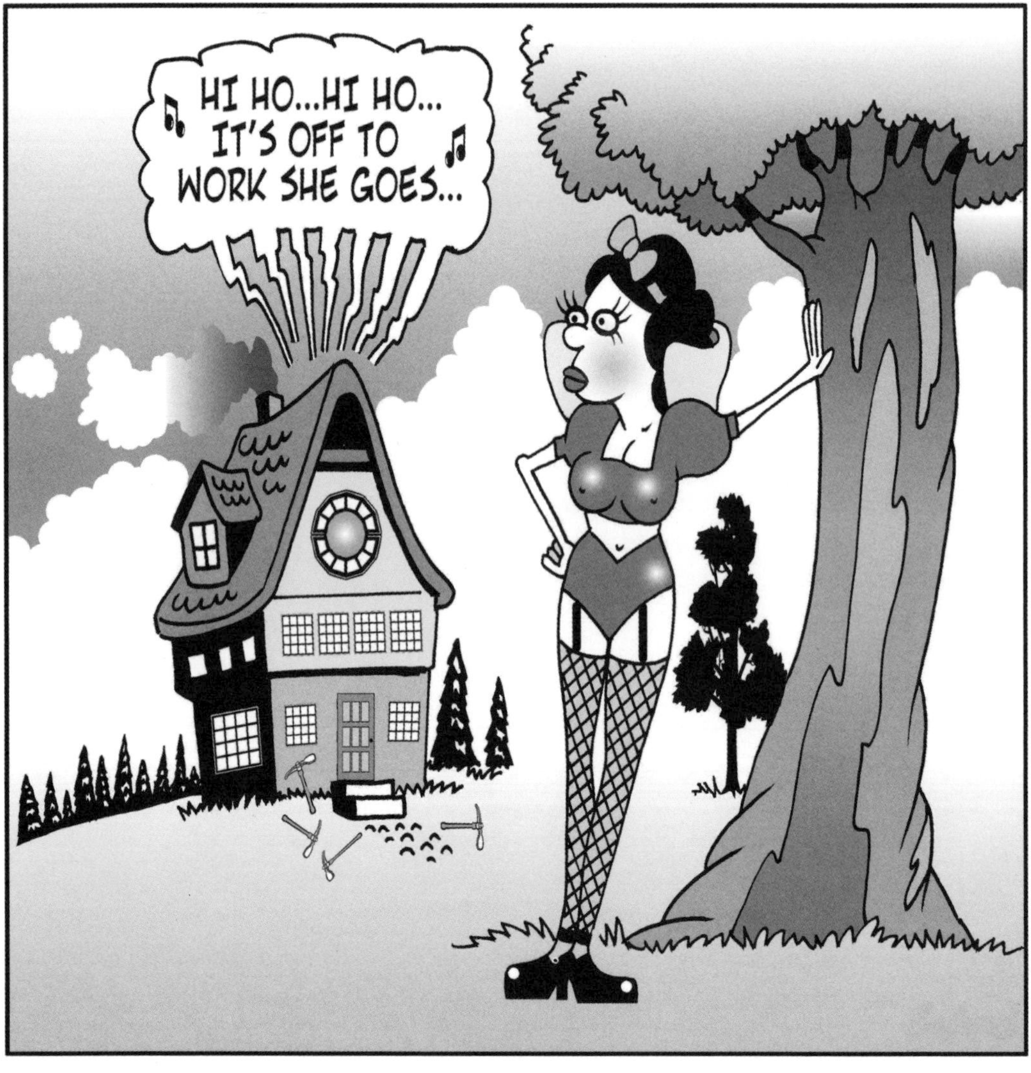
HI HO...HI HO... IT'S OFF TO WORK SHE GOES...

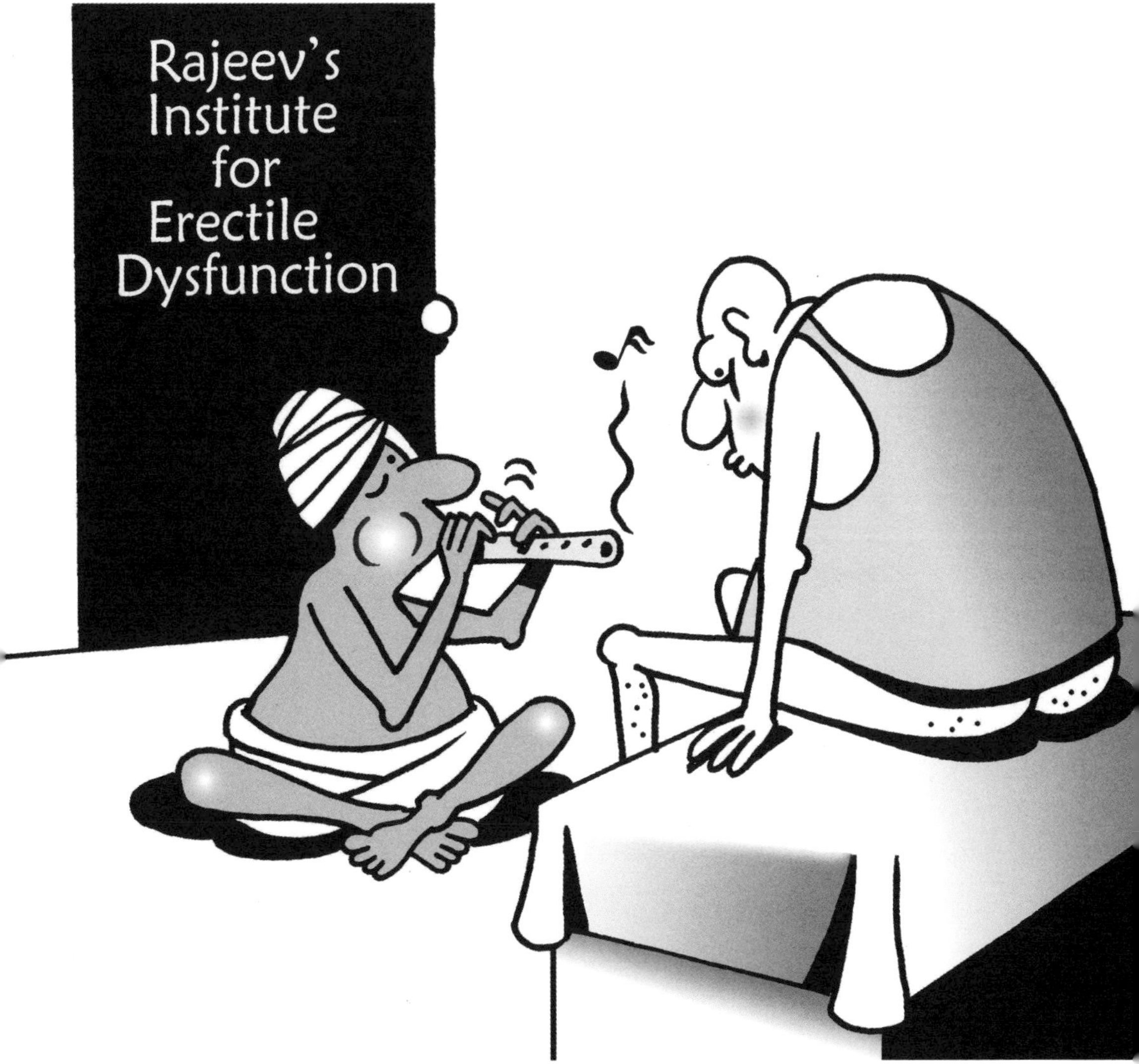
Rajeev's
Institute
for
Erectile
Dysfunction

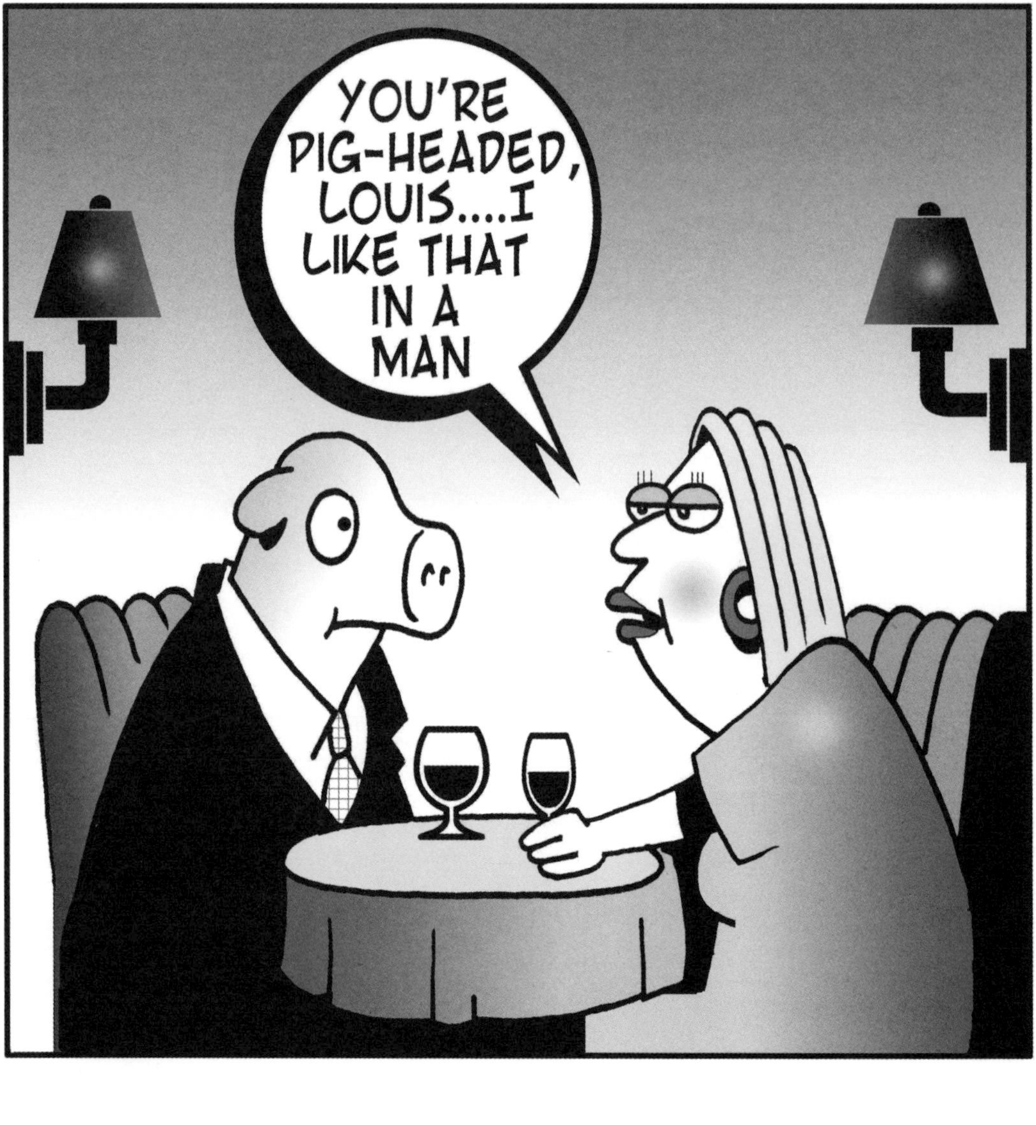
YOU'RE PIG-HEADED, LOUIS....I LIKE THAT IN A MAN

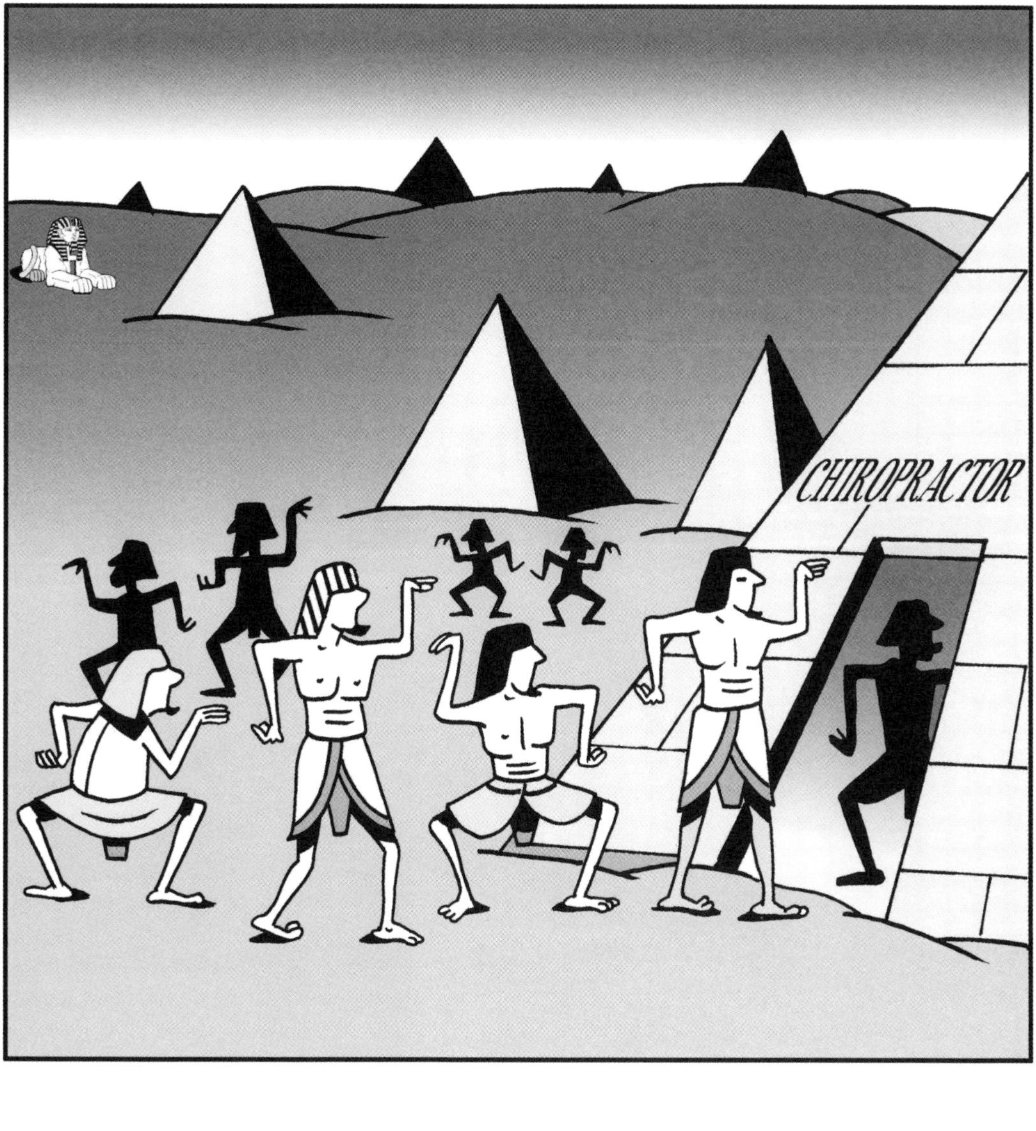
CHIROPRACTOR

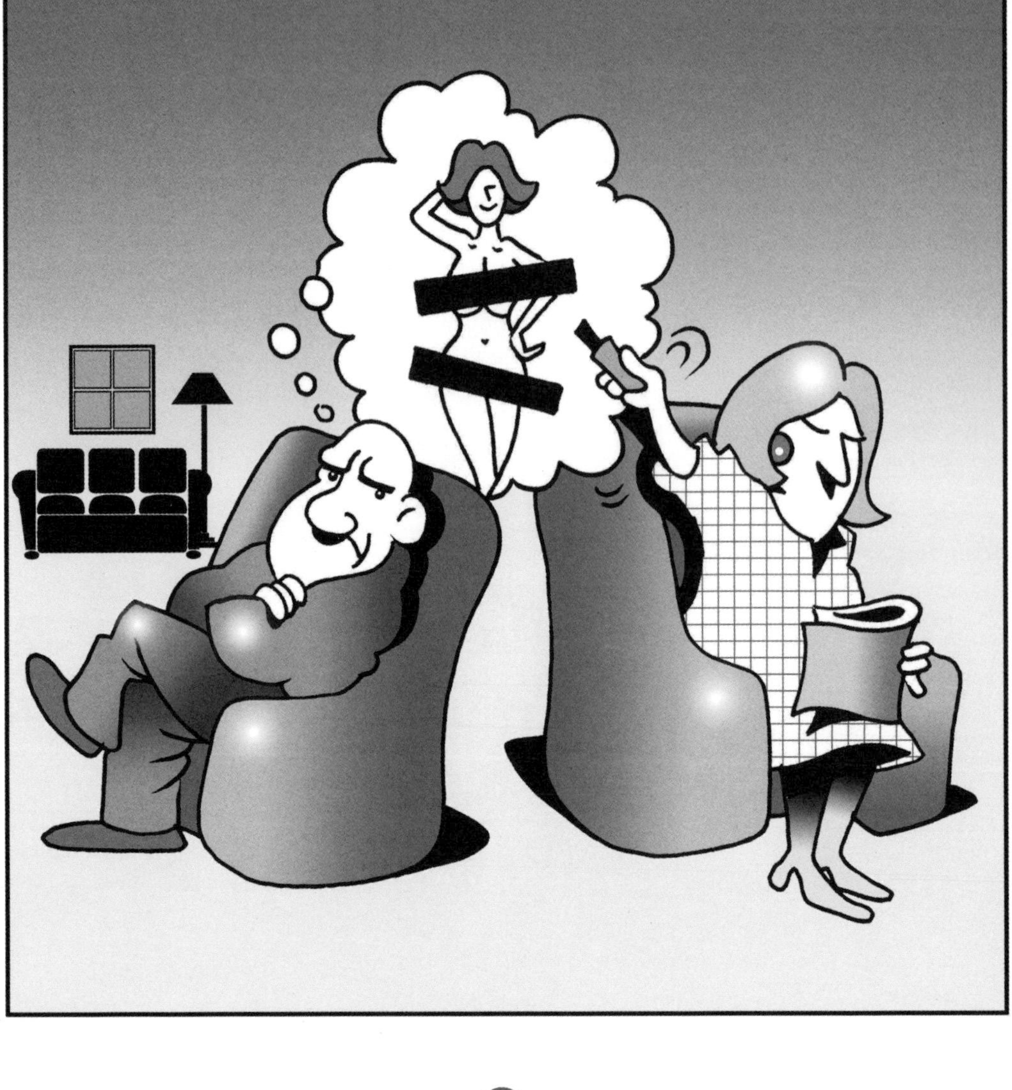

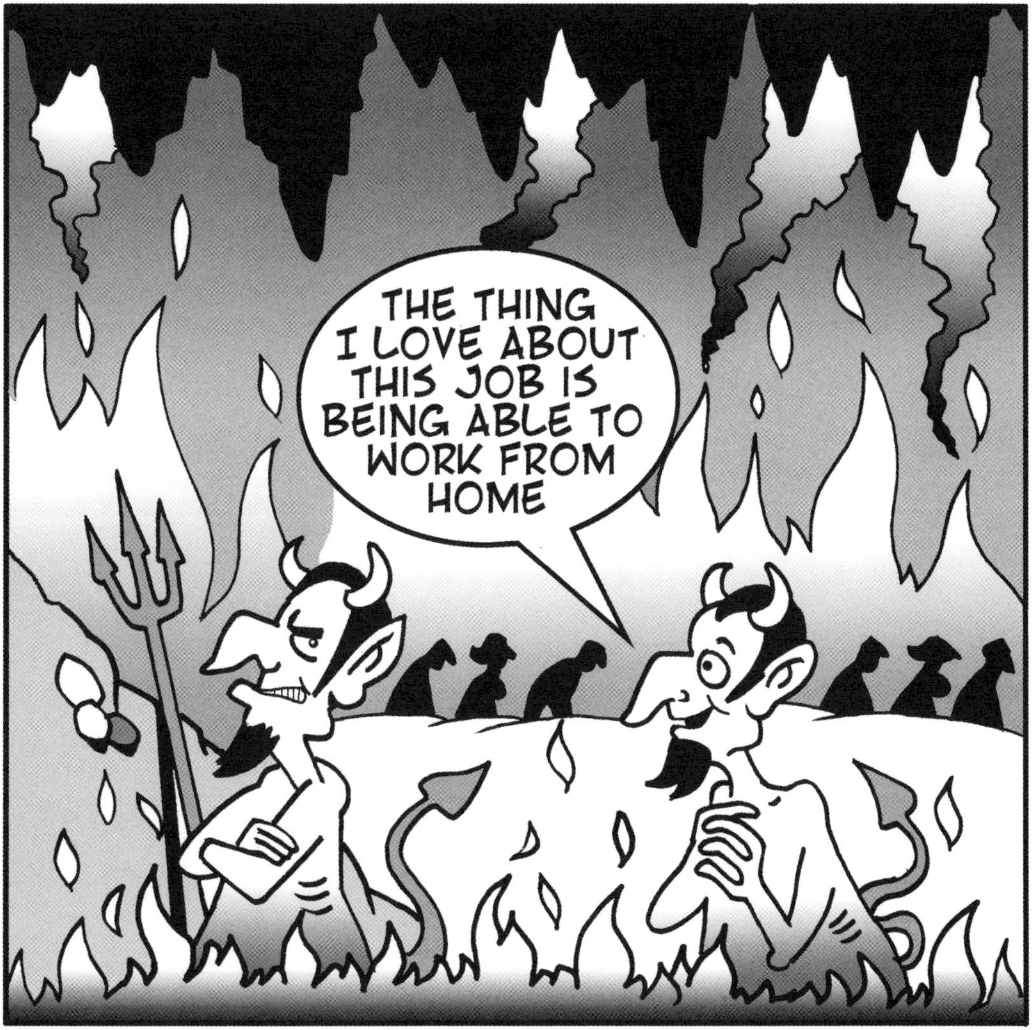
THE THING I LOVE ABOUT THIS JOB IS BEING ABLE TO WORK FROM HOME

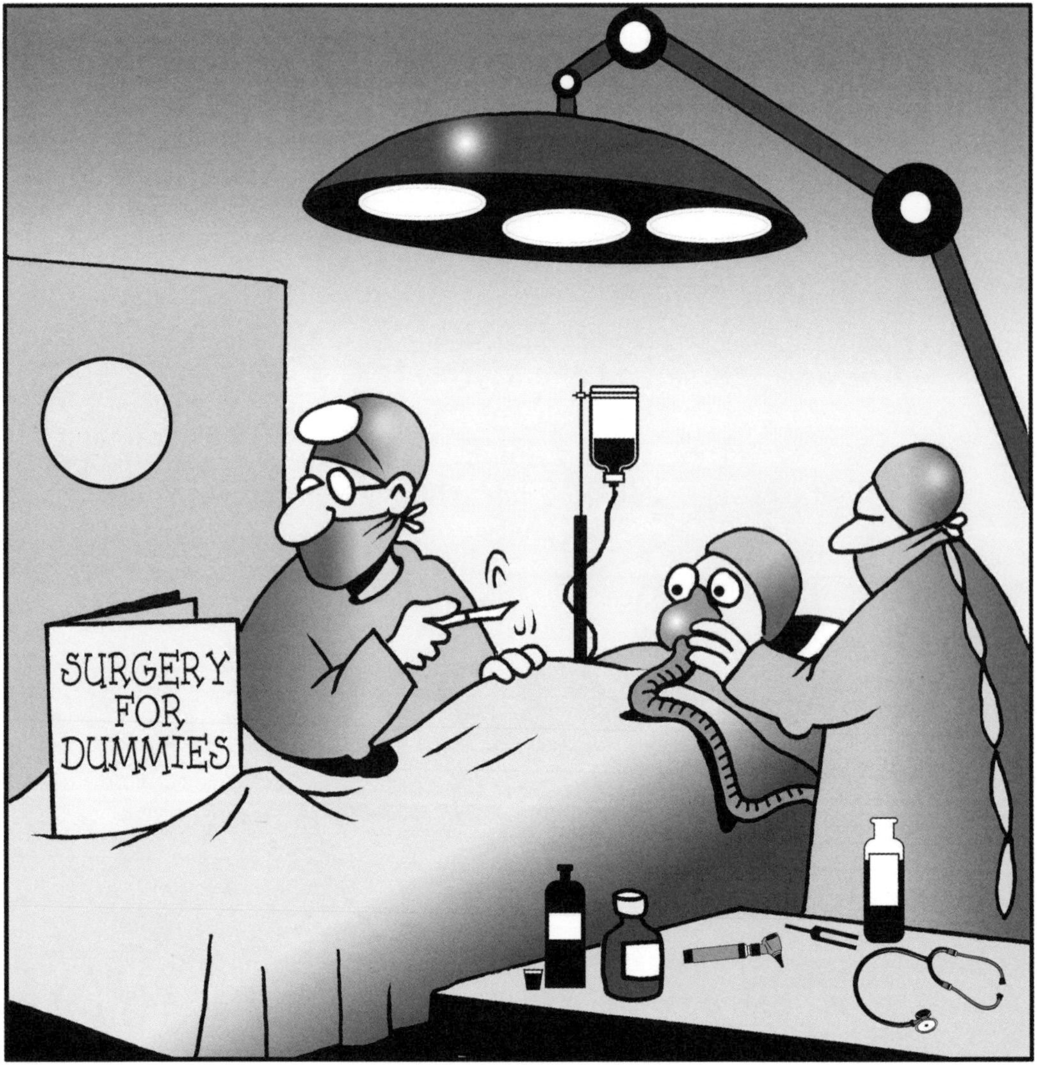
SURGERY
FOR
DUMMIES

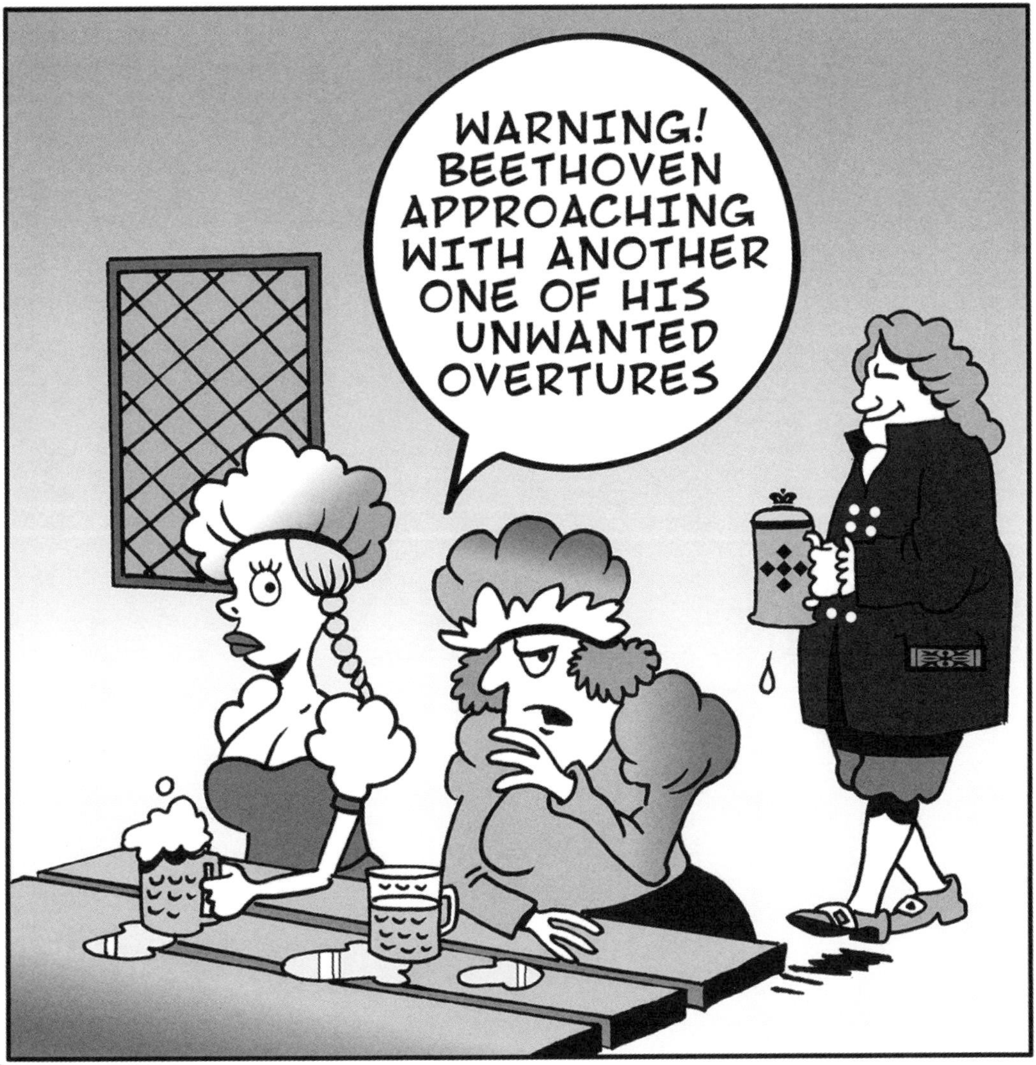
WARNING! BEETHOVEN APPROACHING WITH ANOTHER ONE OF HIS UNWANTED OVERTURES

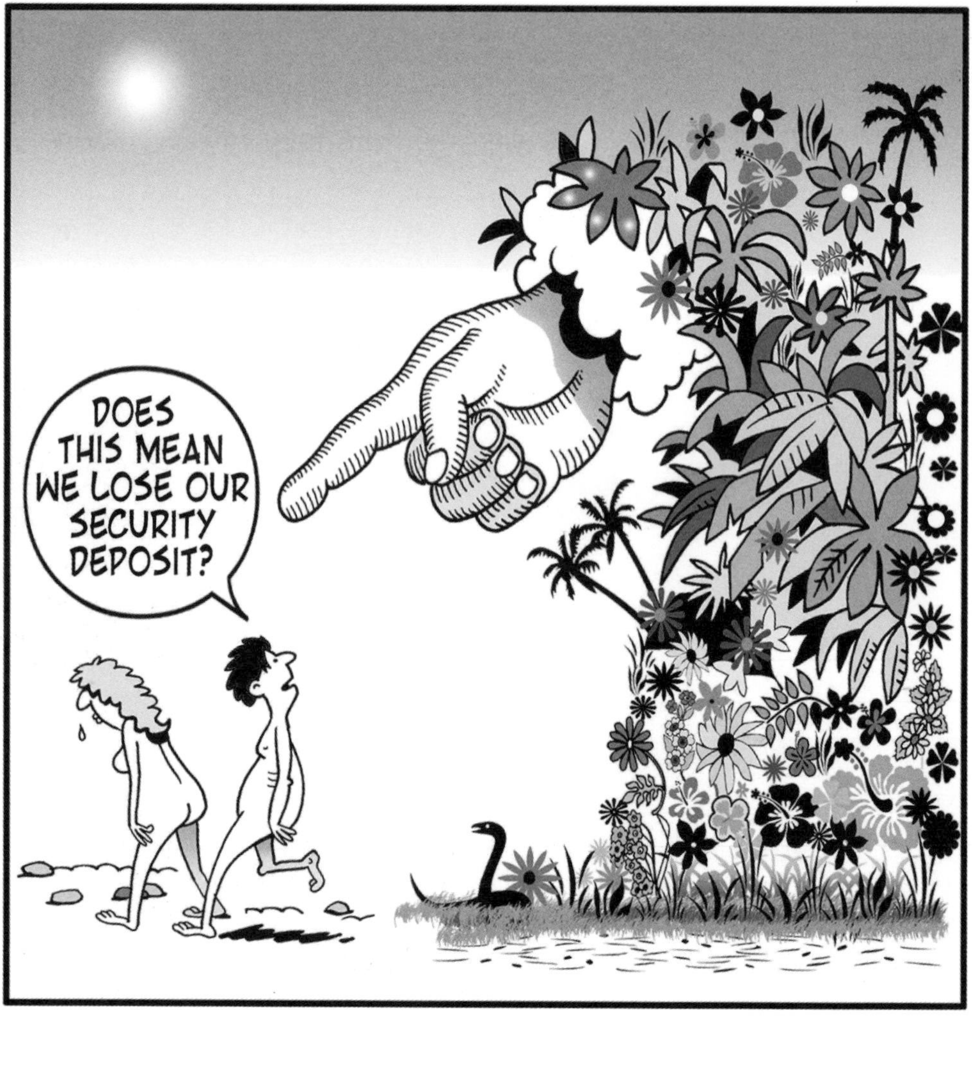
DOES THIS MEAN WE LOSE OUR SECURITY DEPOSIT?

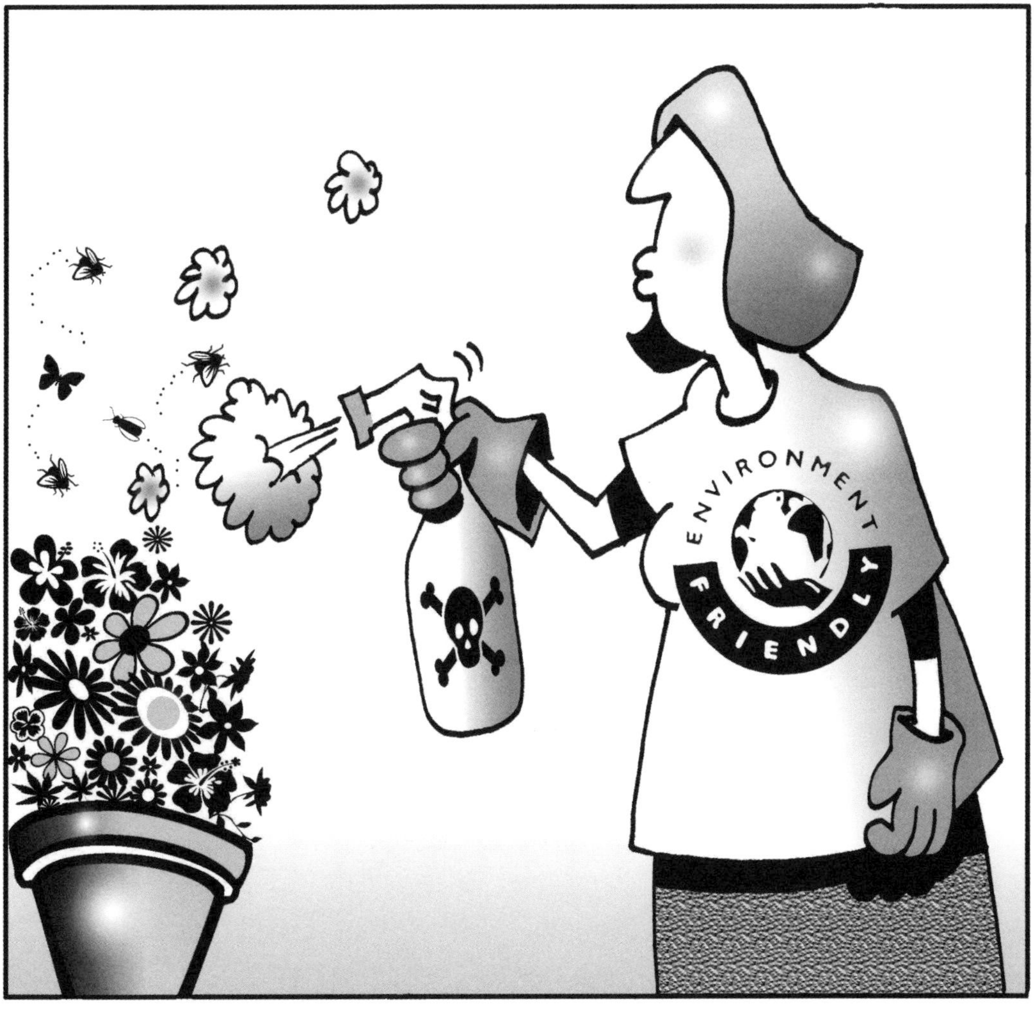
ENVIRONMENT
FRIENDLY

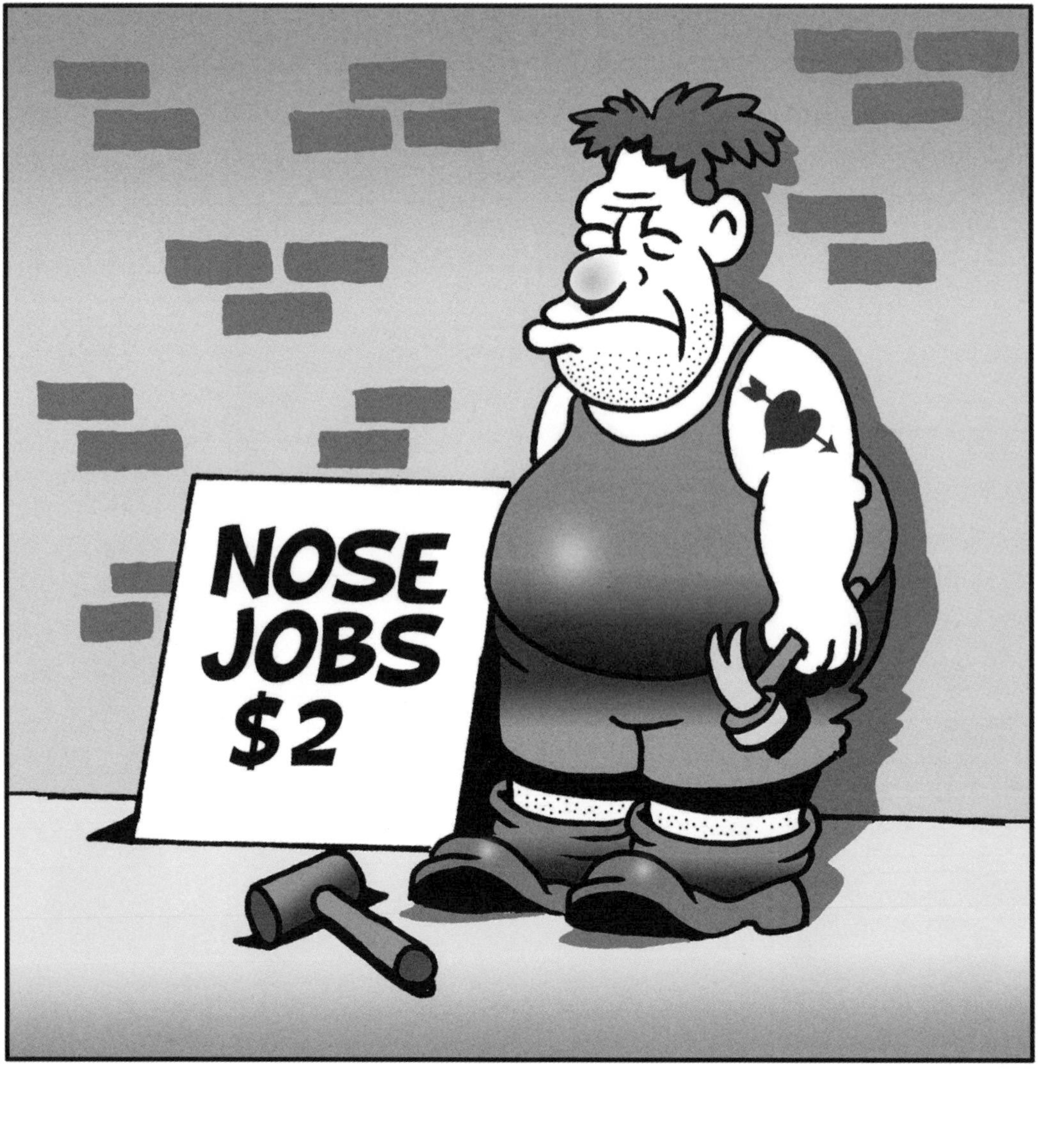
NOSE
JOBS
$2

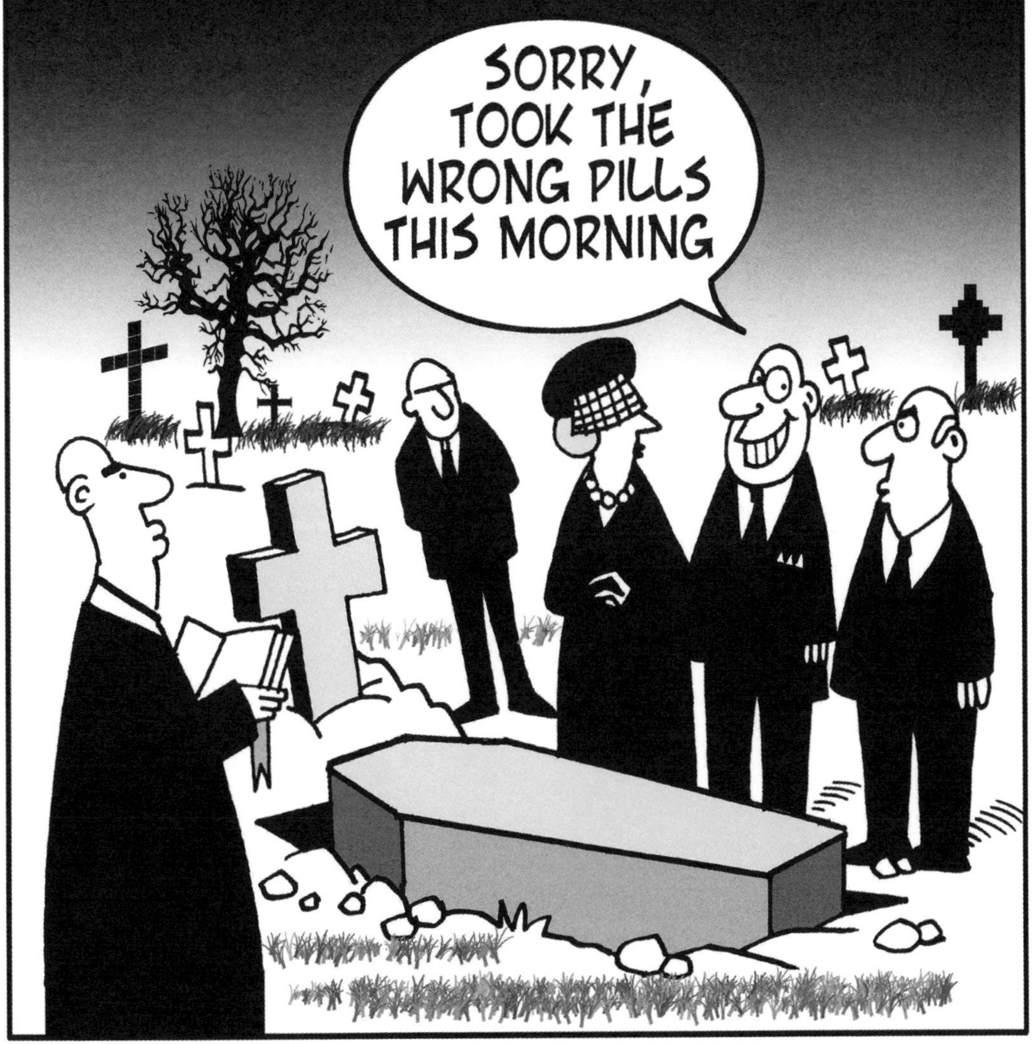
SORRY, TOOK THE WRONG PILLS THIS MORNING

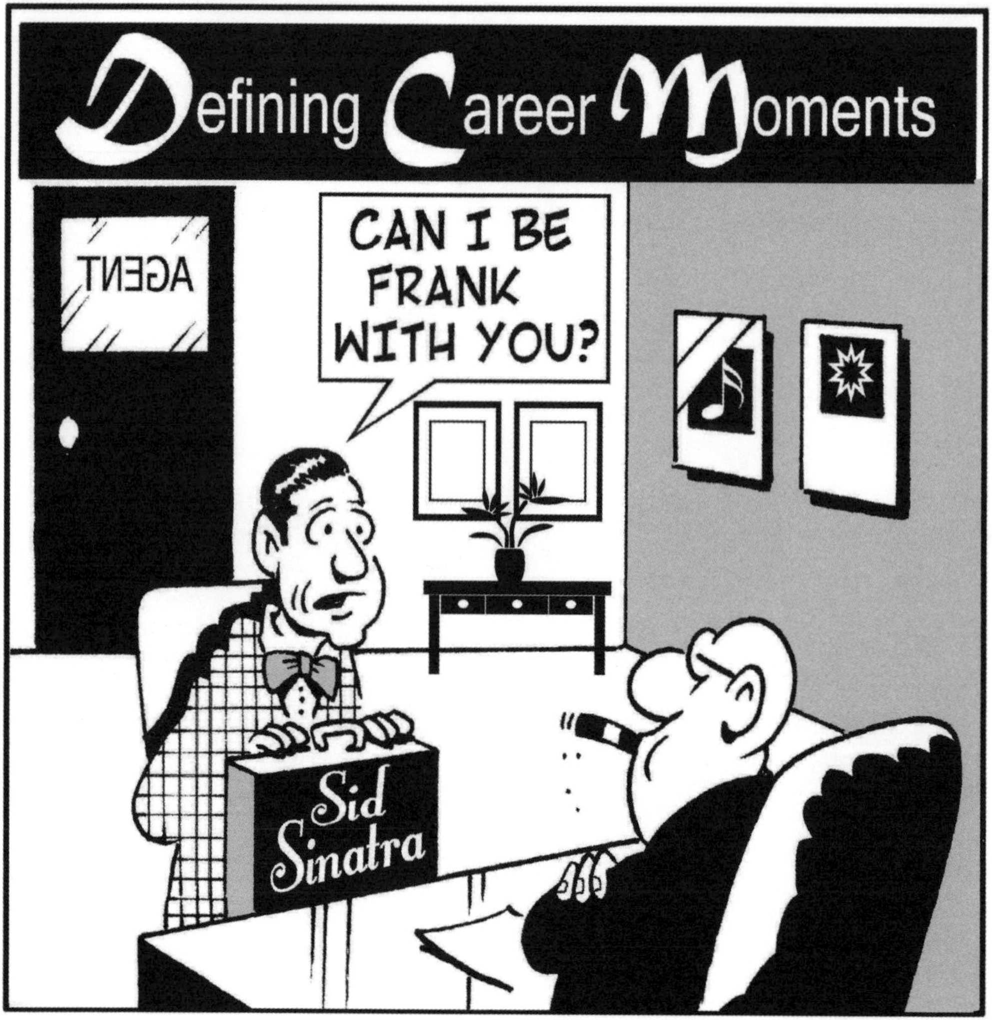

Defining Career Moments
ƎGAT (mirrored)
CAN I BE FRANK WITH YOU?
Sid Sinatra

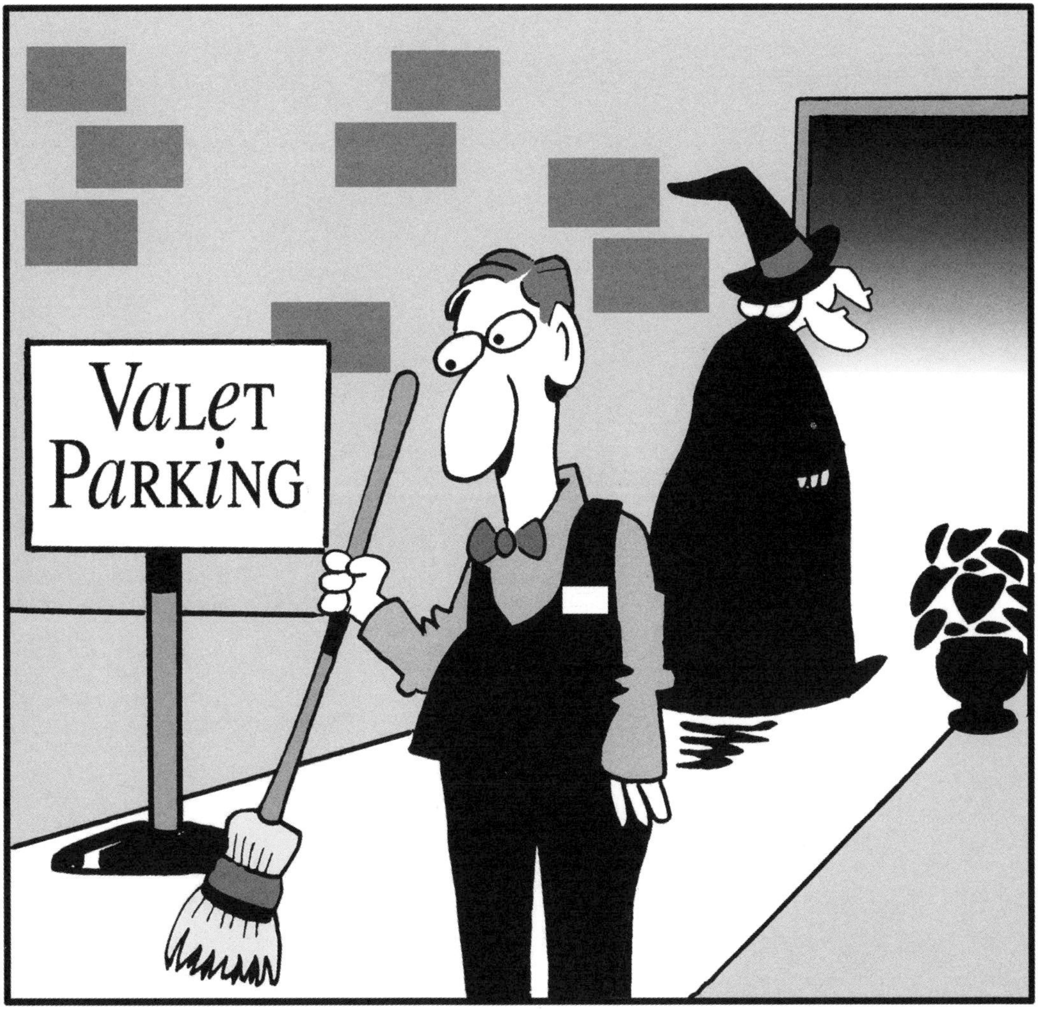
Valet
Parking

First published 2009

Exisle Publishing Limited
'Moonrising', Narone Creek Road, Wollombi, NSW 2325, Australia
P.O. Box 60–490, Titirangi, Auckland 0642, New Zealand
www.exislepublishing.com

National Library of Australia Cataloguing-in-Publication Data:

Lynch, Mark.

Smile / cartoons by Mark Lynch.

ISBN 9781921497278 (pbk.)

Australian wit and humour, Pictorial
Caricatures and cartoons—Australia.

741.5994

Designed by Wendy Farley, anthouse
Printed in China through Colorcraft Limited, Hong Kong

10 9 8 7 6 5 4 3 2 1